EUROPEAN UNIONS

European Unions

Labor's Quest for a Transnational Democracy

ROLAND ERNE

ILR PRESS   an imprint of

CORNELL UNIVERSITY PRESS

Ithaca and London

Copyright © 2008 by Cornell University

First published 2008 by Cornell University Press

Printed in the United States of America

Library of Congress Cataloging-in-Publication Data

Erne, Roland.
   European unions : labor's quest for a transnational democracy / Roland Erne.
      p. cm.
   Includes bibliographical references and index.
   ISBN 978-0-8014-4648-1 (cloth : alk. paper)
    1. Labor unions—European Union countries—Political activity.   2. Labor
movement—European Union countries.   3. International labor activities—
European Union countries.   4. Democratization—European Union countries.
5. Industrial relations—European Union countries.   I. Title.

   HD6658.5.E76 2008
   322'.2094—dc22

2007038142

Cloth printing   10 9 8 7 6 5 4 3 2 1

Pour Lena

Contents

Acknowledgments

This book calls on my two decades of experiences as a unionist, political science student, and labor relations lecturer in Zurich, Berlin, Paris, Brussels, Florence, and Dublin. I cannot list here the names of the unionists, works councilors, colleagues, and friends who supported my research with their experiences and ideas, not to mention practical assistance. Nevertheless, they should all know that I am very grateful for their help.

I also thank those who commented on my work when I presented parts of it at seminars and conferences. I am particularly grateful to Colin Crouch and Philippe Schmitter for the encouragement and advice that they provided from the very beginning of this study and to Stefano Bartolini, Hans Baumann, John Benson, John Geary, Corinne Gobin, Andi Gross, Richard Hyman, Maarten Keune, Heinz Kleger, Evelyne Léonard, Paul Marginson, Guglielmo Meardi, Oscar Molina, Udo Rehfeldt, Bill Roche, Stijn Smismans, Sabina Stan, Franz Traxler, Ulrich K. Preuss, and Valeria Pulignano for many valuable suggestions.

I also thank John Kelly, Nathan Lillie, and Andrew Martin for their very helpful feedback on a preliminary draft of this book and Catherine O'Dea and Julie F. Nemer for helping me prepare the manuscript for publication. Finally, I acknowledge the institutions that provided financial support throughout the course of my research, namely, the European University Institute in Florence, the Irish Research Council for the Humanities and the Social Sciences, the Swiss National Science Foundation, and University College Dublin.

Abbreviations

ABB	Asea Brown Boveri
APA	Alcan-Pechiney-Algroup
BBC	Brown Boveri Corporation
CCOO	Confederación Sindical de Comisiones Obreras (Spain)
CDU	Christlich Demokratische Union (Germany)
CEEP	European Centre of Enterprises with Public Participation and of Enterprises of General Economic Interest
CFDT	Confédération Française Démocratique du Travail (France)
CFE-CGC	Confédération Française de l'Encadrement-CGC
CFTC	Confédération Française des Travailleurs Chrétiens (France)
CGE	Compagnie Générale d'Electricité
CGIL	Confederazione Generale Italiana del Lavoro
CGT	Confédération Général du Travail (France)
CGTP	Confederação geral dos Trabalhadores Portugueses
CISL	Confederazione Italiana Sindacati Lavoratori
COBAS	Comitati di Base (Italy)
CSC métal	Christian Metalworkers' Union (Belgium)
CSC	Confédération des Syndicats Chrétiens (Belgium)
DAG	Deutsche Angestellten Gewerkschaft
DG	(European Commission) Directorate-General
DGB	Deutscher Gewerkschaftsbund
EADS	European Aeronautic Defence and Space Company
ECB	European Central Bank

EEC	European Economic Community
EFBWW	European Federation of Building and Woodworkers
EFTA	European Free Trade Association
EMCEF	European Mine, Chemical, and Energy Workers' Federation
EMF	European Metalworkers' Federation
EMU	European Monetary Union
EMWU	European Migrant Workers' Union (Germany)
ERT	European Round Table of Industrialists
ETUC	European Trade Union Confederation
ETUF-TCL	European Trade Union Federation–Textiles Clothing Leather
ETUI	European Trade Union Institute
EWC	European works council
FGTB	Fédération Générale du Travail de Belgique
FIOM	Federazione Impiegati Operai Metallurgici (Italy)
FNV	Federatie Nederlandse Vakbeweging (The Netherlands)
FO	Force Ouvrière (France)
GATT	General Agreement on Tariffs and Trade
GE	General Electric (U.S.)
GEC	General Electric Company (U.K.)
GM	General Motors
GMB	General, Municipal, Boilermakers and Allied Trade Union (U.K.)
GPMU	Graphical, Paper and Media Union (U.K.)
GWC	Group works council
HICP	Harmonized Index of Consumer Prices
ICF	International Federation of Chemical and General Workers' Unions
IG	Industriegewerkschaft
IG BAU	IG Bauen-Agrar-Umwelt
IIRA	International Industrial Relations Association
ILO	International Labour Organisation
IMF	International Metalworkers' Federation
INFO-Institut	Institute for Organizational Development and Corporate Politics (Germany)
INSEE	Institut National de la Statistique et des Études Économiques (France)
IRES	Institut de Recherches Économiques et Sociales (France)

LO	Landsorganisationen i Sverige
MEDEF	Mouvement des Entreprises de France
MEP	Member of the European Parliament
MP	Member of [national] parliament
NEAT	Neue Eisenbahn Alpentransversalen
NRW	North Rhine–Westphalia
OECD	Organisation for Economic Cooperation and Development
OSE	Observatoire Social Européen (Belgium)
PCF	Parti Communiste Français
PRC	Partito della Rifondazione Comunista (Italy)
RSU	Rappresentanze Sindacali Unitarie (Italy)
SMIC	Salaire minimum interprofessionnelle de croissance (France)
SMUV	Swiss Metal and Watchmakers' Union
SNB	EWC Special Negotiation Body
SNCF	Société Nationale des Chemins de Fer Français
SPD	Sozialdemokratische Partei Deutschlands
TCE	Treaty establishing a Constitution for Europe
TEC	Treaty establishing the European Community
TEU	Treaty establishing the European Union
TUC	British Trades Union Congress
UAEPME	Union Européenne de l'Artisanat et des Petites et Moyennes Entreprises
UGT[P]	União Geral de Trabalhadores [Portugal]
UGT[S]	Union General de Trabajadores [Spain]
UIL	Unione Italiana del Lavoro
UMP	Union for a Popular Movement (France)
UN	United Nations
UNICE	Union of Industrial and Employers' Confederations of Europe
USWA	United Steelworkers of America
VAW	Vereinigte Aluminium-Werke
WCC	World company council
WWC	World works council
WSI	Wirtschafts- und Sozialwissenschaftliches Institut (Germany)

EUROPEAN UNIONS

CHAPTER ONE

Introduction

When the legitimacy of European governance structures is debated, it is generally acknowledged that the European Union (EU) is facing a democratic deficit (Héritier 1999; European Commission 2003b). Conversely, however, it has been argued that the EU cannot be democratized because there is no European society as such, no European network of intermediate social organizations, no European public sphere, no European identity, and no European demos (people).[1] This study of European trade union networks challenges the view that there is no realistic prospect for remedying the EU democratic deficit. Although the making of a more democratic EU does require transnational collective action, our findings suggest that Euro-democratization is more constrained by the technocratic mode of EU governance than by the persistence of national differences.

In addition to citizenship rights and democratic constitutional bodies, a democratic polity needs tight networks of intermediate civil society organizations, such as unions. These offer the possibility of greater citizen participation in the political system and thus an increase in its legitimacy (Lepsius 1993a, 1993b; Skocpol 2003). Citizens' organizations, such as unions, also consolidate political democracy by holding corporations accountable when they subject citizens, as they frequently do, to autocratic rule in the production process or colonize the democratic process by pecuniary means (Sinyai 2006; Foot 2005; Crouch 2004). It follows that the emergence of transnational union networks could contribute to the constitution of a more democratic EU. Consequently, this book addresses two questions. First, has there emerged a European trade union movement that crosses national boundaries in response to the political and socioeconomic EU integration process? Second, to what extent and under which conditions do European trade unions contribute to the making of a more democratic EU?

European Integration, Labor, and Democracy

The political function that trade unions play in established democracies, however, does not necessarily match their role in democratization processes. Moreover, the EU-democratization process differs significantly from previous national experiences. Unlike comparable national processes, it cannot be analyzed as a transition from authoritarian rule to democracy in an established state (Schmitter 2000). For that reason, nation-state-based theories of democracy and democratization can only partially serve as a reference. Furthermore, most European integration theories neglect the concept of Euro-democratization; this is partly due to their output-oriented technocratic understanding of political legitimacy and partly due to their focus on elite EU-level actors. However, the prospects of a more democratic EU are widely discussed in political theory (Habermas 1992, 632–60; Kleger 1997; Abromeit 1998). Although we have already argued elsewhere that a transnational democracy (Erne et al. 1995)[2] would be an essential normative objective, it is much more difficult to explain under which conditions social actors would pursue, consciously or unconsciously, a Euro-democratization strategy. Therefore, this book does not add another more or less sophisticated blueprint of a future Euro-democracy to the debate. Rather, it expresses how one actor, organized labor, may be an agent of Euro-democratization.

Democratic political systems allowed organized labor to shift class conflicts from the marketplace to the political arena, where the workers' strength lies in their sheer numbers (Esping-Andersen and Korpi 1984). But even if unions may have played an important role in national democratization processes (Stedman Jones 1983; Rueschemeyer, Huber Stephens, and Stephens 1992), this does not necessarily promise a similar role for them at the EU level. Because authoritarian regimes typically repress independent union activities, they necessarily channel desires for worker representation into democratization movements. However, the institutional setting of the EU provides alternative options for organized labor. For this reason, this book assesses the various, deliberately chosen or emergent (Stråth 1990), strategies that unions can adopt to influence the transformation of governance in the EU.

Previous Debates and Evidence

Numerous studies emphasize that EU-level trade unionism is primarily based on a union diplomacy, exclusive to union executives and experts (Turner 1996; Dølvik 1997; Gobin 1996; Schulten 2000b; Pernot 2001). The activities of these EU-level unionists were partly successful, given some achievements such as the social protocol of the Maastricht Treaty. These successes may be explained by a compatibility of this type of union action with the technocratic mode of EU governance. Indeed, EU institutions may favor the participation of labor in EU policy making because they require union compliance and expertise to act in some policy fields (Smismans 2004). For this reason, a strategy of what we call Euro-technocratization could be a promising alternative to Euro-democratization for labor.

However, given the impact of neoliberal ideology on the economic policy of the EU, some unions have also opposed the EU integration process as a capitalist project. They have therefore rejected any Europeanization strategies in favor of renationalization.[3] One of two renationalization strategies is a national social-democratic strategy. Despite its internationalist ideology, the history of organized labor is profoundly linked to the nation-state. Diverse national arrangements in the field of industrial relations and welfare have integrated the working classes into their nation-states and provided them with an important set of rights and benefits (Visser 1996). Accordingly, Pasture and Verberckmoes conclude that the unions "cannot afford to reject the appeal of national identity" (1998, 23). However, the national democratic renationalization strategy seems to be losing its viability because national social-democratic policies face firm constraints within an increasingly transnational capitalism (Sassoon 1997; Gray 2000). Instead, unions may turn to a technocratic renationalization strategy characterized by the aim of enhancing national competitiveness (Rhodes 1997; Streeck 1998a). Accordingly, a national-competition state would replace the social-democratic welfare state (Cerny 1990).

The increasing constraints on social-democratic policies at the national level could also motivate the unions to Europeanize their activities. In fact, to some extent a growing Europeanization of rank-and-file union activities can be observed, as demonstrated by the recent increase in demonstrations by European trade unions and global justice movements (Lefébure 2002; Della Porta and Mosca 2007). As political mobilization frequently went from contestation to democracy at the national level (Giugni, McAdam, and Tilly 1998), a similar process is plausible at the EU level too. Democratization requires a feeling of commonality among its citizens. It follows that organized labor could contribute to Euro-democratization if it encouraged European collective action and the rise of a European public sphere (Habermas 1992, 650). People start recognizing that they belong to the same polity as soon as they begin to act together, even if they might contest its policies. European collective action would also contribute to the rise of a European public sphere and to a politicization of the EU integration process (Imig and Tarrow 2001). Likewise, Richard Hyman has argued that supporting the emergence and consolidation of a European civil society and citizenship should be an important task for unions (2001). In short, we have identified four types of strategies that unions may adopt when facing the tensions between national competition and European coordination, on one hand, and democratic and technocratic decision making, on the other.

Research Design

The identification of these strategies provides us with a typology of four possible orientations that actors may take in relation to the European integration process: Euro-democratization, Euro-technocratization, democratic renationalization, and technocratic renationalization. This typology is designed to distinguish among the effects that union strategies can have on the direction of the development of the EU polity rather than to characterize the strategies that specific unions actually pursue. Hence, we do not classify specific unions as more or less European or national and democratic or technocratic but, rather, aim to understand the strategic choices of unions, which are likely to vary in different situations and at different times.

Our typology is applied here in several comparative studies of the contrasting performance of various union networks in central fields of their everyday activities. Hence, this book does not study union declarations— every union rhetorically supports a more social and democratic EU. If a union is pursuing a Euro-democratization strategy, it must be evident in its key activities. Therefore, this book focuses on two areas that constitute the core of union politics, namely, collective bargaining and job protection during company restructurings.

Furthermore, the book avoids a widespread selection bias, namely, that of studying Europeanization at an EU level and renationalization at a national level. Such research designs risk leading to flawed results. For instance, an exclusive research focus on national social pacts ought to find evidence supporting the renationalization thesis; in contrast, an exclusive focus on EU-level social dialog must produce more evidence in support of the Europeanization thesis. However, if there is to be a Europeanization of organized labor, it must take place not only in the EU-level structures but also within the respective national-, local-, and firm-level union organizations. Likewise, if there is any renationalization of union activities, this must also cause corresponding effects at the EU level. This calls for a multilevel enquiry that includes EU-, national-, and enterprise-level union activities.

This study also goes beyond the classical country-by-country comparisons of national union movements. The increasing interdependence of the EU member states suggests the necessity of new methodologies for comparative analysis (Smelser 1995). Often, the failure of unions from different countries to cooperate has been explained by national differences; but this explanation cannot elucidate why the same national unions adopt different European strategies in various situations. Whereas French and German metalworkers' unions joined forces in organizing a European day of action in one case, the same unions failed to cooperate in another case. This suggests that national explanations of failed transnational cooperation must be questioned; but this is only possible if we question the conventional unit of analysis in comparative studies, that is, the nation-state. In order to confront national with competing hypotheses, it is necessary to compare not only nation-states but also transnational units of analysis, such as transnational union networks that are linked to different multinational companies or different economic sectors.

This research project was based on a wide range of research methods, including statistical analysis, document analysis, participant observation, and expert interviews. It also draws on European, German, French, Italian, and Swiss academic and union literature. This variety of sources enables a critical examination of each source in the light of alternative sources (Tarrow 1995). Because of open access to local-, national-, and EU-level union organizations, I was able to include a very wide range of internal documents.[4]

Case Selection and Plan of the Book

The next chapter provides an overview of the Euro-democratization debate and the potential interests of the labor movement in EU democracy. It also develops and operationalizes the typology of the strategic orientations that social actors may follow in response to the EU integration process, including Euro-democratization. However, because social actors often do not view democratization as a goal in its own right, chapter 3 assesses the European power resources of labor in relation to the various strategic orientations that unions could pursue regarding the European integration process.

Part II of this book assesses the tension between Europeanization and renationalization in the field of wage bargaining. There is widespread agreement that national bargaining systems are exposed to increased pressures due to the European Single Market and the European Monetary Union (EMU) (Bieler 2006). However, researchers disagree over whether an EU-wide coordination of wage bargaining represents a viable alternative to its technocratic renationalization—that is to say, competitive corporatism. Hence, chapters 5–7 assess the tensions between national social pacts and the different emergent bargaining coordination policies of the European Metalworkers' Federation (EMF) and the European Federation of Building and Wood Workers (EFBWW).

In so doing, the chapters analyze export-oriented and domestic sectors of the economy because the processes of economic globalization and Europeanization affect the two sectors differently—whereas in the former the Europeanization process is mediated through the free movement of goods, in the latter it is mediated through the free movement of workers and services. The free movement of workers and services may have a considerable impact. Local manufacturing workers are not directly confronted with the workers of competing enterprises, whereas competing foreign construction workers may work even on the same site (Menz 2005a). Hence, our analysis also reveals whether these sectoral differences had a decisive impact on the European strategies adopted by the unions in the field of collective bargaining.

In part III, we examine the tensions between Euro-democratization and Euro-technocratization strategies. Specifically, chapters 8–10 examine activities of labor in two significant multinational company merger cases, namely, the ABB Alstom Power and the Alcan-Pechiney-Algroup merger projects. Given the inaccessible institutional setup of the EU merger control policy, it would be reasonable to suggest that labor has no role whatsoever in this policy field. Nevertheless, workers' representatives have increasingly been trying to influence EU competition policy. Their actual activities, however, have differed considerably: whereas in the ABB Alstom merger the workers' representatives tried to politicize the merger, the Alcan-Pechiney-Algroup workers' representatives adopted a strategy that was compatible with the technocratic approach of the competition policy of the European Commission. Hence, the same European, German, and French metalworkers' unions surprisingly adopted conflicting EU-polity strategies in the two cases: a Euro-democratization strategy in the ABB Alstom case and a Euro-technocratization strategy in the Alcan-Pechiney-Algroup merger case. These different EU-polity strategies did not result from different company policies. ABB and Algroup were controlled by the same Swiss shareholder-value capitalist, Martin Ebner, and Alstom and Pechiney share a similar corporate history and policy as previously state-owned French-ethnocentric multinationals. Moreover, all companies adopted a similar shareholder-value-oriented corporate strategy. Hence, the proposed comparison of the two merger cases represents an almost perfect most-similar-system design. This research design allows us to test the recurrent explanations of diverging union activities within multinational firms on the basis of national differences.

The selected cases provide a good picture of the European trade union movement. All cases cover key areas of union action and also cover a large territorial scope of European trade unionism. The analysis of the emerging European wage-bargaining coordination networks covers almost all EMU countries; the assessments of the two European company merger cases also include an in-depth analysis of related local union activities in Germany and France. Thus, this case selection confronts the two major continental traditions of unionism, namely, the mixture of business and civil society unionism and the mixture of class and civil society unionism (Hyman 2001).

PART ONE
Analytical Framework

CHAPTER TWO

Approaching Euro-Democracy and Its Alternatives

After the fall of most dictatorships in the early 1990s, democracy might seem to be the only uncontested form of government left. However, despite this global resurgence of democracy (Diamond and Plattner 1996), democracy is also facing a twofold crisis. The French political scientist Jean-Marie Guéhenno (1994) has even predicted the end of democracy, given the diminishing autonomy of nation-states in a globalizing capitalist economy and the growing impact of technocratic policy making.

First, many nation-states have delegated competencies in many policy areas to supranational organizations to create and regulate transnational markets.[1] The most obvious example of such an organization is the EU, especially since the introduction of the European currency. To date, however, there has been little participation by citizens in this process, arguably due to the lack of a European public sphere and of democratically accountable institutions at a supranational level. For this reason, it has been argued that the shift of national competencies to the supranational level also causes an erosion of democracy (Grimm 1995).

The second crisis in contemporary democracies lies within the nation-states themselves. Policy makers are increasingly insulated in various ways from accountability to the population affected by their decisions. Whereas some analysts note that technocrats, corporate lobbyists, and disconnected party leaders are determining major policy decisions (Crouch 2004), others detect twin processes of popular and elite withdrawal from electoral politics (Mair 2006). Although more citizens desire to be directly involved in the political process—mirroring the democratization of education and the rise of information and communication technologies (Schiller and Mittendorf 2002; Budge 1996)—there is a widespread feeling that citizens are being pushed into the role of powerless spectators of the political circus. Consequently, there emerges a notion of democracy that is being stripped of its popular component (Mair 2006).

This twofold crisis not only deprives classical democratic theory of its central claim—to obey no laws other than those to which the citizens have given consent—but also questions the foundations of modern democracies: namely, the responsiveness and accountability of political leaders to citizens and, vice versa, the access of citizens to the decision-making process (Dahl 1989). How can governments be responsive to citizens and be held accountable by them if their polity has lost its autonomy? How can citizens have access to political decisions if they are taken outside the realm of the democratic nation-state?

Is a Democratic EU Polity Possible?

If supranational governance structures affect "the conditions for autonomous self-government at the national level" (Eriksen and Fossum 2007, 15), what then are the prospects for democracy in the context of the EU?

Ever since the rejection of the Maastricht Treaty in the first Danish referendum in 1992, official announcements referring to subsequent Inter-Governmental Conferences of the EU have pointed out that the democratic legitimacy of the EU must be strengthened to make it more acceptable; however, many EU politicians use the notion of a Europe of the citizens fairly rhetorically. Although most politicians acknowledge the need for enhanced citizen involvement in EU politics, some also fear that increased citizen participation could threaten their prerogatives and lead to undesired outcomes, such as the rejection of the EU constitution by French and Dutch voters in 2005. It is therefore not surprising that the meaning of the notion Europe of the citizens varies substantially. Whereas for the European Commission even the uniform EU driving license was an element of a citizens' Europe, others request the introduction of EU-wide citizens' initiatives and referenda.[2]

The difficulty associated with EU democratization reflects not only the skepticism of actual EU decision makers, who fear a loss of their prerogatives, but also diverging conceptual approaches to the question of Euro-democracy. Social and political scientists also disagree on how to achieve a more democratic EU. Whereas skeptics argue that only a Europe of the nations could be legitimate, others claim that supranational EU policy making could also be democratic.

The Europe of the Nations

There are perspectives that advocate a renationalization, or rolling back of EU politics to the national level (Lepsius 1993a, 1993b; Grimm 1995). These authors regard EU democracy as practically unfeasible due to the lack of a European public sphere and a European *demos* (people), given the national cultural, linguistic, and political differences within the EU.[3] This section assesses the arguments of the German sociologist Rainer M. Lepsius, who is representative of this Euro-skeptical line of thought.

The institutional order of the EU reminds Lepsius of the constitution of the German Reich in 1871. Like this alliance of princes and Hanseatic towns, the EU was founded by treaties signed by heads of state and not by a constitutional act of the people. In both processes, it can be observed that the accumulation of competence at the Reich or EU level is way ahead of any democratic constitutional development. In addition, the EU, like the former German Reich, can be characterized as a political regime run by bureaucratic elites that the parliament, with its limited competencies, is unable to control. Lepsius now fears that the EU will face constitutional conflicts similar to those of the German Reich because the asymmetrical development of political sovereignty and democratic legitimization will generate critical tensions (Lepsius 1993a).

According to Lepsius, the basic problem is the Janus-faced structure of the institutional order of the EU. He emphasizes that the EU is both an international and a supranational organization, in other words, both a confederation of independent states (*Staatenbund*) and a federation of federated states (*Bundesstaat*). Therefore, a far-reaching parliamentarization of the EU legislation will not be able to avoid the danger of constitutional conflict. Even though strengthening of the competence of the European Parliament parallel to the extension of the competence of the EU would correspond to democratic precepts and to the way in which the European Parliament views itself, this project invariably encounters barriers as soon as the governments of the member states seek to maintain their status as masters of the treaties. According to Lepsius, the *pièce de résistance* of any democratization perspective for the EU lies in the tension produced by this double legitimization structure. Hence, to avoid constitutional conflict, the only solution is to overcome the double legitimization structure of the EU. This implies a choice between national and European democracy.

Even more important, a functioning democracy needs, according to

Lepsius, not only a democratic constitution but also a dense network of intermediate social institutions such as the unions, other citizens' organizations, and a free press. These offer the citizens opportunities to participate in the political system and thus increase its legitimization; but because the standardization of this network across Europe is unlikely to happen, due to the different histories, cultures, and languages of the European nation-states, the nation-state remains for Lepsius, at least for the next decades, the only expression of the democratic will of the people. Because European unification cannot be based on the model of the European nation-state, the parliamentary democratization model of the nineteenth century does not provide a framework for overcoming the double legitimization structure of the EU. It follows, for Lepsius, that the model of a European federal state does not represent a reference for the democratization of the EU because it cannot be created without breaking up the manifold social structures of single European nation-states. This would imply dissolving the legitimization basis of European nation-states, their respective *demos,* because a democratic system is by no means legitimized only through parties, elections, and parliaments (Lepsius 1990).

A more decentralized EU might help to minimize this problem by rolling back some EU competencies to the national level (Lepsius 1993b). However, this solution would only solve the EU legitimacy problems insofar as the remaining market-making and regulating policies at EU level do not entail political choices. Put positively, EU membership could be reconciled with a national understanding of democracy if it involved only functional, problem-solving decisions that made no party worse off (Eriksen and Fossum 2007).

The Europe of Technocratic Efficiency

Although sharing much of the skepticism regarding the feasibility of a genuine EU democracy, several authors have tried to legitimize the EU by its beneficial policy outcomes (Scharpf 1999). Hence, efficiency, and not democracy, assures the legitimacy of the EU. Democratic decision making is even perceived as a problem because it could be in conflict with effective EU governance. Although the European single-market program of 1992 certainly reinforced these technocratic attitudes (Ziltener 1999), it should also be noted that the EU integration process was sponsored by economic interests and enlightened despots from its very beginning (Haas 1968).

Advocates of technocratic EU decision making, such as Giandomenico Majone, acknowledge that this mode of functioning raises the problem of democratic accountability. However, they paradoxically argue that this form of so-called regulatory decision making is, nevertheless, legitimate given the negative consequences of election pressures for the quality of legislation (Majone 1994a). It follows that the existence of an objective and universal criterion of decision-making quality is taken for granted. However, if the citizens have divergent preferences, as they almost always do, this assumption turns out to be problematic—what is a good regulation for one citizen or one country is a bad one for another. The democratic process is essentially a conflict-regulation mechanism and not a means to produce the good.[4] Another core assumption of regulatory decision making that is also questionable is the assumed impartiality of the decision makers. In fact, regulatory agencies tend to be shaped and captured by powerful political actors and ideologies. Joseph Weiler, Ulrich Haltern, and Franz Mayer accurately emphasize that technocratic regulation "often masks ideological choices which are not debated and subject to public scrutiny beyond the immediate interests related to the regulatory management area" (1995, 33).

However, the quality of policy outcomes is important. Thus, Fritz Scharpf (1975) introduces the notion of an output-oriented democracy to describe an efficiency-oriented view of legitimacy. He shares Schumpeter's (1954) view and perceives democracy as an elite selection process that is detached from the aspirations of citizens. Consequently, only elites can guarantee the public good, as critically noted by Jürgen Habermas:

> Because the unspecific and highly aggregated trust of masses of passive voters no longer can determine the policies of the competing leadership groups, only the rationality of the elites themselves, capable of decision and ready for innovation, can guarantee that the administration functions more or less in the equal interest of all. This gives rise to the image of an administrative system that, operating relatively independently of society, procures the necessary mass loyalty and determines political goal functions more or less by itself. (1996a, 332)

Be that as it may, Scharpf's output-oriented democracy is a misleading oxymoron. Either policy outcomes are beneficial because they please a democratic majority (a situation that corresponds to the established input-oriented understanding of democracy) or they are good because they implement decisions made by technocrats in line with predefined objectives (a situation that has nothing to do with democratic politics). According to Scharpf's definition, even a dictatorship could be democratic provided it produced the desired results. Scharpf's desire to use the pleasant word *democracy* is understandable, but he would be better advised to use the term *technocracy*. The term *democracy* loses all its analytical qualities if its definition is extended to include the output-oriented forms of legitimacy. However, given the weak democratic legitimacy of the EU decision-making process, technocratic legitimacy often represents its only saving grace for its supporters. Many EU judges and lawyers—who cannot escape making decisions—often use efficiency arguments to legitimize specific public policies of the EU (Joerges 2001).

The Europe of the Citizens

Ironically, both the EU-skeptical advocates of the Europe of the nations and the technocratic supporters of an efficient EU agree that democracy cannot work at the EU level. Other authors have challenged these pessimistic views and have considered the possibility of a transnational European democracy. Nevertheless, the limited attention paid by social scientists to the possibility of such a transnational democracy is remarkable. Until the mid-1990s, these questions triggered only little attention (Kaufmann 1995). Robert A. Dahl (1989) emphasizes the urgency of a third transformation of democratic theory to adapt it to the age of globalization, and Daniele Archibugi and David Held (1995) speculate about the prospects for a cosmopolitan democracy. By comparison, Habermas's ambition was more modest when he started to explore the potential of a transnational democracy in the European context (Habermas 1996b [1990]).

Habermas argues that in the future a postnational understanding of citizenship will provide the basis for a transnational European democracy. Democratic citizenship need not be rooted in an amalgamated identity of a European *demos*. It demands only, regardless of the variety of forms of social culture, the socialization of all citizens in a common political culture. This socialization could be the result of the political participation of citizens in EU politics.

In contrast to Lepsius, Habermas does not consider the Janus-faced structure of the EU to be a fundamental problem of the EU institutions. The EU should not develop into a centralized state but into a multilingual state of different nationalities. This federation would, in the long run, be similar to a federal state, but "would have to retain certain features of [Charles] De Gaulle's 'Europe of Fatherlands'" (Habermas 1996a, 502). Habermas is, instead, more concerned about the encroachments of administrative and economic power on the public sphere within nation-states and, even more so, above them, as portrayed by the technocratic paradigm of an efficient EU. Indeed, an increasing number of political decisions are made by transnational elites that act as if they were in possession of the truth. In turn, citizens have almost no possibility of influencing these transnational decisions because citizenship has been institutionalized in an effective way, thus far, only at the national level. Nevertheless, Habermas also argues that Euro-technocracy is avoidable and that a gradually developing, postnational European public sphere and citizenship could provide the basis for a new European democracy: "Democratic citizenship need not be rooted in the national identity of a people. However, regardless of the diversity of different cultural forms of life, it does require that every citizen be socialized into a common political culture" (1996a, 500).

Habermas thus abandons the assumption that modern democracy requires a link between citizenship and nation-state. Habermas's deliberative theory of democracy instead allows for a conception of civic autonomy that is not linked to a nation in the sense of an ethnically homogenous community of fate. This conclusion also appears to be plausible because the concept of citizenship was originally tailored to the needs and scopes of city-states and was associated with nation-states only because of the nation-building processes of the eighteenth and nineteenth centuries (Koselleck and Schreiner 1994).

Moreover, the development and democratization of the territorial nation-states during the past two centuries can be seen as the result of a political mobilization of the population and their increased mobility. Because the European integration process would also lead to a greater horizontal mobility of people, it would be justified to make cautiously optimistic conclusions about the democratization of the EU too:

> The European market will set in motion a greater horizontal mobility and multiply the contacts among members of different nationalities. In addition to this, immigration from Eastern Europe and the poverty-stricken regions of the Third World will heighten the multicultural diversity of society. This will no doubt give rise to social tensions. But if those tensions are dealt with productively, they can foster a political mobilization that will give additional impetus to the new endogenous social movements already emergent within nation-states. . . . At the same time, there is a growing pressure of problems that can be solved only at a coordinated European level. Under these conditions, communication complexes could develop in Europe-wide public spheres. (Habermas 1996a, 506)

Economic and political integration processes certainly contribute to an increased mobility of capital, goods, and people. However, Habermas also acknowledges that the conflicts that are likely to be triggered by these processes might favor the development of a European public sphere and democracy only under certain conditions, namely, when there is policy-making capacity at a coordinated European level. Democracy requires not only a people (*demos*) but also binding rules (*kratos*). Democratization processes depend not only on popular political mobilizations but also on the capacity of a political authority to act and to enforce the result of democratic consultations (Tilly 2004).

It has therefore been argued that the EU cannot become a democratic federation because it is not a sovereign state (Eriksen and Fossum 2007). However, a comparison of the EU with past federation processes shows that we should abandon the notion of the nation-state as the only locus of democracy. Shared powers, such as alliances between local and federal authorities, can also implement democratic decisions. Moreover, the EU has already acquired more coercive, legal, and political authority than the Dutch union, the United States, and modern Switzerland in their first fifty years of existence (Goldstein 2001). It follows that Euro-democratization is not primarily constrained by the EU institutions' lacking the capacity to act but, rather, by the difficulties experienced by social and political actors in their attempts to empower otherwise isolated citizens to engage with EU governance structures.

Accordingly, we should read the closing sentence of Heidrun Abromeit's book on Euro-democracy—"Something, at any rate, will have to be done" (1998, 169)—as an invitation to study social actors and their potential involvement in Euro-democratization processes. Indeed, by whom will this something have to be done? Which social and political groups might have an interest in constituting a European polity that would establish a more accountable political system, guaranteeing better access to and more participation for European citizens?

Arguably, the making of a transnational European democracy will not happen without popular intervention. Nevertheless, we should not dismiss the role of democratic ideals in the democratization process, in particular in its early stages. In fact, the opposition of critical intellectuals to authoritarian rule has frequently contributed to the revival of the collective identifications that favors democratic mass movements (O'Donnell and Schmitter 1986). However, although Habermas and others have offered valuable propositions on how to reconstitute democracy in the context of the EU integration process (Eriksen and Fossum 2007; Schmitter 2000), the making of a transnational European democracy requires not only democratic theorizing but also social and political actors that have an interest in Euro-democratization. Accordingly, the next section is inspired by the empirical and comparative democratization literature rather than by political theory.

Exploring Future European Union–Polity Developments

Processes of democratization always require a redistribution of power. Rulers have therefore rarely initiated them. The democratization of the EU is, thus, only likely to take place if social forces, such as political parties and social movements, are willing to work in this direction. Although processes of democratization have been pushed further by grassroots social mobilizations, it is also true that new political and social rights have at times been implemented by rulers. The democratization literature emphasizing the role of elites in such processes is considerable (O'Donnell and Schmitter 1986). The success of a democratic transition often depends on successful pacts between soft-liners in the ruling elite and in the opposition. Ruling elites of undemocratic systems often prove to be much less monolithic than we might think. Indeed, some of the old elite might be willing to change their attitudes because this might also improve their probability of staying in a leading position.[5] Nevertheless, even these top-down democratization processes can be explained as responses to latent social and political protest.[6] Unions and other social movements, for example, played a decisive role in the South African transition to democracy (Adler and Webster 1995).

In the case of the EU, this implies that democratization will be possible only when it becomes a goal toward which social actors work. In other words, the constitution of a democratic EU polity, as postulated by Habermas and others, is only likely to happen to the extent that mass movements come to share this objective. In turn, moderates of the ruling elites could compromise on Euro-democratization in order to consolidate the EU integration process. As stated previously, however, the EU democratization process is not likely to simply follow the known trajectory of national democratization processes (Schmitter 2000).

Likewise, the idea of Euro-democratization has, by definition, no place in intergovernmental international relations and EU integration theories. The EU must be democratic because its member states are democratic (Milward 2000). From this perspective, the democratic deficit of the EU is a myth (Moravcsik 2001). Conversely, the so-called neofunctionalists are afraid of a premature politicization of the European integration process because they fear that this could block further integration (Haas 1968). They see further integration as a product of the incremental political action by elites carried out behind the backs of the European citizens. The prospect of a democratic EU is discussed only in federalist integration theories, although Euro-democracy, in this context, is often a mere utopian claim. Although federalists may reasonably argue for the foundation of a European federation, they find it difficult to explain why such a big bang would be likely to happen. However, it is also worth noting that some federalists adopt a more promising research profile, namely, the comparison of past federation processes with the current EU integration process (Gross 1998; Goldstein 2001). Nevertheless, Euro-democratization still represents a rather underdeveloped research area. This is also the case because Euro-democratization is arguably neither the only possible nor the most probable actor strategy regarding the future development of the EU (Marks et al. 1996).

Strategies to Shape Future EU Development

As already stated, Euro-democratization will be compared with other possible European actor strategies, namely, Euro-technocratization and national retrenchment (renationalization). Whereas renationalization refers to a process in which the powers of the EU are rolled back and reestablished at a national level, Euro-technocratization refers to an expansion of apparently apolitical decision making at the EU level, disconnected from partisan politics. Figure 2.1 clarifies the distinctions between those various strategies.

This typology provides us with an analytical framework that facilitates the analysis of the various strategies that actors can pursue regarding the future development of the European integration process. It distinguishes various strategies based on their effect on EU developments rather than actors, which are likely to adopt different strategies in different situations and times. Real-life actors can hardly afford to pursue a simple clear-cut strategy because real situations are hardly ever clear-cut (Crouch 2005).

It follows that I do not aim to put actors into specific categories because this would necessarily entail the use of stylized evidence to ensure that a specific real-life case fits into the desired box. However, acknowledging these practical incongruencies does not imply the end of clear-cut typologies, as suggested by Dølvik (2001). On the contrary, with clear frameworks it is much easier to explain the varying strategic choices of each analyzed actor. Hence, there is no aspiration to put all actors into a specific Euro-democratization, Euro-technocratization, or renationalization box. My aim

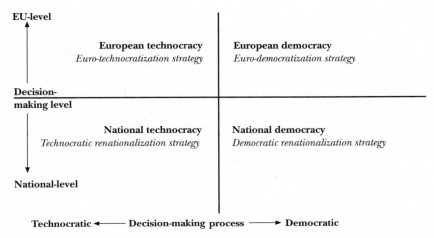

Figure 2.1. European actor strategies leading to alternative EU-polity developments.

is to use the typology as an analytical tool to reveal in each case study the inherent tensions that might trigger institutional change.

No social system is free from incoherencies and contradictions. In the case of the EU, this is even more evident. Its laws and policies mirror compromises among a wide range of various national, social, and political positions. Yet one view typically becomes the dominant one because of joint efforts of dominant economic, social, and political actors, including the courts. For that reason, some authors assert, the dominant technocratic path of EU development does not leave much space for democratic agency. Others, however, maintain that, under the surface of the dominant institutional settings, alternatives always continue to persist. Social and political institutions rarely evolve along a predetermined path, as we understand it today—a fixed, sign-posted road with clear boundaries (Crouch 2005).

Although historical trajectories of economic, social, and political institutions certainly do matter, Colin Crouch suggests that institutional development paths might be rather like medieval pilgrimage routes that included a series of alternatives: "At one point a river might be in flood on the way the pilgrims were using, and local people would tell them when that happened that they had to take a different path through the hills. Or there might be wolves in the hills; in which case another way through was advised" (2005, 1). Crouch not only insists that there are alternative paths of political and socioeconomic development, he also shows that actors are not bound by the gloomy determinism of those who stress the path dependence of institutional and socioeconomic development.

The proposed typology of alternative actor strategies provides, therefore, also a tool to test Crouch's assumptions. Its application in the following empirical chapters shows whether one social actor, namely, organized labor, can leave the dominant technocratic path of EU development. Before that, however, we need to identify the indicators by which we can distinguish our alternative EU-polity actor strategies.

Many authors claim that the activities of EU nongovernmental organizations and interest groups will contribute to a more democratic EU (see Smismans 2006). Their real-life activities, however, do not always fit easily into Habermas's (1992) paradigm of deliberative democracy and civil society. Habermas defines *civil society* as a sphere that is autonomous from the economy and the state, based on deliberation or arguing rather than on political and economic power struggles or bargaining. However, social actors hardly ever conceive of democratization as a goal in its own right. That is to say, they usually favor democratization if they expect that a more democratic polity will provide a framework in which their interests can be better satisfied. Therefore, the Italian Marxist Antonio Gramsci (1992) introduced a concept of civil society that is analytically more useful for the purpose of this study; it acknowledges the interdependence of civil society with the economy and the state and thus sees civil society as an area not only of deliberation but also of economic, political, and ideological struggle (Altvater 1995; Kocka 2000).

This implies that the strategies that actors might adopt to influence the EU integration process are neither simply chosen nor simply structurally predetermined, but also a result of social struggles. Likewise, democracy is not the only outcome of modernization. Technocracy, which is a regime of rational mastery, results from the same process of modernity (Wagner 2001). This claim also raises questions for authors who argue that specific social groups are the genuine proponents of democracy, be it the bourgeoisie, the working class, or the new social movements.[7] In contrast, it seems that the interest of an actor in Euro-democratization, Euro-technocratization, and renationalization depends on the actor's role in the policy-making process; the more access an actor has to decision making, the less the actor's interest in democratization. In order to analyze the various European actor strategies, we must identify the concrete actions that add up to the respective strategies. Hence, it is necessary to operationalize the typology, to use the rather awkward jargon of the social sciences. Therefore, we need to specify the building blocks, or indicators, of each EU-polity actor strategy.

The Euro-Democratization Strategy

Despite their conflicting conclusions about the feasibility of an EU democracy, Habermas and Lepsius concur that social actors contribute to the process of Euro-democratization if they contribute to the rise of a European public sphere. Democracy requires a public sphere in which political leaders are obliged to legitimize their political actions. Governments can be held accountable only if they are obliged to legitimize their actions publicly. The mere existence of a space for communication is not sufficient. The public sphere is more than that. It can be defined as an aggregation of different, publicly accessible, intermediate arenas that include ordinary citizens and the political power. These arenas offer people—mainly via organizations that unite and empower individuals—the possibility to hold government accountable and to participate in the political system. Hence, the realm of the public sphere within a developed Euro-democracy can hardly be limited to the partial public sphere of the 50,000 Euro-professionals (Wolton 1993).

Social actors also promote Euro-democracy if they encourage European collective action. Despite Habermas's questioning of national unity as a precondition of democracy, democracy still requires a minimal feeling of communality among its citizens. EU citizens should recognize that they belong to a common polity. However, the question remains: How can this be achieved? This question can, of course, be answered in various ways, but it is likely that such a common identity is related to collective action. In other words, the feeling of belonging to the same political system will be reinforced if people act together, thus constructing a we-feeling or collective habitus (Büchi 1995). Consequently, citizens' organizations can play an important role in the construction and reproduction of a democratic political community.

Furthermore, actors may contribute to Euro-democracy when they politicize EU-level decision making in a transnational public sphere. This element emphasizes that Euro-democratization is likely to happen only if the process of European integration becomes political in character. If a European political struggle is absent, there is no need to implement democracy as a mechanism of peaceful conflict regulation (Rustow 1970). Accordingly, Thomas Risse and Mareike Kleine (2007) argue that EU policies must become subject to contestation and controversy in the transnational public sphere. However, if actors believe in the availability of national exit options—in alliance with Euro-skeptical parties and groups (Bartolini 2005; Kriesi 2007)—then a politicization of the EU could also lead to a renationalization of EU policies. In this study, however, another indicator captures such a nationalist politicization of the EU, as we will see shortly.

Finally, the development of Euro-democratic convictions will also be an indicator for the adoption of a Euro-democratization strategy. This element emphasizes the importance of Euro-democratic convictions and commitments in the process of democratization. In this sociological study, however, we do not use this indicator because of the widespread rhetorical use of democratic notions, such as the Europe of the citizens.

The Euro-Technocratization Strategy

Whereas Euro-democratization is a process that requires several composite elements, one single indicator can detect the pursuit of a Euro-technocratization strategy. Actors contribute to Euro-technocracy if they support regulatory EU decision making. Actors that have direct access to the regulatory decision making of EU agencies prefer a technocratic form of governance. They do not support the integration of additional actors into the decision-making process because the addition of more voices could reduce the impact of their own activities. This suggests that the status of an actor within the policy-making process is of major significance; whereas insiders generally favor technocratic decision making, outsiders frequently argue in favor of a more democratic form of government.

The Technocratic Renationalization Strategy

By contrast, social actors contribute to technocratic renationalization if they support competition-state nationalism. A technocratic renationalization strategy can be expected if national actors question the feasibility of social-democratic policy making at the national and EU levels, in the context of globalizing capitalism and EU market integration (Scharpf 1999). Its typical sign is a particular design of national corporatist arrangements, not as social-democratic compromises between conflicting class interests but as monistic alliances to boost national competitiveness (Rhodes 1997; Streeck 1998a). As a result, a national competition state (Cerny 1990) replaces the welfare state. However, the adoption of a technocratic renationalization strategy in one policy field (e.g., wage policy) can be compatible with the adoption of a Euro-technocratization strategy in another policy area (e.g., monetary policy).

The Democratic Renationalization Strategy

Finally, actors contribute to a democratic renationalization strategy if they reaffirm the autonomy of the nation-state. Autonomy is the essential precondition of any democratic polity. Democracy as a system of self-determination is possible only if the polity has the capacity to affect the processes that shape the lives of its citizens. Governments can be held accountable only if they can implement the will of the citizens. Correspondingly, an actor that reaffirms the autonomy of the nation-state consolidates the *conditio sine qua non* of national democracy.

Moreover, if actors politicize and reject the EU integration process as a threat to democratic decision making, then they are pursuing a democratic renationalization strategy. In this case, the specific actor still believes in the political decision-making capacity of the nation-state, despite increasing transnational interactions that characterize the ongoing globalization and Europeanization processes.

Table 2.1 restates all indicators identified so far and relates them to the four strategies that social actors may adopt in repose to the EU integration process. This model does not identify a predetermined winning strategy but provides an analytical framework for the following empirical case studies. In summary, social actors contribute to Euro-democratization if they contribute to the making of a European public sphere, act collectively on

Table 2.1. Indicators for actor strategies leading to alternative EU-polity developments

	Actor strategies leading to			
Actor activities	Euro-demo-cratization	Euro-techno-cratization	Technocratic renationalization	Democratic re-nationalization
Creating a European public sphere	**Yes**	No	No	No
Organizing European collective action	**Yes**	No	No	No
Politicizing the EU in the European public sphere	**Yes**	No	No	No
Supporting regulatory EU decision making	No	**Yes**	No	No
Supporting competition state nationalism	No	No	**Yes**	No
Affirming the autonomy of the nation-state	No	No	No	**Yes**
Rejecting the EU integration process	No	No	No	**Yes**

a European level, and politicize the EU integration process in the transnational European public sphere. Conversely, actors that neglect the creation of a European public sphere, that do not participate in European collective action, and that try to enhance the competitiveness of their national economy at the expense of their neighbors are conducting a technocratic renationalization strategy, even if they rhetorically support a social and democratic Europe.

Unions: Actors of Euro-Democratization?

This study examines the strategies that one social actor, organized labor, consciously or unconsciously adopted to influence the EU integration process. The European trade union movement presents an interesting case because it has played a substantial role in national democratization processes (Hobsbawm 1984; Rueschemeyer, Huber Stephens, and Stephens 1992; Florek 1994; Thompson 1994). Moreover, EU integration began essentially as an economic integration process and, as a result, unions were among the first citizens' organizations to be concerned about it (Haas 1968; Gobin 1997; Pasture 2002). Therefore, they might have developed, before other citizens' organizations, a sensitivity concerning the need for the democratization of the EU integration process.

However, even if unions played an important role in past national democratization processes, this does not mean that they will necessarily play a vital role in the Euro-democratization process.[8] In contrast to authoritarian regimes, the EU does not challenge the existence of the unions. As a result, Euro-democratization is not directly related to the most vital interest of the unions, namely, the survival of their own organizations. Whereas the repression of authoritarian regimes impelled unions to support national democratization movements, the EU institutional setting provides different options for labor. Renationalization and EU-technocratization are also seen as available European trade union strategies. Whereas the technocratic renationalization strategy implies that unions, employers, and political leaders have joint national interests, the Euro-technocratization strategy aims to integrate the leading unionists into the existing technocratic EU policy networks.

Despite its internationalist ideology, organized labor is strongly linked to the nation-state.[9] This link has substantive and ideological dimensions. First, specific national arrangements in welfare and labor relations, such as neocorporatist social pacts, integrated the working classes into the nation-state and provided them with an important set of rights and benefits

(Crouch 1993; Esping-Andersen 1990). Second, in the course of the twentieth century, the labor movement often also embraced nationalist ideologies, like most other societal groups (Wets 2000), although the formation of the labor movement has seldom been favored by the state.[10] Nowadays, European nation-states no longer repress the labor movement as they did at the beginning of capitalist expansion in the early nineteenth century. However, this is hardly reason enough to praise the national welfare state as a workers' paradise. The welfare state has negative side effects for labor, too, such as the containment and bureaucratization of unions and the weakening of societal solidarity in the shadow of the national bureaucracies (Narr 1999). Authors who see the nation-state as the safeguard of workers' aspirations usually neglect these points.

Labor history also shows that the labor movement did not start at the national level. The English working class is not alone in having been the product of long and painful historical processes (Thompson 1980). In Germany, for example, the first labor organizations founded by journeymen before 1848 looked like traditional local guilds rather than modern national unions (Schneider 1989). The development of a feeling of communality among workers from different regions was the product of lengthy learning processes. At times, these processes were rooted in tangible acts of transregional solidarity.[11] These arguments are relevant here because they underline the idea that it would be wrong to assume that "the members of national working classes are or ever were homogeneous bodies of Frenchmen, Britons or Italians. . . . All national working classes tend to be heterogeneous, and with multiple identifications, though for certain purposes and at certain times some may loom larger than others" (Hobsbawm 1984, 49). It nevertheless follows that workers' territorial identifications are not eternal. The labor movement is a priori neither local, national, nor international.

The next chapter assesses the question of whether unions could have an interest in Euro-democratization because social actors almost never conceive of democratization as a goal in its own right. There are notable exceptions, however. The Chartist movement in the mid-nineteenth century is one. Although it was undoubtedly a working-class mobilization and probably one of the largest in British history, its demands were exclusively for the democratization of elections. Its supporters may or may not have implied a social program, but Chartism certainly did not have such a program. This provides support for Stedman Jones's (1983) conclusion that early labor activists saw the achievements of political democracy as an end rather than just a means. Hobsbawm supports this view: "since there were very few political democracies in Europe before the very late nineteenth

century, the fight to establish or make effective democratic rights remained primary. By far the most powerful mobilizations of labour on the
continent, e.g. general strikes, were for electoral reform, as in Belgium and
Sweden" (1984, 306). But how can we explain the subsequent shift of organized labor's priorities from political democratization to economic class
struggle? According to Stedman Jones (1983, 178), Chartism lost its appeal because "the labour market and the fate of the producer could no
longer be presented simply as politically determined phenomena." Hence,
it is essential that a study that assesses an actor's contribution to Euro-
democracy emphasizes the actor's interests in such a process. Thus, only if
there is some evidence that Euro-democracy might be congruent with the
material interests of unions does it makes sense to undertake research with
regard to the following question: In what way and under what conditions
do or can European trade unions contribute to a democratization of the
EU?

The behavior of a social organization is not determined only by the aims
of its members; the particular political and socioeconomic context and the
means available also affect its action. This explains why we should describe
contemporary unions as intermediary organizations, as organizations that
attempt to reconcile members' aspirations with general public interests,
external restrictions, and the available power resources (Müller-Jentsch
1986).

CHAPTER THREE

Do Unions Have an Interest in Euro-Democratization?

T he activities that unions adopted in response to the EU integration process reflect two factors: the restrictions of the power of labor in the given political and socioeconomic context and the gains expected by labor that are associated with alternative EU developments. In order to understand the process of union Europeanization, this chapter first discusses the mechanism through which unions generate power at the national and EU levels. Then it confronts the power resources of unions at the national and EU levels with the prospects and dilemmas of the four EU-polity strategies we have identified.

Power Resources of Organized Labor

Mobilization Power in the Workplace

Typically, the workplace is the main power base of unions. Their ability to wage industrial action can be seen as the constitutive power of organized labor; however, although strikes still play a major role in the hagiography of the labor movement, their frequency has declined during the last decades. The growing cross-border mobility of capital provides employers with a wider range of possibilities to counter workplace collective action on the part of labor. Threats to delocalize enterprises have considerably weakened workplace union power, even if capital is not as footloose as is often alleged. The ongoing restructuring processes of the economy have also weakened union power; not only do unions have problems organizing

[29]

new members in the growing service sectors (Dribbusch 2003b), but they are also losing members due to the decline of well-unionized industries.

However, the demise and relocation of the traditional mass-production plants do not necessarily put an end to the union movement. Many emerging companies have a great interest in a highly skilled and motivated core workforce. Therefore, management and labor might cooperate if unions could provide crucial services to these new corporations and their employees, such as lifelong learning. Hence, cooperation between capital and labor would no longer aim to contain industrial conflicts but would focus on the mutual gains of cooperation (Kochan and Osterman 1994). Nevertheless, it would be tantamount to deceit to say that power struggles might disappear in this new world of the postfordist[1] meta-corporation (Sabel 1991). However, these conflicts could take place between the small groups of core workers, who can use their power to extract benefits, and the excluded marginalized peripheral workforce rather than between capital and labor. Even if workers might still be interested in collective organization, this polarization trend obviously undermines worker solidarity and, thus, workers' capacity for collective industrial action within the firm (Hyman 1999).

In Europe, however, the loss of the capacity of labor to wage successful industrial action has been partially compensated by institutionalized forms of workplace labor representation. Examples of this include national laws on union recognition as well as national and EU rules on statutory employee involvement in company governance, for example through freely elected works councils. Legislation and politics seem to be becoming an increasingly important sphere for organized labor. This leads us to the second form of union power—political mobilization power.

Political Mobilization Power

The second source of union resources is linked to the capacity of unions for political mobilization. This resource is generated through either parliamentary or extra-parliamentary channels of influence, mirroring "political and economic institutions, the choices of party and governmental leaders, union identities, and the choices of union leaders" (Hamann and Kelly 2004, 112). In the economic sphere, the power of management frequently overwhelms employees because of the asymmetric relation between these two labor-market actors: the mobility of labor is much more limited than the mobility of capital. Also, economists acknowledge that dismissed employees bear a stigma that makes it difficult for them to obtain another job. It is also very difficult for dismissed employees to exist without employment, putting them into a far more disadvantageous position than the employer who loses only rent from the employee's labor (Stiglitz 2002). However, democratic political systems allowed labor to shift the conflict between employers and employees from the marketplace to the political arena (Esping-Andersen and Korpi 1984). The fact that the number of workers tends to be higher than the number of capitalists provides labor with a structural political advantage. This explains why the European labor movement fought for centuries for the extension of the franchise. Friedrich Engels, for instance, saw democratization as the strongest weapon for the emancipation of the workers and of humankind:

> The revolutionary workers of the Latin countries had been wont to regard the suffrage as a snare, as an instrument of government trickery. It was otherwise in Germany. *The Communist Manifesto* had already proclaimed the winning of universal suffrage, of democracy, as one of the first and most important tasks of the militant proletariat, and Lassalle had again taken up this point. When Bismarck found himself compelled to introduce the franchise as the only means of interesting the mass of the people in his plans, our workers immediately took it in earnest and sent August Bebel to the first, constituent Reichstag. And from that day on, they have used the franchise in a way which has paid them a thousand fold and has served as a model to the workers of all countries. The franchise has been . . . transformed . . . from a means of deception, which it was heretofore, into an instrument of emancipation. (2007 [1895])

Although variable electoral success and emerging oligarchic tendencies in labor parties often frustrated these hopes (Michels 1999 [1911]; Sassoon 1997), the extension of political citizenship rights has undeniably favored the emergence of social rights (Marshall 1992 [1950]). The major achievements of organized labor in Europe, such as the establishment of the welfare state, cannot be explained without highlighting the close interaction between unions and their allied parties (Bartolini 2000). The rule of law and free elections seem to be compatible with mass-market consumerist capitalism, but the issue of democracy is even more central to its social-democratic transformation (Sklair 2001). It should also be noted that the welfare state transformed the labor market not only through labor law, but also by applying a wide variety of social policies and by using its powers as an important economic agent.[2]

Today, there is a heightening tension between labor parties and the union movement (Höpner 2003; Waddington 2003). Many modern social-democratic leaders portray themselves as brokers of economic reform rather than advocates of labor. Some have argued that this trend just reflects declining union membership and, thus, the declining electoral significance of unions (Piazza 2001), whereas advocates of the new labor approach have suggested that union-labor party relations deteriorated due to inflexible union policies (Streeck 2000; Ferrera, Hemerijck, and Rhodes 2000). Yet many European social-democratic parties still owe their strength at least partly to union support.[3] Although the union vote cannot and never could secure an electoral victory, the growing frustrations of unionists might ensure electoral defeat, as recently experienced by the former German chancellor Gerhard Schröder.

Political union power can also be a result of the frequently proven capacity of unions to organize huge political demonstrations and relatively concise political strikes. These can force political leaders to mitigate or even abandon unsocial policies. This political mobilizing capacity is not necessarily linked to high membership figures but, instead, to the capacity of the union movement to galvanize support from public opinion. Examples of the political effects of extra-parliamentary union mobilizations can be found, for instance, in recent Italian history. The first Silvio Berlusconi government completely ignored the unions and paid a high price for this attitude—in 1994 Italy saw one of the largest union demonstrations in its history, a demonstration that was in no small part responsible for the defeat of Berlusconi's pension reform and the fall of his first government. In 2002, the second Berlusconi government provoked several general strikes against its plans to eliminate provisions prohibiting unjust dismissals (Mania and Sateriale 2002). Eventually, the government had to make concessions to win the support of at least two moderate union confederations, CISL and UIL. Similar examples can also be found in France; in 1995 and 2006, massive strike waves prevented conservative governments from changing major social security and labor law provisions (Pernot 2005). Hence, strikes can still be successful even in a globalizing economy (Frege and Kelly 2004). However, because these strikes are typically seeking political concessions from the government rather than economic ones from employers, they represent a case of political rather than economic mobilization power.

Exchange Power

The third source of union power can be described as the capacity to conclude exchanges with employers and/or political leaders. This power resource is ironically linked to a (partial) renunciation of the two previous sources of power, the capacity to wage industrial action and political mobilization. In other words, employers or the government can trade goods in exchange for social consent with unions that could threaten to withdraw it (Pizzorno 1978).

In the economic sphere, unions typically seek to conclude collective agreements with organized capital in exchange for social peace. In recent times, organized labor has also offered employers its collaboration to persuade workers to use controversial technologies, to respect safety regulations, or to retrain. In addition, unions and employers can jointly lobby politicians in favor of their industries. Employers often welcome such collaboration because unions usually possess better connections to center-left politicians. Typical examples of this type of partnership can be found in the German and European chemical and pharmaceutical industry, in which capital and labor often joined forces to counter green policy proposals.

In politics, unions use exchange power when they organize political exchanges with political leaders. Usually unions share the burden of the legitimization of a contested political decision in exchange for union-favorable government policy. For example, unions may accept wage moderation in exchange for union-favorable legislation as regards workplace co-determination rights (Trentin 1994). Sometimes, exchange power can even take a rather symbolic form, in which neither political leaders nor unions exchange any goods but only information, expertise, and legitimacy (Crouch 2000c). In this context, unions are no longer a counter-power but an actor within a neocorporatist policy network that also assumes governmental functions. Even if these exchanges often lead to positive-sum games, neocorporatism can also be risky for labor; the main problems are "an inability to trust" capital and government, inadequate information to judge the nature of an issue, and the "contingent, future nature of gains" in compensation for present sacrifices (Crouch 1993, 44).

However, the paradox of exchange power is its dependence on the capacity of labor to threaten the social consensus. The exchange power of a union depends on its mobilization power. In consequence, exchange power uses—but does not reproduce—mobilization power. The use of exchange power might even cause a decline in union membership that would finally undermine the very capacity to conclude exchanges. If mobilization power is low, then exchange power is low, too. In contrast, high mobilization power does not inevitably generate high exchange power because the latter also requires the capacity of the union to control its membership (Müller-Jentsch 1986).

Union Power Resources within the European Union Polity

Workplace Mobilization Power

The process of economic Europeanization, accelerated by the 1992 single-market program and European Monetary Union, is a strong reason to develop cross-border cooperation among unions, "to keep workers from being played off against each other, undermining wage and labor standards" (Martin and Ross 1999, 312). Although this has been difficult to achieve, the existence of transnational workplace mobilization power has been demonstrated by several Euro-strikes in the manufacturing sector and in the transport sector (Dufresne 2006; da Costa and Rehfeldt 2006). The March 6, 1997, strike against the closure of the Renault-Vilvoorde plant near Brussels especially generated headlines in the press. This strike was supported by almost all of the 4,000 Belgian and by 20,000 French and 5,000 Spanish Renault workers (Langneau and Lefébure 1999). Although it did not prevent the end of car production in Vilvoorde, it was perceived as a success for the labor movement (Vanhulle and Van Grop 1998). First, a court condemned Renault for not having consulted its European works council (EWC) in good time. This ruling also clarified the definitions of information and consultation in the EWC directive (Rehfeldt 1998). Second, the Vilvoorde case noticeably accelerated the adoption of the new EU directive on information and consultation (Bercusson 2002). Third, and most important, the Vilvoorde case confirmed that transnational collective action is possible.

The Vilvoorde case became a paradigm for transnational collective action, and many unionists explicitly referred to it, for instance, during a transnational General Motors (GM) strike against the closure of its Luton plant. On January 25, 2001, the EWC of GM called for a Europe-wide day of action, and about 40,000 European GM workers joined the corresponding strike actions.[4] This strike was quite successful, and the GM management signed a pioneering framework-restructuring agreement to avoid forced redundancies in all European plants (Carley 2001). It is noteworthy that only some months earlier Hancké (2000, 55) concluded, drawing on evidence from GM, that EWCs in the motor industry have "failed to become a pan-European vehicle for trade union coordination." Today, this statement ought to be revised. At least in unionized sectors, EWCs definitely facilitated the transnational coordination of union action (da Costa and Rehfeldt 2006; Pulignano 2006). Apparently, Hancké's view was based on the flawed Olsonian assumption that self-interest and union solidarity must be mutually exclusive (Crouch 1982).

Nevertheless, it would be equally wrong to argue that workplace mobilization power is, today, a significant union resource at the EU level. In addition to the usual dilemmas of collective action and the limitations of the strike weapon in the context of the ongoing capitalist restructuring processes already described, organizers of European workplace mobilizations face the following practical problems. First, the legal rights to strike differ among the EU member states. Whereas, for example, in Germany the right to strike is a collective and highly regulated right, the French constitution defines it as a fundamental individual right. Furthermore, the relevant EU law is ambiguous. Whereas Article 28 of the Charter of Fundamental Rights of the EU recognizes the individual and the collective right to strike, in accordance with community law and national laws and practices, Article 137 (6) of the Treaty establishing the European Community (TEC) explicitly excludes the adoption of directives that would regulate the freedom of coalition and the right to strike. Hence, although the EU recognizes these rights, it has no competence to harmonize them.[5]

The second problem reflects the diverse habits of the different European trade unions, mirroring different state traditions, capitalisms, and cultures (Hyman 2001; Crouch 1993). These varieties of national experiences and traditions question a frequent assumption of the industrial relations literature, that is, the existence of a common workers' interest. Mobilization theory suggests that, even at the local and national level, the transformation of a set of individuals into a collective actor is usually the work of a small but critical mass of activists that convince workers to consider a hitherto accepted situation as unjust (Kelly 1998). Therefore, collective action involves intense discussion processes among activists and workers and, eventually, a high degree of group cohesion. But how can transnational workplace-based union solidarity be forged when local unionists have little chance of communicating with one another? For decades, EU trade union politics was exclusively a matter for a small number of union executives (Turner 1996).

Since the adoption of the EWC directive in 1994, however, the number of unionists who are directly involved in EU affairs has been increasing. In spite of this, the mere existence of an EWC is no guarantee of an internationalist union policy (Streeck 1997). Tony Royle (2000) shows, for example, how McDonalds exploited the numerous loopholes of the EWC directive without difficulty. On the other hand, examples such as the Renault Vilvoorde and the GM cases also allow for more optimistic conclusions. This corroborates Thomas Klebe and Siegfried Roth's (2000) point: EWCs can provide a useful framework for learning and trust-building processes among unionists from different countries, even in the very competitive motor industry. However, these processes would probably not have happened without transnational union contacts that had been established in addition to the official EWC structures.[6] Bob Hancké (2000) correctly underlines that a strengthening of the EWC depends on a strengthening of the links among local branches, national unions, and EWCs.

Finally, the central company management might have an interest in functioning EWCs. The production process increasingly transcends national boundaries (Dicken 2003). This has also led to a concentration of the decision making in multinationals at the EU level and, thus, the rise of Euro-companies (Marginson 2000). Moreover, the just-in-time logistics of postfordist corporations is heavily dependent on a smooth management of its transnational production chains. Therefore, even a strike in a small, but centrally located, plant of a postfordist production network could have a huge impact (Moody 1997). Paraphrasing Lenin, we could argue that a production "chain is only as strong as its weakest link" (Lenin 1917). This explains why some multinationals are advocating decentralized collective bargaining while, at the same time, supporting EWCs (Marginson and Sisson 1996). Although EWCs centralize consultation at the EU level, they are beneficial for the management because the involvement of EWCs "can reduce the potential for conflict and increase the likelihood of employee acceptance of the decisions taken" (European Parliament 2001, 13).

Nevertheless, the workplace mobilization power of labor remains weak at the EU level. This power cannot explain most of the achievements of the European trade unions, such as the social protocol of the Maastricht Treaty that established the social partners' prominent role in the EU social policy. How can we explain that the European employers' associations, Business Europe (the former Union of Industrial and Employers' Confederations of Europe, UNICE) and European Centre of Enterprises with Public Participation and of Enterprises of General Economic Interest (CEEP) concluded legally binding European social-dialog agreements with the European Trade Union Confederation (ETUC)? This question leads us to the politics-based power resources of the European trade unions.

Political Mobilization Power

The essential power resource of unions at the EU level arises from institutionalized political action. From the beginning of the European integration process, the unions tried to use their relations with political leaders to ensure union representation in European institutions, such as the Economic and Social Committee, the European Commission, and the European Parliament (Gobin 1996; Smismans 2000). Moreover, long before the creation of European university institutes, many union officials had acquired intercultural skills due to their exposure to political and labor migration and their work within international labor organizations that allowed them to become civil servants in European institutions (Wagner 2004, 2005). Therefore, the unions hoped to "be able to control the policies of these institutions and to prevent that they would become antagonistic to the workers' interests" (Pasture 2000, 22). However, these activities were hardly ever supported by either the mobilization of rank-and-file unionists or the strong involvement of local and national unions at the EU level.

The political power of EU-level union activities and institutions owes much to the political recognition of the European social partners as co-regulators of social policy by the European Commission during the presidency of Jacques Delors. This policy aimed at mobilizing political resources for the Commission itself, to calm some of the fears that the single market had provoked in European unions, and to help the Commission acquire labor support for its strategies (Martin and Ross 1999). The integration of a social protocol in the Maastricht Treaty institutionalized this recognition. This process led to some achievements, such as the European social-dialog agreements, as well as the European Works Council, the Information and Consultation, and the Posted Workers directives.

Nevertheless, the EU-level union organizations rely heavily on support from the European Commission (Waddington, Hoffmann, and Lind 1997). The European employers' organizations signed the European social-dialog agreements mainly to prevent a probably more constraining initiative of the Commission in favor of a respective EU directive. EU-level union organizations followed a logic of influence in respect to the European Commission rather than a logic of voice, which would have involved political mobilizations (Dølvik 1997; Léonard et al. 2007).

This ambiguous development of EU-level union structures engendered conflicting theses concerning the impact of the EU on European collective action. Corinne Gobin (1997); Andrew Martin (1996); and Jeremy Waddington, Rainer Hoffmann, and Jens Lind (1997) suggest that the ideological, political, and financial reliance of ETUC on the support from the Commission actually hinders the development of transnational union action. Likewise, Jean-Marie Pernot (1998) and Gobin (2005) argue that the rising access of national union delegates to EU politics via the EU-level union structures contributed to the dissemination of a Eurocratic jargon and policy style rather than to the birth of a genuine European labor movement. Lowell Turner (1996) shares this view, but he also argues that the

EU-level union structures could provide a useful framework for transnational union action. The EU-level union structures could open up channels of cooperation among national unions.

Since the mid-1990s, the European unions have been realizing the danger of their dependency on the goodwill of the increasingly free-market-oriented European Commission (Léonard et al. 2007). The more the Commission shifted to the right, the fewer EU directives reflected the concerns of labor. Conversely, unions began to act more independently. In particular, Belgian and Mediterranean unions pressed the ETUC to organize and to support several European rallies. Examples of the latter include the huge *Euro-manif* (demonstration) against the closure of the Vilvoorde plant of 70,000 unionists in March 1997 and, ever since, the recurring ETUC mass demonstrations before crucial European Council and Parliament sessions (Taylor and Mathers 2004; Turnbull 2006). It would be wrong, however, to contrast public actions and political lobbying. The unions use both channels of political influence, which complement and reinforce one another. It is worth mentioning that the European Council, at its Laeken summit, attributed three seats in the EU constitutional convention to the social partners. Incidentally, the day before, the ETUC had just proved its mobilization capacity by mobilizing 100,000 protesters for its Euro-demonstration on December 13, 2001.

The ETUC is a politically pluralistic organization. It does not maintain privileged relations with a specific political group at the EU level, in contrast to many of its national affiliates. Nevertheless, it retains a considerable political influence at the EU level because union support proved to be crucial for the development of the EU integration process. Unions played a decisive role in pro-European referendum campaigns in many countries. It is, for instance, questionable whether the Maastricht Treaty would have been ratified in all EU member states if the ETUC had opposed it. As a result, the ETUC retains political influence, without being linked to a political group in the European Parliament. Instead, it coordinates its EU-level lobbying activities through an intergroup of union-friendly members of the European Parliament (MEPs) from almost all political groups, union-friendly Commission and Council officials, and union-friendly members of national delegations, such as the social attachés in the German and the Austrian embassies in Brussels. This leads us to the third power resource of unions, political exchange power.

Exchange Power

Given the weak European workplace mobilization power, European trade unions have, up to now, used mainly politics-based exchange power.

From the very beginning of the EU integration process, unions frequently used this power resource to influence it.

After the Second World War, labor played an important role in international relations, especially during the Cold War. Union organizations were a major political force virtually everywhere. Inevitably, this close relationship between unions and the political process has attracted the attention of competing superpowers and their intelligence services seeking to influence the political affairs of those countries in which the unions are active. The occupying powers in Germany found that one of the principal problems in the reconstruction of the European political and economic structures was the battle for control of the unions. It follows that Soviet and U.S. agencies sponsored unions in order to support them in their fight for and against communism (Munck 2002). As a consequence, the activities of the international union movement extend far beyond the narrow confines of collective bargaining. "The trades union vehicle is an excellent method of channeling assistance abroad"; union organizations have been, "more than any area outside the military," prime actors in the Cold War (Busch 1983, 262). This political context also shaped the European integration process. The West German trade union confederation (Deutscher Gewerkschaftsbund, DGB) supported the Robert Schuman plan for the creation of the European Coal and Steel Community precisely because its leaders preferred the European steel union to Stalin's Soviet Union.

The Cold War was not the only reason why most social democratic and Christian unions supported the European integration process from its very inception. Their pro-European orientation also reflected the negative experiences of the unions with economic nationalism (Pasture 2002). Not only were they aware of the danger that business interests would capture the European integration process, but most Benelux, German, and Italian unions also believed that the creation of a common market would be a prerequisite for economic growth and, thus, also a prerequisite for the creation of the welfare state. This also explains the paradox, Pasture (2002) argues, of why unions initially did not call for a European social policy.

It should be emphasized that the unions sought tangible compensation from governments for their support of the European integration process. Whereas the German Social-Democratic Party (Sozialdemokratische Partei Deutschlands, SPD) rejected the Schuman plan, the DGB supported the Konrad Adenauer government on this issue.[7] In exchange, the first German member of the High Authority (later, the European Commission) was a former unionist. The DGB also obtained the right to appoint several social attachés for the different German embassies, including in Brussels, and the Adenauer government passed a co-determination law for the coal and steel industries that gave unions equal representation on the companies' supervisory boards in relation to its shareholders. After the DGB announced its support for the Schuman plan, Adenauer declared at a meeting of his Christian democratic party (CDU) that the DGB would never have supported the Schuman plan had it not obtained the co-determination law for the coal and steel industries in exchange (Schönhoven and Weber 1996).

This sort of political exchange became the most important model for EU-level union action. Throughout the whole EU integration process, this political exchange pattern has continued. Unions and the Commission engage in a mutual exchange of legitimacy (Crouch 2000c). Even if economic and political integration put pressure on labor, most unions offered EU leaders their support in legitimizing the EU in exchange for certain advantages, such as the recognition of the ETUC as a social partner.

The Delors Commission rewarded the unions for their support for the EU integration process, especially through its support for the European social dialog. It is noteworthy that the Commission, and not the ETUC, frequently convinced the European employers' organizations to sign European social-dialog agreements (Falkner 2003). It was not that the employers feared the mobilization powers of the unions. They typically signed European agreements only if they feared that the Commission would propose a more restrictive directive in the event of social partners failing to reach an agreement. Correspondingly, the European social dialog ceased to produce major results after the increasingly neoliberal political climate within the Commission restricted the scope and opportunity for an activist European social policy (Léonard et al. 2007).

Because of the European social dialog, the ETUC became a co-regulator of EU social policy, but in this policy field the EU competencies remain very limited (Leibfried and Pierson 2000). In decisive policy fields, namely, economic, monetary and competition policy, the unions remained at the margins of EU-level decision making because the decisions in those areas are not based on partisan politics. The technocratic institutional design of the European Central Bank and other regulatory EU agencies effectively frees these institutions from the pressures of democratic decision making (Majone 1994b).

Which EU Polity Development Would Favor Labor Interests?

When we examine our four alternative EU polity developments—Euro-technocratization, Euro-democratization, technocratic renationalization, and democratic renationalization—we must reiterate that social actors rarely conceive of democratization as a goal in its own right. Therefore, this section first analyzes the relation between the different polity strategies and the union power resources in the given EU context. Then, it considers the gains or losses for the unions linked with these different polity strategies.

Euro-Technocratization

Granted the absence of workplace-based mobilization power and the fragile European political mobilization power, EU-level union organizations, such as the ETUC, base their work on rather weak political exchange power. Union officials sit on relevant EU committees. Within the macroeconomic dialog, for instance, representatives of the European Council, the Commission, the European social partners, and the European Central Bank discuss monetary, budgetary, and wage policy, even if the debates are confidential and no formal conclusions are drawn.

Euro-technocratization could be a possible European trade union strategy. It would legitimize the EU-level union structures, and it might also generate some results. EU institutions favor union participation in EU policy making because they require union expertise and legitimacy in some areas, such as social and employment policy. However, the adoption of a Euro-technocratization strategy also has its costs, namely, a reduction of the social and political objectives of labor. Indeed, unions might increasingly become narrow-minded actors that operate in very limited policy areas, neglecting their broader original values of economic, social, and political emancipation.

Although Euro-technocratization might represent an option for labor, the empirical chapters that follow demonstrate that such a strategy also faces major contradictions. The following thesis drawn from this section is also considered: the greater the impact of EU policy making and the weaker the power resources of the unions, the more labor will pursue a Euro-technocratic strategy.

Democratic Renationalization

If organized labor still has confidence in its national power resources and believes that it can pursue national economic and social policies, it will tend to reject the European integration process as a capitalist project and try to pursue a welfare state renationalization strategy. To some extent, this argument of the traditional anti-European left seems rational, given the pervasive impact of neoliberal ideology on EU economic policy, even if we differentiate between the making of the EU and the transformation processes linked to capitalist globalization (Altvater and Mahnkopf 1999). Another factor that favors a renationalization strategy is rooted in the following perception. Unionists often consider the social and political situation in their own country to be better than the situation in other countries. For instance, some German unionists wrongly concluded from the fact that the chair of the French *comité d'entreprise* is an employer representative that this institution cannot work properly. In reality, French unions and works councils have more power resources than we might expect, especially considering the low level of French union membership. This lack of direct workplace mobilization power is considerably compensated not only by the well-known political mobilization power of French unions but also by highly institutionalized workplace-based power resources.[8]

During recent years, however, this renationalization strategy has lost much of its appeal. The demise of national, egalitarian Keynesian policy and the rise of economic globalization during the last two decades have undermined the prospects of social democracy or democratic socialism in a single country.[9] Moreover, even if left critics of the EU were correct, this would not inevitably provide support for a democratic renationalization strategy. Paradoxically, Richard Hyman argues, "if the pessimistic scenario holds true, and if the scope for effective action at national level becomes systematically reduced, the pressures for effective transnationalism will intensify. There exists genuine scope for strategic intervention" (2000, 81).

Again, it is the task of the empirical chapters that follow to analyze whether and under which conditions organized labor does pursue such a democratic renationalization strategy. The decrease in the national power resources of labor due to increased capital exit options suggests that the prospects of this strategy are declining. Accordingly, we can draw the following thesis from this section: the weaker the impact of EU policy making, the greater the unions' national power resources, and the weaker their expected power gains in both a technocratic and democratic EU polity, the more organized labor will pursue a democratic renationalization strategy.

Technocratic Renationalization

The lack of workplace-based mobilization power and the fragile political mobilization power at the EU level could also lead to the other type of renationalization strategy. If organized labor has lost its confidence in national, egalitarian Keynesian policy but does not believe in a possible social and democratic EU, it could pursue a competition state renationalization strategy, as advocated, for instance, by Wolfgang Streeck (1998a).

The typical expressions of this strategy are corporatist arrangements, such as social pacts, that aim to increase the competitiveness of the national economy while neglecting the question of fair distribution between capital and labor. Hence, these pacts accept wage moderation as an alternativeless imperative and abandon the notion of political choice that is at the heart of democratic politics. Social pacts may eventually encourage international free-floating capital to invest in the particular national economy. At this moment, unions hope that this will also lead to an increase in employment that will compensate the concessions made by labor within the social pact. These hopes may prove illusory, however, because such social pacts could degenerate into a set of competing national beggar-thy-neighbor strategies (Martin 2000). If the neighboring country also reacts with competitive concession bargaining, the competitive advantage of the first country rapidly shrinks. This may lead to a downward spiral of repeated circles of concession bargaining and, thus, to further social dumping and mercantilist races leading to a deflationary spiral that destroys any success achieved on the growth and employment fronts (Noé 1998). This danger exists especially in euroland because flexible exchange rates can no longer compensate extraordinarily high (or low) labor-cost increases by a devaluation (or revaluation). Even if some national economies were winners in such a competition, it might on the whole be self-defeating. This danger has also provoked a countertrend—some unions have started to coordinate their bargaining policy transnationally. Nevertheless, Jelle Visser's (2002) analysis of European wage bargaining trends highlights the resilient tendencies that support the following technocratic renationalization strategy thesis: the weaker the impact of EU policy making, the weaker the national power resources of the unions, and the weaker their expected power gains in both a technocratic and democratic EU polity, the more labor will pursue a technocratic renationalization strategy.

A competing thesis might also sound quite reasonable: the combination of weak EU politics, weak unions, and declining prospects for power resource gains for unions could undermine their capacity to be a strategic actor at all. However, even then, labor still can do something, as shown by the court-oriented litigation strategy of some U.S. unions (Greven 2003). Actually, litigation could also be interpreted as a technocratic attempt that uses the rational logic of the legal system for the benefit of labor, but given the current hegemony of the market logic, we relate technocracy exclusively to the capitalist process of rational mastery (Wagner 2001).

Euro-Democratization

Given the limitations of Euro-technocratization and the limited exit options of renationalization, we might expect an increasing expression of the union voice at the EU level (Hirschman 1970). Indeed, a growth of the union voice can be observed, as demonstrated by the recent increase in Euro-demonstrations. Most of these mobilizations target political aims, such as EU Treaty revisions and EU directives. Likewise, many of the European mobilizations that took place at the company level also focused on political issues, such as more consultation rights for EWCs.

Politics-based mobilization power becomes more effective the more the specific political system provides access and participation opportunities to its citizens. However, under the condition of a remote political system, there is a high probability that such mobilizations will be erratic, if they take place at all. In addition, the logic of political exchange is available only to the extent that the political leaders or central bankers at the EU level need the unions to legitimize, accomplish, or implement political or economic decisions. Nevertheless, the remoteness of the EU institutions and the fact that an important number of decisions at the EU level are treated in regulatory and not political terms allow EU decision makers so far to bypass democratic accountability.

In a more democratic EU polity, this would change. Thus, unions might have an interest in Euro-democratization. Active union support in favor of the democratization of the EU would be consistent not only with union democratic programs but also with realistic attempts by unions to increase their power resources. Given the growing impact of EU policy making, European trade unions could have an interest in a transformation of the EU "from an elitist to a popular project" (Hyman 2000, 81).

The case studies that follow examine whether labor is capable of overcoming the internal and external obstacles of such a Euro-democratization strategy. In line with the preceding discussion, labor is expected to adopt this strategy under the following conditions: the greater the impact of EU policy making, the stronger the power resources of the unions, and the greater their expected gains of power in a democratic EU polity, the more the unions will pursue a Euro-democratization strategy.

This chapter has provided a preliminary discussion of different strategies for organized labor concerning the EU integration process. Are unions to be considered actors of Euro-democratization, Euro-technocratization, or renationalization? At present it is premature to draw any conclusion about these issues, given the conflicting views of the reviewed literature. Whereas Streeck (1998b) recommends the adoption of a technocratic renationalization strategy, others argue that unions understand that, more than ever, there is an urgency to unite across national boundaries; but even authors who question Streeck's views cannot dismiss the

obstacles to a Euro-democratization strategy. These include external obstacles, such as the neoliberal dynamic of the EU integration process that
is built into its technocratic polity framework (Scharpf 1999), and internal obstacles, such as the diversity of national union traditions that make
it difficult to construct a genuine European trade union movement.

PART TWO
European Labor
Wage-Bargaining Strategies

Wage Policy and the European
Monetary Union

The national wage-bargaining systems of Europe are exposed to increased pressures due to the establishment of the single market, the European Monetary Union (EMU), and the process of economic globalization. Whereas we can observe an organized decentralization of wage-bargaining systems in some countries, in others centralized social pacts have been concluded. In both cases, unions seem to be forced to accept less favorable bargaining outcomes, and it is often stated that unions could not pursue alternative bargaining policies beyond competitive corporatism. However, is there really no alternative to concession bargaining to remain, at least, at the negotiating table? Although unions could theoretically limit the competitive pressures on national bargaining systems through a coordination of their wage policies at the EU level, the question remains as to whether this proposal is more than wishful thinking.

The topic is relevant to this study because collective bargaining is still at the core of the activities of organized labor. It follows that union attitudes toward wage bargaining must also affect their actions and emerging strategies relating to the EU integration process. The analysis of labor wage-bargaining policies provides insights not only for the future of EU labor relations but also for the making of the EU polity. It is, however, first necessary to review the wage policy context in the EU, especially in the age of the single European currency. In so doing, the aim is to identify the impact of EU policy making in the field of wage bargaining, to assess the power resources of labor in this field, and to reveal the potential gains and losses that could be expected from each of the four emerging EU-polity strategies identified earlier.

European Politics of Collective Wage Bargaining

Defending labor's share of the national income represents a core objective of any union. It follows that wage policy is a central field of union activities, but unions are obviously neither the only, nor the main, actor in the labor market. In addition, the employers and their organizations, governments, central banks, the traders on the currency markets, and free-trade regimes play important roles in wage setting. Exchange rates, in particular, have often played an important role in adjusting national wages levels in the case of external shocks. This happens not only through devaluation when a national economy becomes uncompetitive but also through revaluation in the opposite case. With the introduction of the EMU, this adjustment mechanism has disappeared within the eurozone. This could be problematic, given the differences of productivity and wage levels within euroland.

In this context, the question arises as to whether there are any alternatives to massive deflation and real-wage reductions when one euroland country is asymmetrically affected by an economic crisis. It is noteworthy that most authors deny the viability of any alternative solutions, such as federal solidarity or increased transnational labor migration (Pochet and Vanhercke 1998). The mainstream literature disagrees only regarding the methods needed to achieve a more flexible labor market.

From a neoliberal perspective, only a complete dismantling of national wage-bargaining systems seems to be promising (Siebert 1997). Even if a centralized system of wage determination would have the ability to impose wage moderation (Calmfors and Driffill 1988), Siebert prefers, as do most orthodox economists, the free-market solution. This would be the only solution, according to the neoliberal orthodoxy, that achieves both low inflation and low unemployment. It seems that the EU integration process has undermined the autonomy of national wage bargaining systems. As a consequence, many have argued that the European social-democratic class compromise has lost its viability. This suggests that any democratic renationalization strategy of labor in the field of wage bargaining would be doomed to fail because national systems are losing their autonomy to regulate an ever more disorganized capitalism (Offe 1985).

The Resurgence of the Technocratic Free-Market Paradigm

This view is disputed by authors who stress the high social and political cost and, in consequence, the unlikely success of radical neoliberal shock therapies in democracies.[1] As an alternative, a new type of corporatist agreement at the national level has been suggested, namely, competitive corporatism (Rhodes 1997). Such arrangements could provide a functional equivalent of devaluation, but from the viewpoint of labor neither the neoliberal nor the competitive corporatist perspective is a priori very promising (Hassel 1999). In contrast to the social-democratic neocorporatism of the 1970s, competitive corporatism accepts the primacy of competitiveness and global capitalism. Moreover, competitive corporatism is basically a nationalistic strategy that transfers the microeconomic logic of competition between companies to the macro level. This leads to the idea of competition between nation-states, or regime competition.

Unions also conclude national social pacts to obtain political aims, but the compensations these pacts offer unions is often smaller than the benefits obtained through the generalized, political exchanges between capital, labor and the state of the 1970s (Marin 1990; Pizzorno 1978). Nevertheless, Crouch argued, the new national social pacts also contribute to a consolidation of the organizational interests of labor in an unfavorable socioeconomic environment and in the context of declining union density and militancy (table 4.1) (2000c). In concluding social pacts, unions usually aim to secure their position as a key actor, not only in labor relations but also in the broader context of economic and social policies. This is often the main compensation such agreements offer unions, but if the power resources of unions are weak, social pacts often become a goal in themselves. To date, examples of social dialog can be found in every Western European country except the United Kingdom. Even in France, the archetypical case of contestation in European labor relations typologies (Crouch 1999), the negotiations between the social partners cover a wide range of issues, from the single work contract to the jointly administered social security agencies.

Social dialog seems to be more stable in countries with weaker, but still effective, labor movements. Unions often adopt national social pacts out of a generalized feeling of weakness, in the belief that there are no alternatives (Bispinck and Schulten 2000) and because of the decline of their national power resources. Lodewijk de Waal, the president of the Dutch union confederation Federatie Nederlandse Vakbeweging (FNV), has stated that an increase in union membership above 35 percent of the workforce would not be good for the Dutch model of social dialog because its

European Unions

Table 4.1. Union density and militancy in Western Europe[a]

	Union density (%)[b]			Militancy[c]		
	1980–1989	1990–1999	Trend	1983–1989	1990–1999	Trend
Austria	52.1	42.1	−	2	4	=
Belgium	50.9	52.7	=	22	32	+
Denmark	77.8	76.3	=	165	180	+
Finland	69.9	77.3	+	413	184	−
France	14.7	10.1	−	76	36	−
Germany	34.2	30.4	−	26	12	−
Ireland	55.0	47.8	−	346	105	−
Italy	44.0	38.8	−	493	129	−
Netherlands	28.8	24.2	−	15	21	+
Norway	57.5	58.1	=	92	86	=
Portugal	46.1	26.4	−			
Spain	10.5	17.3	+	691	351	−
Switzerland	28.9	24.2	−	1	1	=
Sweden	80.0	85.0	+	177	51	−
United Kingdom	46.1	34.4	−	337	32	−
Western Europe	37.6	31.9	−	218	66	−

Sources: Visser (2002); Ebbinghaus and Visser (2000).
[a]−, decreasing; +, increasing; =, no change.
[b]Union density is defined as union membership as a percentage of the total workforce.
[c]Militancy is measured in terms of workdays lost due to strikes and lockouts per 1,000 employees.

success relies on the common feeling of powerlessness that is shared by all three parties: the state, capital, and labor (Boot 2000). All parties should have roughly equal power because this discourages any unilateral action by the most powerful player. Conversely, all actors involved feel the need to cooperate. It follows that social pacts, as with other systems based on co-operation, reflect a situation in which the costs of conflict are higher than the costs of cooperation.

The fewer choices unions have, or the more they are persuaded that sacrifices are essential in order to reach an important socioeconomic or political objective, the more likely they are to support a policy of wage restraint. Good examples of this are the Italian emergency negotiations between employers' organizations, unions, and the government from 1992 to 1995, which aimed to avoid a marginalization of Italy within the EU by securing its EMU membership while the whole political system was deeply involved in the *tangentopoli* corruption crisis. In this decisive period, technical governments used the social partners as a source of their legitimacy because they offered the governments a greater amount of citizen participation and legitimacy than the discredited political parties (Ferrera and Gualmini 1999; Baccaro 2002).

The benefits of bargained wage-restriction pacts are not limited to the reaffirmation of the institutional role of the unions. Given that such pacts are mainly designed to enhance the competitiveness of the economy of one country, they may encourage international free-floating capital to invest in the particular national economy. However, competitive social pacts are riskier for labor than were the capital-labor compromises of the 1970s. In addition to the classic trust problem of corporatism (Crouch 1993)— will the agreed wage restraints really lead to more employment or only to increased profits?—there is another, unpredictable variable, namely, the reaction of unions and employers in other countries. If they also react with concession bargaining, the competitive advantage of the first country rapidly shrinks. This may lead to a downward spiral of repeated circles of concession bargaining and thus to social dumping. Even if some economies might be winners in such a competition, such a downward spiral would be self-defeating for the workers of all countries. This illustrates the limits and risks of any technocratic renationalization strategy of labor in the area of wage bargaining.

Toward the Europeanization of Collective Bargaining?

The only hope of breaking the described cycle of the downward spiral of concession bargaining may be to supranationalize the practice of corporatism (Grote and Schmitter 1999). Therefore, corporatism must increase its scale to cover all of Europe and extend its scope to include a broad range of social citizenship rights. However, Jürgen Grote and Philippe Schmitter (1999) also argued that supranational corporatism functions only if it also meets the two ideal-typical clusters of conditions highlighted by the neocorporatist literature of the 1970s, namely, a strong enforcement capacity on the part of the participating social partners and a balance of class forces between capital and labor (Schmitter and Lehmbruch 1979).

First, in order to produce enforceable results, ideal-type neocorporatism requires particular associational properties, namely, a monopoly of representation of the participating associations, a hierarchic coordination between them, their official recognition by the state, quasi-compulsory membership, and some degree of heteronomy with regard to the selection of leaders and the articulation of demands. Second, typical neocorporatism is based on particular decision-making characteristics, such as parity between capital and labor representation, privileged access for capital and labor representatives to legislative deliberation, active and concurrent consent and not just majority voting as the usual democratic decision rule, regular interaction in functionally specified domains, and devolved responsibility for policy implementation (Grote and Schmitter 1999).

If we could find these ideal-typical properties of neocorporatism at the EU level, then Euro-corporatism could theoretically become a routine practice and even "an important component of its (eventual) democratization" (Grote and Schmitter 1999, 40). Indeed, classic neocorporatist arrangements of functional interest representation and territorial systems of parliamentary democracy do not exclude one another (Schmitter and Lehmbruch 1979; Baccaro 2002).[2] In contrast to competitive corporatism, classical neocorporatism not only acknowledges the existence of competing social and political interests, but also requires a balance of power between capital and labor. In this case, neither side can force the other to do anything through threat of sanction. In such a situation, only the force of arguments can be relied on. Hence, if management and labor represent the two opposing groups in a debate and if the power resources of these two groups effectively neutralize one another, neocorporatist arrangements could effectively be described as a form of functional democracy. Unsurprisingly, however, any author who shares the classic view of Philippe Schmitter and Gerhard Lehmbruch (1979) regarding the necessary preconditions of neocorporatism must come to the conclusion that its Europeanization presents a very unlikely scenario.

Although it would seem logical that a wage-determination system should similarly operate at the same level as the monetary system (Crouch 2000b), the Euro-corporatist vision is usually dismissed as not being feasible. As a matter of fact, wage bargaining is explicitly excluded from the scope of the European social dialog (Article 137 (5) TEC), which is the tool used by the Commission for bringing about EU-level collective bargaining. Likewise, there are also no signs that the European employers' organizations are willing to engage in negotiations about wages at the EU level (Léonard et al. 2007). In contrast, many employers supported the EMU precisely because they hoped that these economic Europeanization projects would undermine the role of unions in the area of wage determination. For instance, the deputy chairman of the Banque Nationale de Paris and a director and board member of the Dresdner Bank frankly stated as far back as 1997, at a Franco-German business round table, that the unions would "lose their role in wage negotiations" after the introduction of the EMU. The two bank directors expected that national wage-bargaining systems would lose their functionality and, thus, that unions would lose their *raison d'être* within the eurozone.[3]

The Strategic Wage-Bargaining Dilemmas of Organized Labor

Although the lack of an EU wage-bargaining policy and the declining autonomy of national wage-bargaining systems are obvious, authors disagree on the lessons that labor should learn from these developments. Whereas Streeck concludes that the unions must direct their focus again to the nation-state (Streeck 1998a, 1999), Grote and Schmitter (1999) argue that a Europeanization of wage bargaining is nonetheless a scenario well worth simulating and stimulating. These opposite views are not a result of different interpretations of the past (Streeck and Schmitter 1991) but of different visions of the future. Streeck (1999) believes that we are witnessing a replacement of redistributive[4] or social solidarity between the rich and the poor by a competitive solidarity between producers in nations or regions, whereas Schmitter (2000) argues that precisely these competitive pressures make a democratization of the EU and the development of EU social policies and European social rights even more urgent.

More fundamentally, however, it is questionable whether we can assess the possibility of EU-level wage-bargaining coordination and social policy making on the basis of national yardsticks. Euro-corporatism will never have the same properties as its national equivalent. To paraphrase Grote and Schmitter (1999), Sisyphus would certainly have to push his huge boulder up a much steeper and higher cliff to reach the top of Euro-corporatism, but, precisely because he may never reach that top, he does not have to start all over again. In contrast, national corporatist arrangements frequently tend to collapse when they reach their high point. In other words, even in a fragmented polity, corporatist arrangements might be viable. In the real world, we can find some empirical cases that are still labeled neocorporatism, even if they differ considerably from Schmitter and Lehmbruch's (1979) ideal-type. One example of this is Switzerland. The Swiss polity and labor movement fall short of the centralized and hierarchical structures that are at the base of the neocorporatist ideal-type (Fluder et al. 1991; Kriesi 1995; Fluder 1996). Therefore, it might be equally misleading to conclude from the absence of robust EU-level state structures that Euro-corporatist arrangements are neither possible nor desirable (Streeck 1998a) because less robust governance structures are also able to change and respond to new situations.

One first step in the Euro-corporatist direction could be the establishment of a supranational, or at least transnational, coordination of national wage-bargaining policies. Given the interest of capital in low wage costs, the initiative for such a European coordination must come from labor. It follows that national unions face difficult choices. Should they accept wage restraint and pursue a technocratic renationalization strategy that might encourage a race to the bottom in wage levels across Europe? Or should they try to limit transnational wage competition through the adoption of an EU-level wage-bargaining benchmark even if some other unions might act as free-riders and conclude wage agreements below the agreed EU-level wage-bargaining norm (Mermet 2001)?

Finally, unions face an additional dilemma because Europeanization and renationalization of collective bargaining are not the only possible scenarios in the field of wage policy. The EMU could also unleash a dynamic that would be more likely to result in an Americanization or deregulation of wage-setting structures than in either of the two alternatives. Such a development would also entail crucial political implications because the weakness of labor is a major contributor to the poor quality of democracy and the weak democratic control of capitalism in the United States. Therefore, an Americanization of EU labor relations "would be yet another way in which the chosen construction of EMU will deepen the democratic deficit in European integration" (Martin 1999, 32).

Although it would be wrong to say that U.S. unions have lost the capacity to act, as demonstrated by recent organizing successes in new urban battlegrounds (Turner and Cornfield 2007), EU trade unions are nevertheless tempted to accept almost anything to avoid a further erosion of multi-employer wage-bargaining structures. The next chapter reviews wage developments in fourteen EU member states. Can we observe a general trend toward wage restraint in the EU? If so, is this practice a result of union wage policy within the framework of national competitive corporatism?

CHAPTER FIVE

The Rise of National
Competitive Corporatism

Since the adoption of the Maastricht Treaty in 1993, we can observe a real wage trajectory in Western Europe that fails to fully match the growth of productivity. Does that mean that European trade unions have actively supported wage-moderation policies? It would be wrong to argue that wage moderation, as such, is an indicator of a technocratic renationalization strategy, but if unions did accept low wage increases to support competition state nationalism, then they would have adopted a technocratic renationalization strategy in the field of collective wage bargaining.

Unions have adopted wage-moderation policies in the past, for instance during the resurgence of neocorporatism in the 1970s, but these arrangements were social-democratic compromises between conflicting class interests rather than monistic pacts in favor of national competitiveness. Therefore, this chapter reviews not only wage statistics but also labor wage bargaining policies in all Western EU countries except Luxembourg. For the same reason, this chapter relies primarily on statistical data that have actually been used by union experts, even if alternative academic data sets might have provided more accurate pictures of European wage trends.

Real Wage and Productivity Developments
in the European Union

In 1999, Emmanuel Mermet, the European Trade Union Institute (ETUI) economist in charge of ETUC wage-coordination policy, pre-

European Unions

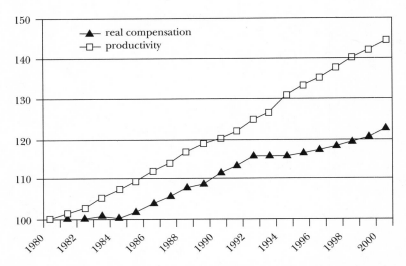

Figure 5.1. Real compensation and productivity in the EU 15 (the fifteen old EU member states).

Source: European Commission, *European Economy,* cited in Mermet (1999).

sented data that confirmed that real compensation obtained by employees did not track the increase in labor productivity. Using Commission statistics, Mermet compiled the indexed evolution of real compensation and labor productivity per head from 1980 to 1999 in the fifteen old EU member states. These cumulative index-based figures played an important role in convincing unions that a European coordination of wage bargaining was urgent.

Figure 5.1 reveals an increasing disparity between productivity and real compensation growth. After 1993, real wages stagnated while productivity increased considerably. Hence, figure 5.1 seems to confirm the thesis that the European single-market program of 1992 and the coming into force of the Maastricht Treaty in 1993 favored wage moderation due to increased transnational competition.

The labor share of the national income, or the adjusted wage ratio as a percentage of GDP to factor costs, is another indicator used by trade union experts to assess wage trends (Schulten 2002a). The wage ratio is linked to the development of real compensation and productivity in the following way. The labor share of the national income increases if real wages increase at a higher rate than productivity, and vice versa. Therefore, an equal development of real compensation and productivity rates has a neutral effect on the distribution of wealth between labor and capital. Table

Table 5.1. Adjusted wage share in the European Union, 1961–2000

	1961–1970	1971–1980	1981–1990	1991–2000
European Union	73.6	75.3	73.0	69.7
Austria	76.7	78.8	80.0	76.4
Belgium	70.4	75.8	74.3	72.2
Denmark	75.2	77.7	70.3	68.3
Finland	73.1	72.5	71.9	66.5
France	75.3	76.6	75.4	69.3
Germany[a]	71.6	73.7	70.9	67.9
Greece	86.1	70.7	74.0	67.2
Ireland	79.3	77.3	72.5	63.7
Italy	75.5	76.7	74.3	70.5
Luxembourg	57.7	65.5	66.5	64.5
Netherlands	69.4	74.8	68.1	65.9
Portugal	67.8	81.2	74.0	73.1
Spain	77.3	79.1	73.0	68.8
Sweden	72.3	74.1	70.5	68.9
United Kingdom	72.6	73.2	72.7	73.6

Source: European Commission, cited by Schulten (2002a). Aggregate wage share as a percentage of GDP at factor costs.
[a] 1961–1991 values are for West Germany.

5.1 indicates that until the 1970s the growth in real wages almost everywhere in Western Europe fully matched the growth in productivity. This not only satisfied the workers who could enjoy an equal share of the general rise in prosperity, but was also instrumental in the mid-century compromise between capital and labor, which was based on the parallel growth of mass production and mass consumption. After 1968, most unions even briefly succeeded in obtaining pay gains above inflation and productivity increases (Schulten 1998, 1999a). By contrast, in the 1980s and the 1990s, there is a significant decrease in the average annual wage share. Only in the United Kingdom did the adjusted wage ratio remain stable during the 1980s and the 1990s, whereas a considerable decrease in the wage ratio can be observed in most of the other countries, especially in Ireland and Spain.

This overview indicates a general trend away from productivity-oriented, solidaristic collective wage-bargaining polices (Schulten 2002a). This general picture remains the same, even if we include the reduction of yearly working hours in the calculation (Schulten 1999a). Incidentally, the working-time reductions were also higher during the 1960s and 1970s than during the 1980s and 1990s, despite successful union campaigns for the 35-hour working week in Germany and France. Obviously, this general trend must be caused by more fundamental reasons than simply the need to adjust the economy of one country with regard to the EMU. Nevertheless, we cannot exclude that the unions in the 1990s deliberately adopted a nationalistic competitive wage-bargaining policy. Thus, in the following section the annual growth of real wages compared to the rise in productivity is analyzed country by country. If we can observe a continuing increase in the disparity between real wages and productivity during the 1990s, we can conclude that this might be a product of general wage trends resulting from rising unemployment figures rather than a result of a competitive collective wage-bargaining policy. On the other hand, an abrupt change in the trend would support the competition state renationalization thesis because such a change implies active involvement on the part of the unions in the reorientation of wage policy. The latter thesis seems even more probable if the abrupt change occurred after the conclusion of a specific social pact.

We can distinguish the following three patterns of organized-labor wage policies and compare them to national productivity and real-compensation developments:

1. If the share of labor (or the adjusted wage ratio) as a percentage of GDP to factor costs is not declining over time, then unions are not engaged in competitive concession bargaining and the renationalization thesis is proven false.

2. If the share of labor (or the adjusted wage ratio) as a percentage of GDP to factor costs is constantly declining over time, then wage moderation is likely to be a result of structural factors. This suggests that unions cannot act strategically at all, and therefore the renationalization thesis is proven false.

3. If the share of labor (or the adjusted wage ratio) as a percentage of GDP to factor costs is declining significantly after a policy change by organized labor (e.g., after the adoption of a social pact), then wage moderation is likely to result from a strategic decision on the part of unions. In this situation, the renationalization thesis is confirmed.

This classification is outcome-oriented, in contrast to other, more institutionalist typologies of national bargaining policies.[1] Such an outcome-oriented classification is more appropriate here, given that different institutions can produce functionally equivalent outcomes and given the action and outcome-oriented research question of this chapter: Are the unions actively supporting wage moderation? A country-by-country review

Table 5.2. Post-Maastricht Treaty wage-moderation types

No wage moderation	United Kingdom, Denmark, Sweden, Greece, Portugal
Structural wage moderation	France, Spain
Bargained wage moderation	Ireland, The Netherlands, Italy, Belgium, Finland, Germany, Austria

of Mermet's real-compensation and productivity data leads us to distinguish among three types of wage policy outcomes in the 1990s (table 5.2):

- *No wage moderation.* In some countries, real wages tracked productivity development. This suggests that unions in these countries did not effectively apply wage moderation and, hence, did not support any technocratic renationalization strategy in the area of wage bargaining.
- *Structural wage moderation.* In other countries, we see an increasing gap between real wages and productivity that does not seem to be related to any change in union wage bargaining policy. This suggests that unions have no impact on wages and that wage restraint seems to be a result of structural changes, such as high unemployment, rather than a result of a technocratic renationalization strategy of unions to increase the competitiveness of the country.
- *Bargained wage moderation.* Finally, in most Western EU countries we observe abrupt changes in real-wage trends relative to productivity after the conclusion of specific social pacts or in the framework of an enduring neocorporatist industrial relations system. This suggests that the unions in these countries actively supported wage moderation and adopted a technocratic renationalization strategy.

No Wage Moderation

Denmark, Sweden, and the United Kingdom: The Eurozone Outsiders

The British, Danish, and Swedish data suggest that, surprisingly, in the 1990s there was no wage moderation in these non-EMU countries (fig. 5.2). Given that the wage-setting mechanisms differ quite substantially in these three countries, the absence of wage moderation in all three coun-

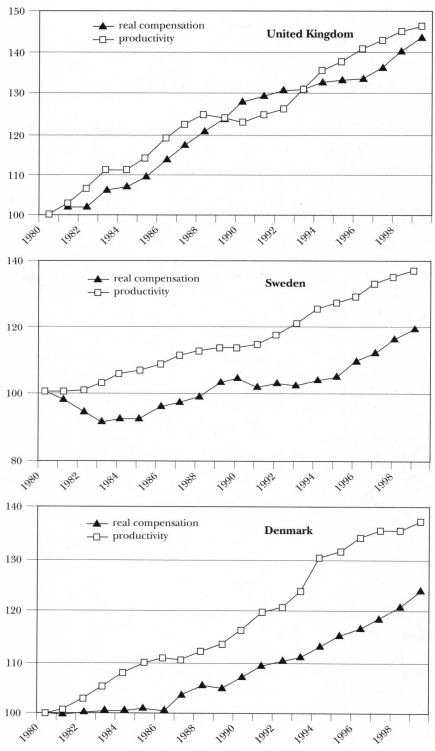

Figure 5.2. Real compensation and productivity in the United Kingdom, Denmark, and Sweden.
Source: European Commission, *European Economy,* cited in Mermet (1999).

tries confirms the view expressed by scholars that the shift to moderate wage policies in the 1990s was a consequence of EMU (Martin and Ross 2004; Crouch 2000a; Pochet 1999b).

The British development is especially surprising, at least from a neo-classical point of view. The roughly deregulated industrial relations system did not lead to wage moderation; real wages closely followed productivity during the 1980s and 1990s. This confirms the findings of Coen Teulings and Joop Hartog's (1998) and Franz Traxler's (1998) comparative studies regarding the macroeconomic effects of coordinated wage-bargaining structures. Apparently, it is much easier to reduce the adjusted aggregate wage ratio by corporatist structures on a macro level than it is for "real-life labor markets, dealing with limited information and contractibility" on the micro level (Teulings and Hartog 1998, 192). This argument is also supported by the aggregated U.S. wage development, which corresponds to the U.K. pattern of no general wage moderation. Although U.S. real wages also lagged behind productivity since 1980, they did so to a lesser degree than in the EMU countries (Flassbeck and Spiecker 2000).

Other statistical data indicate, however, that the destruction of the co-ordinated wage-setting structures during the 1980s had a considerable impact on wealth distribution in the United Kingdom. Crouch (1999) points out that in the 1980s and 1990s the relative income positions of the 10 percent of British earners with the lowest incomes sharply deteriorated, whereas the incomes of the top-decile earners leapt ahead considerably. Accordingly, the decentralization of wage bargaining is likely to lead to a decline in real wages in the lower-wage sectors, but it also excludes any compromise on wage moderation in general, due to the dismantling of multi-employer collective wage-bargaining structures. The radical eradication of multi-employer wage agreements did not, however, lead to a complete elimination of union activities at the local level. Even though the coverage of collective wage agreements has dramatically dropped since 1979, in 1998, 34.5 percent of British workers were still covered by collective agreements (Fulton and Lefresne 1999). It follows that local union pressure and the lack of qualified employees lead to considerable real-wage increases in some sectors of the economy. The Bank of England did not welcome such excessive wage developments, but local employers and unionists did not take note of the macroeconomic concerns of the Bank. Ironically, Margaret Thatcher's deregulation policies also had positive side effects for some unions and employees if they worked in a booming sector of the economy and if they managed to consolidate their power resources in their enterprises. In this case, they could negotiate real-wage increases that they would hardly have been able to obtain through national-level col-

lective wage bargaining because the decentralization unchained them
from the obligation to take into account any macroeconomic considerations. Hence, the British unions never developed a technocratic renationalization strategy in the field of wage bargaining. Whether this outcome
mirrors primarily the reluctance of the unions or the employers to engage
in corporatist arrangements is of little concern in this context (Hyman
2001; Crouch 1993).

The Danish data indicate a period of wage moderation during the early
1980s. Possibly, this trend is due to the end of the automatic indexation of
pay to inflation in 1981 and the decentralization during the 1980s of the
bargaining structure from the national intersectoral to the sectoral level.
However, in 1986 this period of wage moderation suddenly ended. Figure
5.2 shows that an almost parallel development of real wages and productivity occurs afterward, although the former indicator increased in the
early 1990s slightly more slowly than the latter. Hence, we do not observe
the adoption of a competition bargaining policy by the Danish unions in
the 1990s.

Nor does the Swedish situation show signs of continuing wage moderation. The late 1980s and 1990s saw an almost parallel development of real
wages and productivity. Only during the two economic crises of the early
1980s and 1990s do we observe phases of wage moderation that included
a reduction of purchasing power. This stop and go policy is an indicator
for the adjustment capacity of the organized Swedish industrial relations
system. International comparisons also play an increasingly important role
in wage setting. In the industrial sector, social partners virtually agreed in
1997 that the Swedish average hourly labor cost should not increase faster
than in the rest of Western Europe. At the same time, the Swedish blue-
collar union confederation (Landsorganisationen i Sverige, LO) reframed
its wage policy to ensure low inflation as well as real-wage increases as much
as possible (Mermet 1999); but this did not lead to a generalized wage
moderation trend.

Greece and Portugal: The Two Low-Wage Euro-Countries

The comparison of the Greek and Portuguese real-wage and productivity trends suggests that also in these states no wage-moderation policies
have been adopted (fig. 5.3).

Figure 5.3 suggests that the Portuguese unions did not pursue a technocratic renationalization strategy in the field of wage bargaining; Portuguese real wages followed productivity. Despite this, Portugal fulfilled
the Maastricht criteria, to the surprise of the European Commission

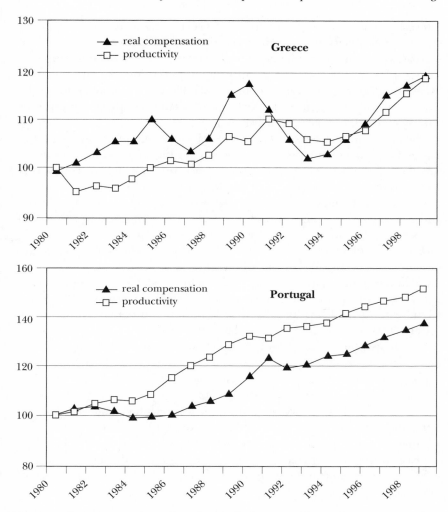

Figure 5.3. Real compensation and productivity in Greece and Portugal.

Source: European Commission, *European Economy,* cited in Mermet (1999).

(1998). The government sponsored a tripartite concerted action program, with the objective of reducing the extremely high inflation rate through a wage policy that aimed to keep pay increases in line with anticipated inflation. However, only the smaller UGT(P) union confederation signed the Strategic Concerted Action Agreement 1996–1999, whereas the larger CGTP rejected it. The left-wing CGTP obviously preferred a decentralized approach, based more on power relations and the immediate interest of the workers, whereas the UGT[P] based its wage policy on macroeconomic arguments. However, the UGT[P] also sought real-wage increases covering the anticipated productivity gains. This claim was partly successful. Portugal consolidated its position as the country with the highest adjusted aggregate wage ratio in the EU. However, this position is relative, given the considerably lower level of Portuguese purchasing power compared to all other EU states (Pernot 1999).

The Greek unions also seem to have rejected wage moderation. In the 1980s, Greek real compensation increased at a higher rate than the almost stagnating productivity. As productivity improved during the 1990s, real compensation followed. In contrast, during the 1960s and 1970s the average annual changes in the wage ratio were very negative, namely, −10.1 and −8.6 percent. Hence, up to now Greece has almost never followed the Western European trend; this is not surprising given the long-lasting impact of authoritarian corporatism and industrial conflict in Greek employment relations. In contrast to most other EU countries, the government and the social partners failed to conclude a stable wage-moderation agreement. Consequently, it was not so easy for Greece to meet the Maastricht criteria. To keep inflation down, the government had to employ different ad hoc measures, for example consumption tax reductions. Nevertheless, Greece also joined the eurozone in 2001. Subsequently, some authors argued that Greek unions would come under pressure because they "have not given any detailed considerations to the far-reaching implications of EMU on standards of living, employment prospects and the scope of collective bargaining; nor have they come up with any detailed proposals" (Mouriki 1998, 181). Nevertheless, the Greek unions adopted a rather self-assured position in the EU-level union debates on wage coordination; international comparisons indicate that labor-unit costs in Greece were still lower than in most other EMU countries (Mermet 1999).

Structural Wage Moderation: France and Spain— Wage Moderation without Union Involvement

In the French and Spanish cases the comparison of the real-wage and the productivity development suggests that wage moderation has been a result of structural factors rather than of a corresponding policy of organized labor (fig. 5.4).

As figure 5.4 indicates, French real-wage development stopped mirroring productivity as early as 1983. Hence, we can observe wage moderation

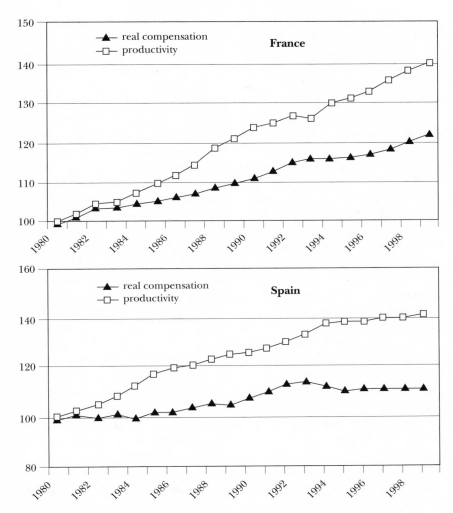

Figure 5.4. Real compensation and productivity in France and Spain.

Source: European Commission, *European Economy,* cited in Mermet (1999).

ever since the end of President François Mitterrand's initial socialist policy. It would be wrong, however, to conclude that the French unions have actively chosen a competition state renationalization strategy. Although most French employees are protected by collective bargaining agreements,[2] this does not signify that the unions have a considerable impact on wage determination. In the private sector especially, it is hardly possible to distinguish bargained wage increases from those unilaterally put forward by the employers and the state. Most collectively agreed-on pay settlements differ not only from one enterprise to another but also geographically, from one *département* to another. This implies in practical terms that unions have to build up separate negotiation power at the level of every single company unit; this is a very difficult task. Consequently, the state effectively sets the wage patterns, first, via its statutory minimum wage (Salaire minimum interprofessionnelle de croissance, SMIC) and, second, by setting the salary increases for the public service, which accounts for a quarter of the French workforce (Barrat, Yakubovich, and Maurice 2002).

According to French labor law, the SMIC is indexed to compensate for inflation and to follow the general wage trend. Additional SMIC increases are possible but, again, only if the government votes a decree. At the beginning of 2000, the statutory SMIC wage was in almost 80 percent of all cases above the lowest wage fixed in private-sector collective agreements registered by Ministère des Affaires Sociales, du Travail et de la Solidarité (2001). This had no practical consequences because employees benefited from the higher SMIC wage level. It shows, however, that unions were not able to negotiate any wage increases in large parts of the private sector. The French practice of wage moderation is not a product of social partnership but a result of structural factors, namely, the weak workplace power resources of French unions. Increasing national competitiveness is an issue for the French state, but not for the French labor movement. Ironically, the weakness of French unions in the area of wage setting prevented them adopting a competitive wage-moderation policy.

The Spanish case is similar to the French one. Spanish trade unionism is also characterized by politically divided union confederations that are organizationally rather weak at both the sectoral and the shop floor level (Molina 2006). Moreover, the extremely high level of unemployment weakened the bargaining power of the Spanish unions, and this further undermined their impact on wage setting. The Spanish government unilaterally deregulated the labor market after it failed to sponsor a social pact in 1994. Enjoying a clear parliamentary majority, it did not need any additional legitimizing of its policies by the social partners, in contrast to the technical Italian governments during the 1990s. Even if the social partners managed in 1997 to conclude three intersectoral agreements, the conservative José María Aznar government and the employers still favored neoliberal solutions that included measures that considerably lowered the wages of certain groups (Miguélez 2000). Hence, it is not surprising that the two union federations, Union General de Trabajadores (UGT[S]) and

Confederación Sindacal de Comisiones Obreras (CCOO), interpreted a small real-wage increase as a success (Gutiérrez and Martín Urriza 1998).

In conclusion, it is accurate to say that in France and Spain unions did not actively support national wage moderation. Given their weak power resources and the decisive role of state policy, however, their support was also not necessary for the implementation of wage moderation. It follows that both French and Spanish unions did not adopt a technocratic renationalization strategy. This does not, however, reflect a conscious strategic decision but, rather, the incapacity of French and Spanish unions to play any strategic role in national wage bargaining.

Bargained Wage Moderation

The Netherlands and Ireland: Long-Lasting Social Partnership

In the Irish and Dutch cases, the comparison of real-wage and productivity trends also suggests that wage moderation has been a result of structural factors rather than a result of policy changes on the part of labor. In both cases, no sharp reorientation of the wage policy developments can be observed over the last two decades (fig. 5.5). Nevertheless, in both cases it is very probable that unions actively supported wage-moderation policies and, thus, contributed to the growing disparity between productivity and real-wage development. The only reason we do not observe a radical shift in the real-compensation development in figure 5.5 is that the Dutch and Irish social pacts had already been adopted in the early 1980s.

The Wassenaar Agreement, signed in 1982 by Dutch social partners and the government, was the starting point of a long-lasting policy of wage moderation. Although the annual changes in the wage ratio in the 1960s and 1970s were very high compared to other EU countries, namely, +6.0 and +5.2 percent, respectively (table 5.1), figure 5.5 indicates an increasing gap between productivity and real-wage development in the 1980s and 1990s. Furthermore, the constant development of both variables is a sign that the EMU cannot be seen as its main cause. Although the press often praises the Dutch case as the most U.S.-style economy of the continent, the Dutch development does not reflect a recent increase in market conformity but rather a long-term interaction between the social partners (Visser and Hemerijck 1997).

In Ireland, the adoption of social pacts also dates back to the mid-1980s, when extremely high levels of unemployment, forced emigration, and

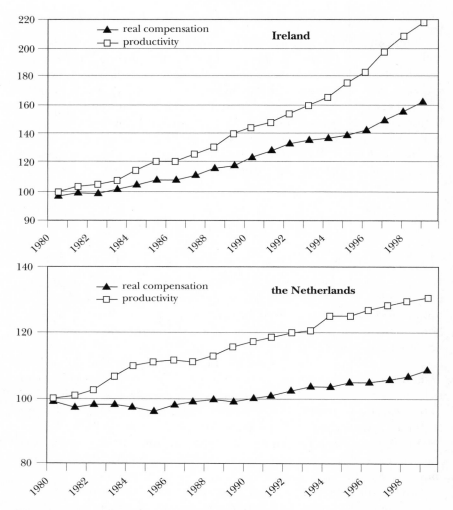

Figure 5.5. Real compensation and productivity in Ireland and the Netherlands.

Source: European Commission, *European Economy,* cited in Mermet (1999).

poverty characterized Irish society. In the 1990s, the situation changed and Ireland profited from the highest growth and productivity gains in the EU. Although many other factors are relevant to the emergence of the Celtic Tiger, the central wage-moderation agreements also played a crucial role in attracting more foreign investments (Hardiman 2000). The various tripartite social partnership agreements did not link real wage to productivity trends but only to inflation. Correspondingly, the Irish wage-profit ratio dramatically declined from the highest level in the EU (82.0 percent) in the 1960s to the second lowest in the 1990s (65.9 percent). Only Dutch labor has a lower share of the national income. Moreover, low pay remains an important issue of current debate (Erne 2006) despite Irish economic development because Ireland is still characterized by a very high degree of income inequality (Nolan and Smeeding 2005). Accordingly, Allen (2000, 2007) and Kirby (2002) present very critical accounts of the Irish miracle, whereas Hardiman (2001) emphasizes that restoring high profitability was a precondition for the expansion of output and employment. Whatever the case, it is evident that the Irish unions actively supported wage moderation. Therefore, social partnership in Ireland can best be understood in terms of competitive corporatism (Roche and Cradden 2003).

In conclusion, both Dutch and Irish unions seem to have pursued a technocratic renationalization strategy. Even though improving the competitive position of the national economy became, in both cases, a major objective, this development was not linked to the EMU. In the Netherlands and Ireland, wage moderation was at the outset a means to overcome the deep economic crisis of the 1970s and 1980s, but then gradually led to the competitive corporatism of the 1990s.

Germany and Austria: Gradual Shift to Wage Moderation

In Germany and Austria, we observe a gradual reorientation of wage policy after 1993, that is, after the adoption of the Maastricht Treaty (fig. 5.6). In Germany, real compensation followed productivity gains quite well until 1993, as indicated by figure 5.6. Afterward, real-wage increases were increasingly contained. This shift to wage moderation is not only a result of the increasing decentralization and gradual erosion of sectoral collective wage agreements (Artus, Schmidt, and Sterkel 2000).[3] It also mirrors the reduction of additional pay over and above the collectively agreed-on wages (Bispinck and Schulten 2002). But, even though the German wage-moderation policy was not caused by a national social pact, it is true to say that the unions supported this policy throughout the 1990s. The moderate German wage-bargaining results find an additional explanation in the informal mutual contacts between the Bundesbank and the social partners. The social partners concluded moderate agreements to encourage a less monetarist Bundesbank policy; albeit, Lars Calmfors and John Driffill's (1988) precondition for bargained wage moderation—namely, fully encompassing wage-bargaining structures—does not exist in Germany (Crouch 2000b).

The Austrian data also indicate a clear change in the relationship be-

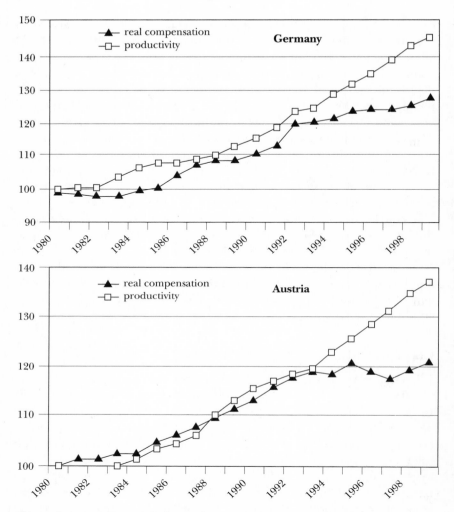

Figure 5.6. Real compensation and productivity in Germany and Austria.

Source: European Commission, *European Economy,* cited in Mermet (1999).

tween productivity and real-wage trends. Both indicators developed in parallel until 1993, but real-wage growth virtually stopped following the productivity increases in 1994. This is a clear indicator of wage moderation. Is this wage moderation a result of a union renationalization strategy wage policy or is it a result of structural changes? The beginning of the Austrian wage moderation does not coincide with a widely publicized social pact. Therefore, the Austrian case is frequently neglected by the literature, even though social partnership is deeply rooted in this country. It is, indeed, very likely that the unions stopped negotiating real-wage increases in order to meet the Maastricht inflation criteria.

In conclusion, given the well-established position of both the Austrian and German unions, especially in the wage-pattern-setting metal industry, and considering that both the German and Austrian wage moderation started suddenly in 1993, we can conclude that the unions supported wage moderation in both countries.

Italy and Finland: Abrupt Shift to Wage Moderation

The Italian and Finnish wage developments are marked by an abrupt shift to wage moderation subsequent to the adoption of their respective social pacts (fig. 5.7). The Italian data clearly reveal the impact of the fundamental reorientation of Italian income policy following the abolition of automatic wage increases to compensate for inflation in 1992 and the social pacts of 1993 and 1998. Despite the famous conflict-oriented image of Italian industrial relations, the three representative Italian union confederations—the left-wing Confederazione Generale Italiana del Lavoro (CGIL), the Catholic CISL, and the moderate UIL—did not develop their neocorporatist behavior overnight. Whereas in the agitated post-1968 period all Italian unions conducted a maximalist and egalitarian income policy, by 1978 they were already prepared to exchange short-term goals for long-term objectives (Hege and Rehfeldt 1999; Crouch and Pizzorno 1978).

The same pattern reemerged in the early 1990s, when the economy was in deep disarray and the Italian elite was in the turmoil of the *tangetopoli* corruption crisis. The Italian 1993 social pact gave the unions better access to the social policies of the government (especially in the field of pension reform) and introduced recognized union structures within firms, the Rappresentanze Sindacali Unitarie (RSU) (Pulignano 2006). In exchange, the unions supported wage moderation to secure Italian EMU membership. Therefore, the Italian social pacts could still be described as neocorporatist political exchanges rather than monistic alliances to enhance national competitiveness (Molina 2006). However, even if competitiveness was not a stated objective of the Italian unions with regard to the 1993 social pact, the shift to wage moderation definitely improved the competitive position of the Italian economy. Because wage moderation did not create employment (Megale, D'Aloia, and Birindelli 2003), it is equally not surprising that the Italian social pacts were not welcomed by all workers. This contributed to the emergence of new, radical, autono-

European Unions

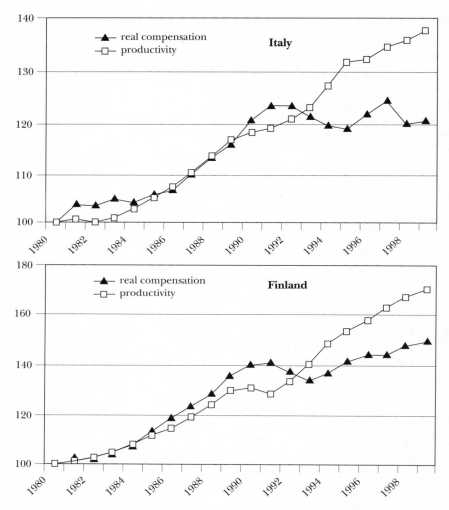

Figure 5.7. Real compensation and productivity in Italy and Finland.

Source: European Commission, *European Economy,* cited in Mermet (1999).

mous unions called Comitati di Base (COBAS), in particular in the public sector.

In Finland, real-wage growth paralleled productivity increases until 1991. Then, a deep economic crisis (1991–1993) and the increase of mass unemployment from 3 to 18 percent had a strong impact on the wage claims of the unions (Sauramo 2000). Subsequently, Finnish unions, employer organizations, and the government agreed on a wage-moderation policy in two centrally negotiated agreements (1995 and 1997). Nevertheless, the Finish social pacts continued to adhere to solidaristic wage policy principles insofar as low-wage employees still received proportionally higher pay increases than the others.

Belgium: State-Imposed Shift to Wage Moderation

In Belgium, real-wage development is also marked by an abrupt shift to wage moderation. In contrast to the other EU countries, this shift cannot be explained either by the adoption of a particular social pact or by structural weaknesses of the labor movement, as in the French and Spanish cases (fig. 5.8).

Like the general EU trend, the Belgian data show first a stagnation of real wages in the 1980s, then a phase of real-wage increases (even above the rate of productivity increases), and finally, after 1994, a real-wage development again below productivity growth. This is a clear indicator of wage moderation, but in this case the government rather than the social partners initiated the transformation of wage trends to a competition state pattern. In 1989 and in 1996, the Belgian parliament passed two laws on industrial competitiveness that tied domestic wage developments to the hourly wage cost developments of France, Germany, and the Netherlands.[4] As a result, every 2 years the social partners are still able to negotiate a wage

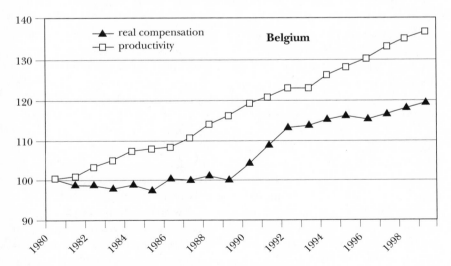

Figure 5.8. Real compensation and productivity in Belgium.

Source: European Commission, *European Economy,* cited in Mermet (1999).

increase norm, but they are also constrained to respect the comparative ceiling set by the law on competitiveness. If the social partners fail to define a wage norm, the government imposes a settlement, as in 1996. Even if the Belgian unions have not favored the establishment of a competitive wage policy, they are barred from concluding wage settlements that would lead to a greater increase in hourly wage costs than in Germany, France, and the Netherlands. Consequently, Belgian unions have been at the forefront of establishing a wage-bargaining policy coordination group made up of the Benelux-German trade union confederations and some of their most important sectoral unions, the Doorn group, in order to overcome the straightjacket of the Belgian competitiveness law (Pochet 1999a).

Conclusion

This chapter has tested the technocratic renationalization union strategy thesis in the area of collective wage bargaining. It attempted to answer the following empirical questions. Can we observe wage moderation in the EU member states since the adoption of the Maastricht Treaty? If yes, did the unions actively support it or was wage moderation, rather, a product of structural causes, such as high unemployment? In the latter case, wage moderation would be a general trend; in the former case, wage moderation should start and end in line with specific union policy shifts, such as the adoption of specific social pacts.

First, the chapter has revealed that the French and Spanish unions might not be an essential factor in the implementation of wage moderation. Although these findings do not exclude the possibility that the French and Spanish unions also might have welcomed wage moderation, it seems that structural reasons rather than union policies were the crucial factor in this development. Indeed, it is an open question as to whether the French or Spanish unions were in a position to shape changes in wage trends at all. It is reasonable to argue that the Spanish and French unions did not pursue any strategy in the area of collective wage bargaining.

Second, this chapter has shown that in five EU member states wage moderation was not a feature in the 1990s. British, Danish, Swedish, Portuguese, and Greek unions did not pursue a wage-moderation policy after the adoption of the Maastricht Treaty in 1993. It follows that labor has not adopted a technocratic renationalization strategy in these countries. It is also impossible to link the wage-bargaining policies to one of the two Europeanization strategies, namely, Euro-democratization and Euro-technocratization because the unions in these countries neglected the European dimensions of wage bargaining. The British, Danish, and Swedish unions could do so because they had, for different reasons, no pressing concerns about the introduction of the euro. Conversely, Greek and Portuguese unions did not perceive any transnational competitive pressures favoring the introduction of wage moderation because their wages were already the lowest in the eurozone.

Nevertheless, the British, Swedish, and Danish industrial unions are increasingly concerned with the competitiveness of their country (Due et al. 1998). In the context of increasing transnational economic integration, British, Danish, and Swedish unions are facing an increasingly difficult choice, namely, to choose between national sovereignty (which is seen as a cornerstone of their national welfare states) and the desire for stronger and more social EU regulation. Whereas the Swedish, Danish, and British unions continue to be among the most Euro-skeptical organizations within the ETUC (Dølvik 1999), a gradual Europeanization of their bargaining policies is taking place. In 1999 and 2000, for instance, the Danish unions of the export-oriented sectors took steps to apply the principles enshrined in the Doorn agreement of the Benelux and German unions and the bargaining coordination guidelines of the EMF (see chap. 6). Nevertheless, it should also be noted that the opposition to closer European cooperation is still vigorous in many Danish, Swedish, and British unions, especially in the domestic sector (Bieler 2006; Due et al. 1998). In fact, the unions of the three EU countries outside the eurozone are split on the European currency issue, especially in Sweden, where a majority of the unionists rejected Swedish EMU membership in the 2003 referendum.[5]

These observations highlight the fact that the relations among the different EU-polity strategies are dynamic. In the area of wage bargaining, the adoption of a democratic renationalization strategy by a union is closely associated with the degree of economic integration into the eurozone of its country of origin. It follows that the more the economic EU integration process progresses, the more the democratic renationalization strategy will lose its appeal. However, it would be wrong to assume a constant, teleological development, as emphasized by the clear rejection of the EMU by the Swedish electorate in autumn 2003. Likewise, it seems that organized labor will change its EU-polity strategies only if major structural changes, such as the introduction of the euro, make such changes necessary.

Finally, this chapter has shown that in seven of the fourteen EU member states analyzed organized labor actively supported the adoption of wage-moderation policies. This is an unexpectedly small number of cases if we recall the very assertive argumentation of the advocates of competitive corporatism (Rhodes 1997; Streeck 1998b, 1999). Nevertheless, the review of the national wage-bargaining policies confirms that the Austrian, Belgian, Finnish, German, Italian, Dutch, and Irish unions at least partially embraced the paradigm of competitive corporatism. Thus, it seems reasonable to argue that labor adopted a technocratic renationalization strategy in the field of collective wage bargaining in these seven EU countries.

This conclusion applies especially to the Italian case, in which the change in wage moderation occurred not only after the adoption of a specific social pact but also in a situation in which the unemployment rate remained stable (Zagelmeyer and Schulten 1997). This suggests that the abrupt decline of the wage share in Italy is an outcome of organized industrial relations rather than simply the result of market forces. Increased competitiveness, however, was not always the explicit policy objective of the unions concerned. Even in the Netherlands, Finland, and Ireland, which for many are exemplary cases of competitive corporatism, wage moderation was initially not directly connected to the question of international competitiveness but, instead, to a severe national economic and political crisis. However, we can only prove the competition bargaining or the technocratic renationalization thesis wrong if we witnesses an international agreement on a coordinated European collective wage-bargaining policy.

Ironically, however, unions only attempt European coordination of their wages policies if there is a need for it, or, in other words, if they believe that international wage competition bargaining is actually taking place. As long as unions believe in the autonomy of national wage-bargaining systems, they are hardly likely to attempt any European coordination of their wage policies. Hence, in contrast to the established understanding, competitive corporatism should not be seen as a static antithesis of any Europeanization of collective wage bargaining. Although it would be wrong to believe in a linear development of the EU-polity strategies of organized labor in line with the classic functionalist European integration theories (Haas 1968), it is credible that the four competing EU labor strategies are related to one another. As the declining autonomy of national systems made the contradictions of the democratic renationalization strategy apparent, it was likely to be replaced by a technocratic renationalization strategy. In contrast, the conflicts produced by such a technocratic renationalization strategy might also mobilize forces that would eventually lead to its demise because the tendency of competitive corporatism to set off self-defeating cycles of concession bargaining might be an effective catalyst for a Europeanization of labor wage-bargaining policies. Incidentally, the president of the ETUC and the Austrian trade union confederation started to highlight the dangers of a competitive wage policy as he realized that wage moderation—which he had hitherto supported—might also engender adverse consequences (Verzetnitsch 2000). This does not contradict the preliminary finding of this chapter, namely, that the unions in seven Western EU countries adopted a technocratic renationalization strategy, but the preceding remarks do emphasize the need to further assess these results in the light of the emerging attempts at European wage-bargaining coordination.

CHAPTER SIX

European Wage-Bargaining Coordination Networks

Insights from the Manufacturing and the Construction Industry

Since 1993, real wages have stopped following productivity growth in almost all eurozone countries. Chapter 5 shows that many unions accepted this development either to confront an economic crisis or to increase the international competitiveness of their own economy. However, by the end of the 1990s some unions started to question the merits of such a competitive wage-bargaining strategy. Whereas the labor share of national income declined considerably in most EMU countries, the expected compensations for labor, such as job creations, did not materialize.

Already in 1993, the Economic and Social Research Institute (WSI) of the German trade union confederation DGB had commissioned research on the likely effects of the EMU on collective bargaining (Altvater and Mahnkopf 1993; Busch 1994). These studies emphasized the danger of the EMU stimulating a downward spiral in wages, but wage bargaining became a European issue only after the adoption of the euro. Hitherto, most unions supported the EU integration process for political reasons, without bothering too much about its implications. However, the increased pressures on wages in the late 1990s encouraged several unions to explore the possibility of a cross-border coordination of their wage policies.

On September 5, 1998, Belgian, Dutch, German, and Luxembourgian unions adopted the Doorn declaration in the Dutch town of Doorn. Specifically, the unions committed themselves to seek, in their national bargaining negotiations, increases that fully offset national inflation and productivity growth. It was the declared aim of this objective to exclude a competitive race of wages to the bottom and to keep the labor share in the national income stable. If the total value of a collective wage-bargaining agreement matches the sum of inflation and productivity increases, then the distribution of the national income between capital and labor remains stable.[1] Consequently, the Doorn declaration designated the sum of inflation and productivity increases as the target wage increase for national collective bargaining (Kreimer-de Fries 1999). At its collective bargaining conference on December 9–10, 1998, the EMF also adopted an equivalent European coordination rule for national bargaining (Schulten and Bispinck 2001; Gollbach 2000; European Metalworkers' Federation [EMF] 1998). Finally, in December 2000, the ETUC also adopted a corresponding European collective bargaining coordination initiative (Mermet 2001; Traxler and Mermet 2003). By contrast, the European Federation of Building and Wood Workers (EFBWW) pursued a different European wage coordination approach, whose primary aim was to defend the autonomy of national collective bargaining.

This chapter assesses the European collective bargaining coordination initiatives of the EMF and the EFBWW in relation to our four EU trade union strategies. Do these initiatives question the democratic renationalization strategy thesis? If the answer is yes, we would expect the unions to acknowledge the end of the autonomy of their national wage-bargaining policies. Do they challenge the technocratic renationalization strategy thesis? If yes, we would expect an end to the concession bargaining that was typical of the monistic pacts between capital and labor in the 1990s. Or is EU-level wage coordination an element of an emerging Euro-technocratization strategy? If yes, we would expect European wage-coordination policies that are compatible with the regulatory approach that governs EU economic and monetary policy. Or are these initiatives part of an emerging Euro-democratization strategy? If yes, we would expect an EU-wide discussion of these benchmarks in the union press and among union activists, joint European collective actions, and a politicization of the regulatory approach that governs EU economic and monetary policy. The analysis here is also designed to be cross-national and cross-sectoral. This makes it possible to see whether the conflicting wage-coordination approaches are country- or sector-specific (Marginson, Sisson, and Arrowsmith 2003).

Wage bargaining is arguably one of the most important activities of unions. The autonomy of unions and employer organizations to conclude collective agreements is also a recognized principle in all EU member states. Therefore, many have argued that national unions would never sacrifice their autonomy in the area of wage bargaining. For this reason, we would expect unions to always affirm the autonomy of their national bargaining systems and, therefore, pursue a democratic renationalization strategy. In this chapter, this democratic renationalization thesis is put to the test.

The Rise and Demise of Euro-Corporatism

The Tripartite Attempts of the 1970s

The call for a transnational coordination of collective bargaining has a longer history than we might think. As far back as 1967, André Gorz suggested that

> the working-class cannot avoid being forced to shoulder the burden of oligopolist competition unless it can . . . coordinate its demands, especially in the case of contract renewal negotiations. Only in this way is it possible to avoid the eventuality that labor victories in one country, relating to wages, hours, vacations, and restrictions on the profit trade, may be exploited by the manufacturers of another country in order to take over a part of the former's markets. (1967, 183)

This, however, did not convince Gorz to propose European-level collective bargaining either because the European Economic Community (EEC) would be "nothing more than the technocratic emanation of States in which the working-class holds no power whatsoever." He fears that the working class would "cut itself off from the masses by entering into a confidential relationship with technocracy and representatives of big business" at the EEC level (185). However, political participation would make sense if the EEC were controlled by democratic, representative assemblies. Therefore, Gorz also rejects the sterile attitude of simply rejecting the EEC integration process without doing anything else. Instead, he proposes a leapfrog tactic,

> in which the labor movement of each country fights for the advantages won by the labor movement of another country, so that each labor movement spurs on the other movements because one of them will always be ahead of the others in the advantages it has won relating to one or another aspect of the work situation. The coordination of demands does not in effect imply their perfect identity. On the contrary, heterogeneity should be maintained as a source of perpetual ferment and agitation. (185)

Gorz's vision did not engender any immediate union response. However, in 1973 union confederations of the EEC and European Free Trade Association (EFTA) countries set aside their differences and founded the ETUC. This event is important for our discussion because a coordination of bargaining policies could only occur if the different national unions possessed a European forum to discuss and foster joint policies.

In the mid-1970s, the ETUC tried to find a joint European response to the economic crisis. In 1975, it successfully lobbied the Council of Ministers to create a tripartite conference of capital, labor, government, and European Commission representatives (Barnouin 1986). This was not easy for the ETUC, given the reluctance of some national unions vis-à-vis both neocorporatism and the EEC. The British Trades Union Congress (TUC) was careful not to surrender its national autonomy to European tripartite bodies. Nevertheless, the ETUC agreed, in 1976, to influence the tripartite conference in order to achieve the objective of full employment by 1980. The main goal of this campaign was a general reduction of working time, namely, the 35-hour working week, and 5 weeks of paid vacation.[2] Until 1978, national governments, the Commission, employers' organizations, and the ETUC participated in four tripartite conferences in which a whole range of neocorporatist solutions to the economic crisis were discussed. These European discussions also included policies that clearly belonged to the realm of national collective bargaining and policy making, such as working-time reduction, wage moderation, creation of employment in the service sector, and alternative public investments. However, in November 1978 these tripartite negotiations finally failed. The ETUC was no longer willing to participate in these meetings, given that their results were nonbinding due to employer resistance (Gobin 1996). Despite an intervention by then German Chancellor Helmut Schmidt and the Commission to reconsider this decision, the ETUC remained firm on this issue (Barnouin 1986). Then, with the election of Margaret Thatcher on May 3, 1979, and the free-market-oriented EEC Commission chaired by Gaston Thorn in 1981, any revival of neocorporatist bargaining at the EEC level definitely became unrealistic. As a result, collective bargaining policy disappeared for a long time from the EU-level union agendas, apart from declamatory congress resolutions and informal information exchanges, for example within the collective bargaining committee of the EMF (1993).

Until the 1990s, collective bargaining effectively remained a national issue, despite the adoption of the European Single Act in 1986 that launched the European single-market program of 1992. Streeck and Schmitter (1991) highlight the structural obstacles to explain the absence of any Europeanization of collective bargaining, such as the absence of a European central bank, the lack of centralized collective bargaining structures, and the incompatibility of existing national industrial relations systems. Moreover, most unions believed until the early 1990s that they could pursue an autonomous national collective bargaining policy. Therefore, they displayed little interest in a genuine Europeanization of collective bargaining.[3]

Hence, it is safe to argue that, until the adoption of the Maastricht Treaty, unions still believed in the autonomy of national bargaining systems. This explains the demise of Euro-corporatism in the 1970s and suggests that unions were pursuing national strategies, despite the occasional adoption of ETUC resolutions that stated the contrary.

The Symbolic Euro-Corporatism in the 1990s

In the mid-1990s, some believed in a new beginning for European collective bargaining because the adoption of the social protocol of the Maastricht Treaty constituted a legally defined social-dialog procedure at the EU level (Dølvik 1997; Lo Faro 2000). Within precisely defined fields of social policy, social-dialog agreements between the EU-level organizations of capital and labor could even become legally binding, if endorsed by the Commission and Council. This provision has been supported not only by the ETUC but also by its counterpart, Business Europe (formerly the Union of Industrial and Employers' Confederations of Europe, UNICE). It is open to question, however, whether these negotiations should be called collective bargaining. German unions, for instance, perceived the European social dialog as negotiated legislation rather than collective bargaining. In fact, the European social dialog covers only limited fields of social policy and explicitly excludes one core issue of collective bargaining, namely, wages (Articles 137 and 139 TEC). Moreover, it can hardly be considered a genuine case of collective bargaining because the unions possess rather limited means to exercise pressure on employers at EU level, except the threat that the EU legislators might enact a more constraining directive if the social partners fail to adopt a common position. Nevertheless, it is also true to say that the social dialog led, for the first time, to negotiations between employers' organizations and unions at the EU level, even though they only came to pass in the shadow of the law (Bercusson 1994).

So far, the European social dialog has produced only four interprofessional agreements: paternal leave, part-time work, fixed-term contracts, and telework (Falkner 2003; Léonard et al. 2007). Nevertheless, these agreements set standards that improved the social protection in several EU member states (Kowalsky 2000). Moreover, the Maastricht social protocol also supports social-dialog negotiations at the sectoral level. This process has also yielded some results; the number of sectoral agreements reached continues to grow (Léonard et al. 2007; Dufresne, Degryse, and Pochet 2007; Keller 2003; Dubbins 2002). However, most sectoral agreements are not binding. They usually set only recommendations that subsequently need to be interpreted, specified, and enforced at the national or company level. Moreover, European social-dialog agreements covered far less contentious topics, such as vocational training, in contrast to the typical collective bargaining on distributive issues such as wages. Occasionally, however, sectoral agreements also led to binding EU directives.[4]

Nevertheless, the European social dialog convinced the national unions to increase the authority of their European confederation. In 1995, the ETUC changed its statutes in order to create an effective bargaining order. The ETUC statute now states that the decisions about both a negotiation mandate and its outcome should have the support of at least two-thirds of the organizations directly concerned in the negotiations. This reduced the autonomy of its individual affiliates, which can no longer veto ETUC decisions. All ETUC affiliates supported the abrogation of the unanimity principle because the adoption of the new clear-cut rules also guaranteed national ETUC delegates better involvement in and control over ETUC policy (Dølvik 1997). Nevertheless, for grassroots unionists, problems of democratic legitimacy still exist. As in decision making by the Council, in which national executives (i.e., government ministers or their envoys) act as legislators at the EU level, the national union executives have the last word within the ETUC and the sectoral EU-level union federations.

It remains very difficult for local and national union constituencies to hold the ETUC decision makers accountable. This is especially true if the ETUC executives and national union leaders find it objectionable to discuss openly the contents of a European social-dialog agreement prior to its ratification by the ETUC executive.[5] As long as ETUC decisions entailed only limited consequences, this did not matter too much. In contrast, the more important EU-level union federations become, the more the question of internal transparency and democracy grows in significance.

In conclusion, the ETUC and the sectoral EU-level union federations gained a quasi-public status as co-legislators with the development of the European social dialog. Despite its limited scope, which reflects the incapacity of the unions to credibly threaten industrial or political conflict at the EU level, the development of the European social dialog is of importance for this discussion. Jon Erik Dølvik concluded his study of EU social dialogue referring to the following points made by Gary Marks and Doug McAdam: (1) the "causal arrows from union-building to state building go in both directions" and (2) it makes sense to conceive of the "modern polity as the outcome of a prolonged and, above all, mutually interactive process of political restructuring" (Marks and McAdam 1996, 98). Whereas Dølvik finds solid evidence for the second part of the equation, namely, that the making of EU-level unions has been strongly influenced by the EU state building, he acknowledges that it is much more difficult to find evidence for the reverse part of the equation. Even so, Dølvik (1997) argues, the establishment of the European social dialog by the Maastricht Treaty was the result of prior union pressure that emanated in response to the earlier relaunch of social dialog by the Delors Commission.

With the benefit of further hindsight, it is also true to say that the European social dialog contributed considerably to an increase in ETUC authority and to an increased participation of national union leaders in EU politics. However, the aspect of the Maastricht Treaty that did most to encourage a Europeanization of national unions was not the establishment of the EU social dialog but the introduction of the EMU. Until the EMU exhibited its negative impact on national wage trends in the late 1990s, the Europeanization of unionism had been advocated mainly by European idealists, for example, from the Italian CISL and the French Confédération Française Démocratique du Travail (CFDT) (Pernot 2001; Ciampani 2000; Dølvik 1997; Gobin 1996).

In the mid-1990s this situation changed as unions started to realize that European pressures were increasingly affecting national wage bargaining. However, the corresponding reorientation from a Euro-idealistic to a more realistic European trade union policy started outside the symbolic Euro-corporatist framework of the social dialog (Schulten 2000b), at the level of the sectoral EU-level union federations and bilaterally between the German and Benelux unions within the so-called Doorn process.

Setting European Benchmarks: The European Metalworkers' Federation Approach

Decades after its original publication, union researchers from the German WSI rediscovered Gorz's (1967) visions in a project on collective bargaining in the EMU that was commissioned by the EMF (Schulten, Bispinck, and Lecher 1998). That Gorz's thesis is still considered relevant reflects the fact that European coordination of wage bargaining continues to be an unsolved problem. However, whereas Gorz's leapfrogging tactics were meant to set off an upward contest for better working conditions, the contemporary coordination rules aim to prevent downward competition. Moreover, whereas Gorz does not question the autonomy of national unions, the EMF questions the autonomy of its affiliates by setting a European benchmark:

> The key point of reference and criterion for trade union wage policy in all countries must be to offset the rate of inflation and to ensure that workers' incomes retain a balanced participation in productivity gains. The commitment to safeguard purchasing power and to reach a balanced participation in productivity gains is the new European coordination rule for coordinated collective bargaining in the metal sector all over Europe. (EMF 1998a)

The EMF benchmark—and the Doorn and ETUC benchmarks that abide by the same rule of rate of inflation plus gains in productivity—recognizes that the national unions keep their full autonomy with respect to how they use this distributive space for the improvement of wages and working conditions. This flexibility mirrors the fact that the various national bargaining structures differ considerably; and this situation virtually excludes any nominal harmonization of collective bargaining at the EU level in the near future. Nevertheless, the Doorn, EMF, and ETUC benchmarks restrict the autonomy of national unions by setting an EU convergence criterion. This criterion concerns the key variable of collective bargaining: the actual quantity of the distributive space that the negotiations should secure. This leads to a puzzling question that even the ETUC official in charge of the EMU could not answer at the time (Coldrick 1998): Why should national unions voluntarily accept a supranational benchmarking target that limits their autonomy in their most important policy area?

This question is even more striking when we consider the actual substance of the benchmark. Given its distributive neutrality, it is surprising that the EMF benchmark has been perceived as pro-labor. In actual fact, the benchmark effectively abandons a traditional collective bargaining goal of labor, namely, that of a distribution of profits in favor of employees.[6] Hence, the fact that unions seem to be happy with the defense of the status quo would appear to be a good indicator of their current estimation of the balance of power between capital and labor.

Likewise, the Doorn declaration was not inspired by theoretical considerations. Without the constraints of the 1996 Belgian law that aimed to restore national competitiveness, the Belgian unions would hardly have sought any cross-border cooperation with the unions from neighboring countries. As discussed in chapter 5, this law linked the Belgian wage increases to those in Germany, France, and the Netherlands. It follows that, paradoxically, Belgian workers depend above all on the strength of the unions in their neighboring countries.[7]

In this situation, the Belgian unions accepted the demise of their national autonomy. This is remarkable because they also had the option of defending the autonomy of collective bargaining against government intervention. Likewise, the director of the international department of the German IG Bauen-Agrar-Umwelt (IG BAU) union, Frank Schmidt, could not understand why the Belgian unions did not challenge the law on competitiveness because it arguably violated legally binding core conventions of the International Labour Organisation (ILO) on free collective bargaining and independent trade unionism. Arguably, the Belgian unions avoided an open confrontation with the government because they feared that the government would abolish the statutory indexation of wages to compensate for inflation in the event of any conflict. The choice of the Belgian unions to accept the law linking wage bargaining to international benchmarks also suggests that they no longer believed in the national autonomy of bargaining.

All German, Italian, French, and Belgian metalworker unionists interviewed during this study accepted that national wage bargaining is losing much of its autonomy in the eurozone. However, my interviews also show that this feeling of diminishing national autonomy differs from country to country. It is greatest among Belgian unionists and weakest among Italians (see also Marginson, Sisson, and Arrowsmith 2003), but even the Italian Federazione Impiegati Operai Metallurgici (FIOM)-CGIL union, which in the 1970s conceived wages as an independent variable, accepts that wage levels are increasingly affected by transnational trends. The EMF thus agreed to set up a monitoring system, the European collective bargaining database, called Eucob@, which assesses the national wage-bargaining trends.

Certainly, the EMF possesses no coercive power to enforce its coordination benchmarks (Keller 2000). However, the fact that its affiliates voluntarily accepted the EMF benchmark suggests that they no longer believe in the national autonomy of wage-bargaining systems. This means that they are not pursuing a democratic renationalization strategy. Nevertheless, the question of compliance with the EMF benchmark is certainly important (and it is discussed in the following section assessing the coordination attempts in the context of the technocratic renationalization thesis).

Other industrial EU-level union federations had also adopted similar coordination benchmarks. The graphical section of UNI-Europa has also adopted a wage-coordination rule based on inflation and national productivity with the objective of obtaining as large a share of the productivity increase as possible. Moreover, it also approved—like the EMF—an annual maximum working-time target of 1,750 hours (EMF 1998b; Gennard and Newsome 2001). The benchmark of European Trade Union Federation–Textiles Clothing Leather (ETUF-TCL) also follows the EMF example, although its wage target allows for exceptions (Dufresne 2006). The European Mine, Chemical, and Energy Workers' Federation (EMCEF) adopted the least demanding benchmark, calling only for compensation for inflation (Dufresne 2006; Le Queux and Fajertag 2001). This low wage-coordination target corresponds to a much lower level of transnational union cooperation in the chemical and pharmaceutical industry. Without a doubt, the oligopolistic and ethnocentric character of the major players in the industry hindered cross-border cooperation because national unions represented not only different national but also different corporate interests.

Eventually, a discussion on the objectives of coordinating national collective bargaining at the EU level also began within the ETUC. A certain spillover to the ETUC of the discussions among the Doorn and the EMF unions took place. The ETUC Congress held in Helsinki in June 1999 adopted a resolution that highlighted the need to coordinate wage-bargaining policies because of the arrival of the euro. In consequence, the ETUC Executive Committee, in September 1999, set up the ETUC Collective Bargaining Coordinating Committee and urged the ETUC research and training institutes to assist the committee with scientific expertise and the organization of training courses for national union officials (Cochet 2002). At the December 2000 Executive Committee meeting, the ETUC agreed to a resolution on coordination of collective bargaining, which— like the Doorn and the EMF benchmarks—defined the national inflation plus productivity rate as the target for national collective bargaining. It was also agreed to collect quantitative and qualitative data on national collective bargaining, relate them to the target, and assess the data in an Annual Report on the Coordination of Collective Bargaining in Europe that will be discussed by the ETUC Executive (European Trade Union Confederation [ETUC] 2001a).

Today, the ETUC benchmark is accepted as a yardstick for national collective bargaining in Europe. Even union confederations that initially did not welcome the benchmark answered the ETUC questionnaires (Keune 2004, 2005, 2006; ETUC 2001a, 2002b). As a result, even the most powerful national unions, such as the German ones, lost their autonomy regarding the interpretation of bargaining results. The ETUC benchmark introduced a clear criterion that counteracts the common practice of presenting every bargaining result as a success.

Hence, the adoption of European benchmarks represents a change of the collective wage-bargaining strategies of labor. Although national criteria clearly dominated the bargaining agendas until the introduction of the euro, the adoption of the Doorn, EMF, and ETUC wage-increase targets indicates that most unions accept that national wage bargaining is no longer an autonomous national matter. This effectively rules out the pursuit of a democratic renationalization strategy, which depends on national autonomy. However, before we draw any general conclusions, it is necessary to discuss the alternative bargaining-coordination approach that was propagated by the EFBWW. In contrast to the ETUC and the EU-level union federations in the manufacturing sector, the EFBWW approach defended the national autonomy of collective bargaining.

Reestablishing National Autonomy: The European Federation of Building and Wood Workers' Approach

Instead of adopting a European wage-coordination target, in the early 1990s the EFBWW started a bottom-up approach that aimed to protect the autonomy of national wage bargaining in the context of an increasingly European labor market (Köbele and Leuschner 1995; Baumann, Laux, and Schnepf 1996; Wiesehügel and Sahl 1998). The completion of the European single market and the fall of the Iron Curtain led to enhanced transnational competition in various local labor markets in Western Europe (Menz 2005; Hunger 2001). For instance, since 1990 the local labor market in the building sector in Berlin was characterized by a huge influx of foreign posted workers. In contrast to classic migrants, these posted workers were usually not employed by domestic companies; they remained employees of foreign companies, even if they were actually working in Germany. Several German construction firms set up their own Portuguese daughter companies to bypass German collective bargaining agreements. This practice was made possible by the establishment of the free movement of services by the European Single Act. Under these conditions, German wages and working-condition standards came under huge competitive pressures, although both the German government and the EU adopted regulations in the 1990s to protect national labor standards in the construction sector.

As far back as 2000, long before the enlargement of the EU to Central and Eastern Europe, only 23,000 construction workers in Berlin were residents, that is, mostly German and Turkish workers who were actually living in the city for decades. The majority of the Berlin construction-sector workforce, however, was composed of 30,000 posted workers from Western Europe and 30,000 posted workers from Central and Eastern Europe, according to data provided by local IG BAU officials. These numbers are even more impressive if we take into account that approximately 30,000 resident workers lost their jobs since 1990. Although this situation is exceptional, a consequence of the fall of the Berlin wall and the extraordinary post-reunification construction boom, the Europeanization of the construction market put huge competitive pressure on domestic wage agreements.[8] It became increasingly difficult for local unions to enforce local working and living conditions. How is it possible for a German union to monitor the compliance of a company with the German wage-bargaining agreement if the company actually administers and pays in Portugal the wages of its Portuguese employee that it sent to Germany?

In response, the EFBWW and its member unions from the high-wage countries, such as the German IG BAU, adopted a European strategy that aimed to restore the autonomy of national collective bargaining. However, although the intended effect of this effort is clear, it would be problematical to characterize the corresponding strategy as a form of renationalization. The construction workers' unions involved aimed to defend their national autonomy in the area of collective bargaining, but they equally realized that national institutions had lost their capacity to guarantee this autonomy. The unions learned that any restoration of the autonomy of national wage bargaining could be achieved only through processes of Europeanization, by organizing transnational cooperation among unions and by politicizing their demands by directing them to EU institutions—exactly by the kind of action that constitutes a Euro-democratization strategy.

Correspondingly, in 1995 the EFBWW lobbied the EU to adopt the posted-workers directive,[9] which obliges employers of posted workers to comply with the working conditions in the workers' host country. Likewise, in 2006, several high-profile labor disputes in Sweden, Ireland, and Finland, and huge European labor demonstrations against attempts to set in train a race to the bottom in terms of pay and conditions of employment, politicized the debates about the EU service directive (Donaghey and Teague 2006). These mobilizations eventually compelled the European Parliament to amend the draft directive and to exclude the controversial country-of-origin principle[10] proposed by the neoliberal EU commissioners for the internal market, Frits Bolkestein and Charlie McCreevy. The revised draft aims to ensure that the free movement of services across the EU cannot be used to undermine labor standards in the country in which a service is provided.

The capacity of a European trade union federation, such as the EFBWW, to unite its affiliates across Europe is astonishing given recurrent neoliberal slanders of union opposition as anti-immigrant welfare protectionism (Woolfson and Sommers 2006). The EFBWW, however, did not urge its affiliates to protect their members through a closure of national labor markets. On the contrary, it insisted on increased transnational cooperation among unions from different countries (Cremers and Donders 2005; Baumann, Laux, and Schnepf 1996; Schnepf, Laux, and Baumann 1997). For instance, in practical terms, the German IG BAU concluded several bilateral agreements with the construction workers' unions from Austria, Switzerland, Portugal, Italy, and Poland to facilitate transnational union assistance for posted workers (Dribbusch 2003a; Gottschalk and Laux 2000; Schulten 1999b). These agreements include a mutual recognition of union membership rights, information exchange, mutual assistance for the transnational enforcement of working conditions, and the exchange of national union officials.

In particular, transnational exchanges of local union officials proved to be very valuable. Until 1999, the Berlin branch of IG BAU did not organize posted workers. This situation changed after a 6-month union official exchange between the Swiss Gewerkschaft Bau und Industrie union (now part of Unia), which had long experience with the organization and integration of migrant workers, and IG BAU Berlin (Steinauer and Von Allmen 2000; Schiesser 1999). Eventually, IG BAU Berlin also adopted a more open attitude toward the organization of posted workers, not least because IG BAU officials understood that the survival of the union was increasingly dependant on its capacity to organize posted workers. Moreover, IG BAU started to cooperate with community associations of foreign workers in Germany, such as the Polska Rada Społeczna (Polish Social Council), even if noticeable tensions between the two organizations continued to exist due to the ambiguous position of IG BAU toward the organization of undocumented migrant workers.

On the one hand, many IG BAU members regarded the migrant workers as competitors employed to undercut existing pay rates (Dribbusch 2004); on the other hand, unions can hardly afford to alienate migrant workers—because once they are in the country, it is essential to organize them (Castles and Kosack 1973)—even if an increase in labor supply doubtlessly has a moderating impact on pay. Unions will succeed in integrating migrant workers only when they recognize that this requires not only a policy shift at the top of a union but also a profound change in union organizational culture (Penninx and Roosblad 2000; Cachón and Valles 2003). Migrants tend to be sympathetic to unionization efforts because they have a lot to gain from union membership, but the building of an inclusive union movement requires not only organizing victories against employers that are exploiting immigrants but also a change in the "institutional life of unions so that immigrants are at the vital center" (Milkman and Wong 2001, 128).

For this reason, in 2004 the IG BAU leadership sponsored the creation of the multilingual European Migrant Workers' Union (EMWU). It aspired not only to better reach migrant workers but also to contribute to a better understanding between domestic and migrant workers. Certainly, the creation of the EMWU did not remove all tensions between domestic and migrant workers. It did, however, provide the IG BAU with an additional tool to improve the situation of migrant workers and to enforce the agreed-on minimum wages for construction workers.[11]

The EFBWW approach to supporting specific cross-border union contacts was even more successful in the case of the biggest European construction site, that is, the Neue Eisenbahn Alpentransversalen (NEAT; transalpine tunnel) project across the Alps in Italy and Switzerland (Baumann 2000). The effective and ongoing cooperation between unions of various countries that this engendered also ensured the joint representation of the whole multinational workforce vis-à-vis the employers.[12] This cooperation not only facilitated the enforcement of Swiss wages and bargaining agreements for the posted foreign workers, but also helped organize a successful strike against unhealthy working conditions in the Lötschberg tunnel segment of the NEAT project.

Formally, the EFBWW approach of increased transnational exchanges does not question the autonomy of the actors involved. Nevertheless, it seems that the EFBWW-sponsored exchanges have set off important transnational and intercultural learning experiences. Hence, the transnational exchange of information and experiences among unionists might have a greater Europeanization effect than we might expect. Nevertheless, it is very difficult to assess systematically the impact of such cross-border exchanges, as is demonstrated by the necessarily rather anecdotal accounts of the effects of these exchanges in other sectors.[13]

Dufresne (2006) depicts the Doorn and the EMF inflation and productivity wage-bargaining coordination norm as a German paradigm. She supports her claim by pointing to the important role German unionists played in adopting such a wage coordination benchmark within the EMF and other EU-level union federations. However, this assessment neglects the fact that German unionists also heavily influenced the EFBWW approach, which differs fundamentally from the EMF approach. Hence, the different strategies of the EMF and the EFBWW mirror the different Europeanization and globalization trends in different economic sectors rather than the predominance of German preferences.

Whereas in manufacturing the Europeanization process is mediated through the free movement of goods, in the construction sector Europeanization is mediated through the free movement of workers and services. Whereas in manufacturing local unionists are not personally confronted with workers on competing production sites that are located aboard, in construction transnational wage competition takes place locally on the same site. It follows that divergent sectoral situations require different Europeanization strategies on the part of labor (see also Anner et al. 2006). In consequence, the EMF approach became the dominant European wage-bargaining coordination approach merely because of the dominant position of the manufacturing unions in the labor movement.

This, however, also implies that the dominant EMF wage-bargaining coordination approach does not necessarily provide the best answers to the challenges that the unions are facing in the new European economy. In the service sector, which arguably employs the majority of the European workforce, a generalization of the EFWBB bargaining coordination approach might indeed produce better results than the EMF approach. This analysis would also be consistent with the recent successes of U.S. unions regarding innovative strategies for revitalizing the labor movement. Although Lowell Turner and Daniel Cornfield (2007) present a gloomy picture of U.S. industrial unionism in the new global economy, their case studies of several successful service sector union campaigns in several cities in the United States hint at the emergence of a new form of urban unionism.

Combining European Frameworks and National Autonomy

This chapter has assessed the EMF and the EFBWW approaches to European bargaining coordination in the light of the democratic renationalization strategy thesis. In sectors where the Europeanization processes of the economy need to be enforced locally, such as in construction, domestic collective bargaining approaches continue to be essential. In fact, the EFBWW combined national and European elements in its wage-coordination policy. On the one hand, EFBWW unions aimed to secure the autonomy of national bargaining systems against the competitive pressures of the single market; on the other hand, the EFBWW also realized that labor standards could only be defended if EU legislation and European cooperation between the unions supported this goal.

Accordingly, the construction workers' unions not only successfully mobilized workers across Europe for the EU posted-workers directive and against the initial draft of the EU services directive, but also sought bilateral union exchanges that contributed to transnational learning processes at the local level. The transnational politicization, mobilization, and exchange activities of the EFBWW are instances of the kind of action our model describes as Euro-democratization. What the construction-sector unions accomplished arguably made a more substantial contribution to democratizing the EU polity than the Europeanization of targets that the metalworkers' unions brought about.

Nevertheless, the prevailing ETUC strategy in the field of wage bargaining has been determined by the EMF, not by the EFBWW, even though the ETUC did take the same stance as the EFBWW in the case of the EU services directive. Union confederations always favor certain interests and neglect others (Hyman 1999). This axiom also applies to the ETUC[14] and the Doorn group. The ETUC and Doorn approaches to the European coordination of wage bargaining have been shaped by the pattern-setting metalworkers' unions, which exercise a crucial influence, especially in the field of collective bargaining coordination.[15] This situation mirrors not only the relative strength of the manufacturing unions within the European labor movement but also the different Europeanization and globalization processes that take place in different economic sectors.

The adoption of joint European benchmarks shows that most unions acknowledged the demise of national autonomy in wage bargaining after the introduction of the euro and the single market. This indicates the development of a European conceptual framework for wage bargaining; however, this also suggests the decay of any democratic renationalization strategy that requires national independence.

Nevertheless, some unions might also have agreed to the EMF and ETUC benchmarks to assess the competitive standing of their own bargaining policies. It follows that only a thorough review of national bargaining policies will allow us to discern the pursuit of a Europeanization strategy on the part of labor. Only at that stage will it be possible to confidently falsify the competitive corporatism or technocratic renationalization thesis. Because the EFBWW did not adopt any European wage-bargaining benchmarks, the next chapter focuses especially on the performance of the German, French, and Italian unions in relation to the EMF and ETUC benchmarks.

CHAPTER SEVEN

Beyond Competitive Corporatism?

Insights from Germany, France, and Italy

The unions of the Doorn group, the EMF, and the ETUC agreed to joint European wage-bargaining benchmarks in order to limit downward pressures on wages. However, it is still possible that some unions are pursuing a technocratic renationalization strategy to enhance the competitive position of their own countries, despite their promises to honor mutually agreed-on European wage-bargaining targets. This chapter puts the technocratic renationalization strategy thesis to a final test to find out whether this competitive wage bargaining trend is continuing, despite the adoption of the European bargaining targets. First, the recent wage, inflation, and productivity data of selected EU member states are analyzed to assess whether the national wage developments are in line with the ETUC European benchmarks. Second, this chapter reviews the recent wage-setting policies in Germany, France, and Italy, the three most important eurozone countries in economic terms, accounting for 70 percent of the eurozone Harmonized Index of Consumer Prices (HICP).[1]

Analyzing the German, Italian, and French cases is also appealing because pattern bargaining seems to be the only probable scenario for European wage coordination—a movement toward wage bargaining at the EU level is very unlikely (Léonard et al. 2007). Calmfors (2001) identifies the German unions as the natural candidate for the setting of an EU-wide pattern, but he also believes the French, Italian, and Spanish unions might oppose such a German wage leadership, in contrast to the Austrian, Belgian, and Dutch unions. This represents another argument for a detailed assessment of the German, French, and Italian cases.

European Benchmarks and National Competitiveness

According to the ETUC (2002b), nominal wages in the EU rose in 2001 by more than the ETUC benchmark (inflation plus productivity), whereas the 2002 data mark a return to the typical pre-2001 situation, when wage rises were below the target. The ETUC also notes that wage increases in the eurozone fell short of the target, whereas in the EU as a whole they were above the benchmark in 2001 and matched it in 2002. Thus, the ETUC claims that its wage coordination target "has certainly had an effect on negotiations" (ETUC 2002b, 4). But this statement turned out to be premature, as shown by its subsequent reports that evaluated wage tends over a longer period of time (Keune 2004, 2005, 2006).

Table 7.1 relates the average real-wage growth since 2003 to productivity growth in selected EU countries. A negative score in the table means that real-wage growth is below the ETUC wage-bargaining target, and a positive score means that real-wage growth is above the ETUC wage-bargaining target. The table shows that since 2003 real-wage growth has remained below productivity improvements everywhere in Europe, with the

Table 7.1. Average real-wage growth compared to the ETUC bargaining target[a]

	Total real-wage[b] increase minus productivity[c] increase (%)				
	2003	2004	2005	2006 (est.)	Cumulative 2003–2006
Poland	−2.5	−3.6	−5.7	—	−11.4[d]
Germany	−0.7	−2.1	−2.8	−3.3	−8.6
Netherlands	0.9	−2.2	−3.1	−2.6	−6.9
Sweden	−2.7	−1.1	0.2	−2.4	−5.9
Spain	−0.8	−1.4	−1.8	−1.9	−5.8
Belgium	−1.4	−2.1	−1.2	−1.1	−5.7
Slovenia	−0.2	−1.6	−0.9	−1.2	−3.8
France	−0.5	−1.6	0.4	−0.6	−2.3
Hungary	4.5	−5.9	−0.6	—	−2.3[d]
Denmark	−0.1	1.0	−2.1	−0.8	−2.0
Czech Republic	2.2	−1.0	−1.2	−0.8	−0.8
Italy	0.7	−0.1	−0.2	−0.7	−0.3
Finland	0.6	0.4	1.6	−0.7	1.9

Source: ETUC Questionnaires cited by Keune (2006).
[a]ETUC, European Trade Union Confederation.
[b]Data for Belgium, Germany, Denmark, Italy, the Netherlands, and Sweden refer to wages per hour; data for the remaining countries refer to wages per person.
[c]Data for Belgium, Germany, Finland, the Netherlands, Poland, and Sweden refer to productivity per hour; data for the remaining countries refer to productivity per person.
[d]The cumulative figures for Hungary and Poland refer to 2003–2005.

Table 7.2. Collectively agreed-on real-wage growth compared to the ETUC target

	Real increase of collectively agreed-on wages minus productivity[b] increase				
	2003	2004	2005	2006 (est.)	Cumulative 2003–2006
Slovakia	−9.4	−8.8	0.1	−3.2	−19.9
Slovenia	−3.8	−4.1	−2.9	−3.7	−13.7
Poland[c]	−2.7	−4.4	−5.3	—	−11.9[d]
Czech Republic	−0.3	−3.8	−2.8	−3.9	−10.4
Sweden	−4.0	−2.4	−0.9	−3.0	−9.9
Netherlands	0	−3.7	−3.4	−3.0	−9.8
Belgium	−1.1	−1.6	−0.6	−1.1	−4.3
Germany	0.2	−0.5	−1.9	−2.2	−4.3
Hungary[e]	0.7	−4.0	−0.5	—	−3.8[d]
Finland	−0.5	−1.0	0.3	−1.8	−3.0
Denmark	−0.4	1.2	−1.6	−0.8	−1.6
Spain[f]	0.1	0	0.2	−1.3	−1.0
Portugal	0.4	−0.5	0.1	−1.0	−1.0
Italy	0.7	−0.1	−0.2	−0.7	−0.3

Source: ETUC Questionnaires cited by Keune (2006).
[a]ETUC, European Trade Union Confederation.
[b]Data for Belgium, Germany, Finland, the Netherlands, Poland, and Sweden refer to productivity per hour; data for the remaining countries refer to productivity per person. ETUC, European Trade Union Confederation.
[c]Data for Poland are affected by the National Tripartite Commission proposals for wage increases. In 2003, 2005, and 2006, no agreement was achieved and the government established the guideline.
[d]The cumulative figures for Hungary and Poland refer to 2003–2005.
[e]In the data for Hungary, 2004 includes only agreements of the MSZOSZ union and 2006 includess the agreement in the National Interest Reconciliation Council.
[f]Data for Spain include the effect of the revision clause, except for 2006.

exception of Finland. It is noteworthy that in the 2003–2006 period German real-wage growth lagged 8.6 percent behind the ETUC target and Polish real wages remained 11.4 percent behind productivity trends in the shorter 2003–2005 period. Average real-wage growth, however, might not be the best indicator to assess union wage-bargaining strategy, given the decreasing coverage of collective wage agreements in some European countries. For this reason, table 7.2 relates the average real-wage increases resulting from collective bargaining to the ETUC wage-bargaining target.

It is clear from table 7.2, however, that the collectively agreed-on real-wage increases did not to meet the ETUC targets either. This difference is highest in Central and Eastern Europe (CEE) due to huge productivity growth rates. In the CEE countries, the unions not only had enormous difficulties in negotiating real-wage increases in line with productivity trends, they also failed to obtain wage increases in line with average real-wage growth (table 7.1). CEE economic policies are determined by a radical variant of neoliberalism (Bohle 2006), but multinationals that relocate their production to CEE countries will arguably not find themselves in heaven eternally because economic growth and labor emigration are improving the bargaining position of CEE workers (Meardi 2006).

In Germany, the collectively agreed-on wage increases tend to be higher than the average wage increases; this suggests that unions do still matter. Table 7.2 also suggests that the ETUC target played no role in the wage-setting process in Germany, as in most other EU countries. Only the Italian developments seem to be roughly in line with the ETUC target, but this is only due to very low productivity increases. This makes it very difficult to claim that the ETUC benchmark shaped EU wage developments, unless we can prove that the benchmarks were implemented differently in different countries.

The German Case

According to ETUC annual bargaining reports, average German wage increases remained considerably below the ETUC target during the whole 2000–2006 period. In 2001, 2004, and 2005, nominal wage increases remained even below the inflation rate (Keune 2005). It should also be noted that the collectively negotiated wage increases in Germany were higher than the average wage rises. However even the negotiated wage rises remained below the ETUC benchmark. In 1999 only, the unions managed to obtain increases that were 1.7 percent above the ETUC benchmark (ETUC 2001a). Hence, the German unions were among the most unsuccessful agents of the ETUC wage-bargaining coordination policy. This result is puzzling, given that the German (manufacturing) unions were among the strongest supporters of the ETUC benchmark.

Real-wage growth in Germany ceased to follow the productivity increase in 1993. German unions tacitly supported this wage moderation trend, although this did not imply an absence of industrial conflicts. The unions used collective action as a means to restore social rights (e.g., fully paid sick leave) cut back by the conservative CDU government rather than as a tool to secure substantial wage increases. After the victory of the social-democratic SPD in the general election of 1998, the situation changed, at least initially. The unions declared an end to their false modesty and urged wage increases that made full use of the neutral distributive margin. The new German finance minister, Oskar Lafontaine, and his Euro-Keynesian advisors, Claus Noé and Heiner Flassbeck, not only supported this claim, but also actively encouraged the European wage-coordination attempts of the unions.[2] Likewise, Oskar Lafontaine and his French counterpart, Dominique Strauss-Kahn, promoted an EU-wide project for the coordination of economic policy, the intention of which was to provide a Euro-Keynesian revival of the EU economy (Dufresne 2002).

In this context, IG Metall managed in spring 1999 to obtain real-wage increases that went beyond the Doorn and EMF bargaining benchmarks. The same trend could be observed in the other countries of the Doorn group. When union representatives from Belgium, Germany, Luxembourg, and the Netherlands met in September 1999 to evaluate the 1999 bargaining rounds, they concluded that the Doorn bargaining coordination attempt would be a success because the negotiated wage increases in all countries were meeting the benchmark of the Doorn declaration (Bispinck 2000).

In 2000, wage policy became a very contentious issue within the German union movement because the confederal DGB leadership accepted wage guidelines within the tripartite Alliance for Jobs, Vocational Training, and Competitiveness pact that did not match the Doorn, EMF, and ETUC bargaining targets (Bispinck and Schulten 2000). Even if many sectoral unions, including IG Metall, declared that they would not accept any interference by the Alliance wage guidelines in their bargaining autonomy, the bargaining results in the following years fell short of the labor European wage-coordination targets.

The incongruity between the 1999 and the subsequent bargaining rounds corresponds to conflicting (social-democratic) policy orientations. Until Oskar Lafontaine resigned from all of his offices in 1999 in protest against Chancellor Gerhard Schröder, Euro-Keynesian thinking dominated the economic policy of the German social-democratic government. Real-wage increases were in vogue, given their supposed positive effects on consumer demand. Afterward, however, the Schröder government declared an end to the Euro-Keynesian approach and advocated the adoption of a competitive supply-side bargaining strategy.

Correspondingly, Streeck, a leading advisor to Schröder's new center social democrats, argued in 1999 that in an age of global competition firms could no longer afford to allow unions to redistribute resources.[3] Streeck dismissed classic social-democratic egalitarian paradigms because they presuppose an "economy tolerant of slack" and attacked the unions for securing employment for less productive workers in overpaid jobs. In other words, unemployment resulted not from flawed economic policies, as the Euro-Keynesians argued, but from labor costs that were too high.

Streeck's arguments influenced the SPD and the German trade union movement. Moreover, the introduction of the euro also increased the prospects of a competitive wage-moderation strategy for Germany because low wage increases could no longer be counteracted with a corresponding revaluation of the deutsche mark (DM). It follows that the real driving force of wage dumping in the eurozone might not be the former weak-currency countries, but the countries of the former DM zone, which could—after the introduction of the euro—join the wage-moderation race without fearing that a revaluation of their currency would counteract this strategy.[4]

These conflicting social-democratic policy orientations led to ambiguous union policies. While Streeck's positions provoked virulent opposition from some union leaders,[5] the unions simultaneously tried to fit their policies into the supply-side-oriented framework of the Alliance for Jobs, Vocational Training, and Competitiveness.[6] Although German unions supported the Doorn, EMF, and the ETUC benchmarks, they were at the same time seeking an agreement with the German employers and the government to enhance the stance of the *Standort Deutschland*. This led to the pursuit of a logically inconsistent, but nevertheless visible, double strategy. The unions accepted the competitive logic of the Alliance, but they simultaneously tried to overcome it. The assessment of the German bargaining rounds since 2000–2001, however, suggests that the competitive wage-moderation objectives prevailed over the union commitments in favor of a European coordination of collective bargaining, despite the failure of the Alliance in 2003 due to major differences among the government, the unions, and employers concerning controversial labor market and social security reforms.

In January 2000, the pattern-setting IG Metall started its bargaining round, demanding a considerable increase of 5.5 percent. The union justified its claims on the grounds of an assumed inflation rate of 1.5 percent, a predicted productivity growth of 3.5 percent, and a redistribution component of 0.5 percent, reflecting the high profitability of the metal industry. Hence, the IG Metall claims were completely in line with the EMF benchmark. However, in March 2000 new wage agreements were concluded, first in the chemical sector and then in the metalworking sector, that clearly conflicted with the EMF and Doorn benchmarks. In March 2000, the North Rhine–Westphalia (NRW) branch of IG Metall signed a biannual pilot agreement with the regional branch of the employer organization; this agreement foresaw low wage increases in comparison to productivity and inflation increases, even with the inclusion of an additional 0.3 percent relating to the introduction of a new early retirement scheme (Schulten 2000a).

The Schröder government, the employers' associations, the European

Central Bank (ECB), and the mainstream media celebrated this moderate bargaining result as a major success for the Alliance. In contrast, several union leaders voiced their frustrations about it. Whereas the IG Metall president defended the NRW agreement, the head of the federal collective bargaining department of IG Metall openly criticized it. He accused the negotiators of signing the NRW pilot agreement without the consent of the federal IG Metall bargaining department just a few hours before the traditional pattern-setting Baden-Württemberg branch of IG Metall was meant to go on strike. This highlighted the failure of a divided IG Metall leadership to coordinate union activities across its regional branches that represented not only different industrial structures but also different political orientations (Karch 2000).

The head of the IG Metall NRW branch, Harald Schartau, was one of the first IG Metall officials to establish cross-border links with neighboring Belgian and Dutch metalworkers' unions (Gollbach 2000), but he also belonged to the minority of union officials who publicly disapproved the adoption of the "academic" EMF benchmark (Schartau 1998). In addition, Schartau could be sure that many DGB leaders would not interpret the European benchmarks too literally (Putzhammer 1999). Other union officials, however, used the benchmarks when they criticized the moderate bargaining outcome of the 2000–2001 negotiations (Bispinck and Schulten 2002).

The moderate German collective bargaining results were also criticized by several European trade unions, such as those from Belgium (Dufrense 2006; Confédération des Syndicats Chrétiens [CSC] 2000). However, neither the ETUC nor the EMF criticized the German unions for their meager bargaining results. On the contrary, the EMF deputy general secretary thanked IG Metall for its financial support, without which the EMF would not have been able to continue the Eucob@ project beyond spring 2000 (Samyn 2001). Furthermore, the EMF was not telling the entire truth when it asserted that the German increases came very close to its benchmark (EMF 2001a, 2001b).

With the notable exception of the 2007 and the 2002–2003 bargaining rounds (Schulten 2002b; Bispinck 2007), IG Metall only obtained wage increases that were below the EMF target. Accordingly, after the 2000–2001 bargaining round, the German wage trends generally followed competitive wage-bargaining patterns. However, this reflects not only moderate wage bargaining results, but also an increase in company outsourcing activities, a decline in additional payments above the collectively agreed-on wage rates, cuts in the unemployment benefits system, and thus a declining pattern-setting capacity of German wage agreements (Doellgast and

Greer 2007; Menz 2005; Bispinck and Schulten 2003; Dribbusch 2003b; Artus, Schmidt, and Sterkel 2000).

The German unions, and especially IG Metall, never abandoned their European wage coordination objectives. Whenever the unions were disappointed by the lack of compensation from the government or the employers for moderate wage increases, they reasserted their European commitments (Bispinck and Schulten 2002). In the course of the 2002–2003 round, for example, IG Metall invited more than twenty leaders from other EMF metalworkers' unions to Frankfurt to support its industrial action for a new contract. In so doing, IG Metall responded, on the one hand, to an explicit warning from the ECB (Duisenberg and Noyer 2002) and demonstrated, on the other, that it was still committed to the EMF benchmark (Schroeder and Weinert 2003; Schulten 2002b). Likewise, the European union leaders adopted a joint Frankfurt declaration, in which they not only reasserted the EMF target as a tool for fighting against wage dumping in Europe but also agreed to closer transnational cooperation (IG Metall and European Metalworkers' Federation 2002). Although these attempts do not signal robust European wage-bargaining coordination policies, they confirm that national unions feel a moral obligation to explain their policies within a European framework (ETUC 2006; Schroeder and Weinert 2003). Finally, the declining pattern-setting capacity of German wage agreements and the comparisons of German wage trends with wage developments in other courtiers also forced German unions to see the wage-setting systems of other countries more positively. This contributed to a remarkable policy shift on the part of the German unions in favor of statutory minimum wages (Schulten, Bispinck, and Schäfer 2006). Accordingly, in October 2006, the Doorn group declared, "where a minimum wage does not exist [namely in Germany] it must be introduced as a matter of urgency" (ETUC 2006, 1).

The French Case

The ETUC bargaining reports reveal that French average real-wage growth came closer to the ETUC target than the German case. It was only in 2002 that the average wage increases remained considerably below the benchmarks. This result is surprising, considering the marginal role of French unions in the wage-setting process and given their lack of enthusiasm for subscribing to these benchmarks (Dufour and Hege 1999). Nevertheless, this development did not happen accidentally. It was the result of a political choice by the French wage-bargaining pattern-setter—the government.

The French compliance with the ETUC benchmark is related to the staged introduction of the 35-hour working week by the socialist government between 1998 and 2000. According to an *ex-post* evaluation published by the French statistical office, Institut National de la Statistique et des Études Économiques (INSEE), the working-time reduction created up to 350,000 additional jobs (Gubian et al. 2004). This reduced the average productivity per worker. As a result, the share of wages as a proportion of GDP remained stable. However, it remains to be seen whether this development has been influenced by the European wage-coordination benchmarks.

The French unions had been associated at an early stage with both the Doorn initiative and the EMF discussions on wage coordination, but they remained at the margin of these two processes. This situation changed only after French Euro-Keynesian economists and the French government developed an interest in the matter. The Christian Belgian union confederation (Confédération des Syndicats Chrétiens, CSC) initially tried to involve the French unions in the Doorn process, but this proved to be difficult. The moderate French union confederation CFDT did not manifest much interest and the union-related Institut de Recherches Economiques et Sociales was not very sympathetic to the Doorn and EMF wage coordination approaches either (Dufour and Hege 1999). The German unions did not want to involve the French postcommunist union confederation Confédération Général du Travail (CGT) in the process prior to its affiliation to the ETUC in March 1999. Thus, the German and Benelux unions eventually set up the Doorn group without any French involvement. Nevertheless, the German and Benelux unions did not mind the French absence because their involvement would probably not have facilitated the adoption of the Doorn benchmark.[7]

The French bargaining system is characterized by a pattern-setting role of the state and decentralized wage-setting structures at the company level, even though sectoral bargaining structures have never been dismantled, in contrast to the British case (Jobert 2000). Likewise, some observers have argued that multi-employer bargaining is still prevalent in France (Traxler and Mermet 2003), but this categorization is problematic, given that the minimum wages stated in many collective agreements are below the statutory minimum wage (Ministère des Affaires Sociales 2003b).

Nevertheless, this double wage-setting structure by the state and by collective agreements seems to please many unionists. Even the CGT, which issued central wage claims in the past, abandoned this policy during the last decade. Incidentally, the CGT general secretary, Bernard Thibault, could not indicate a wage-rise target in a television debate on the 2000–

2001 bargaining round. Instead, he argued, rises in pay would be determined by the action of the workers in the individual enterprises. In contrast, the secretary of the French employers' association Mouvement des Entreprises de France (MEDEF), Denis Kessler, had surprisingly no problem predicting an average pay increase of 5 percent.[8] Also, the Alstom CGT and EWC delegate, Francine Blanche, argued that wage bargaining should reflect the actual *rapport de force* in each company establishment. According to many CGT officials, the most combative workers should also be rewarded with the greatest pay rises. Hence, shop-floor activists rather than central union officials should define bargaining policy.

This decentralization trend reflects, first, the weak capacity of the French unions to win major improvements through sectoral agreements. In the 1970s, the ineffectiveness of sectoral bargaining frustrated many unionists, especially in large concerns that were comparably well unionized, such as PSA-Peugeot, Renault, and Alstom.[9] Consequently, in 1982, most unions welcomed the *lois Auroux* labor reform of the first socialist government of François Mitterrand, which introduced mandatory annual negotiations on pay, working time, and work organization also at the local company level. Moreover, the increase in decentralized bargaining also reflects an ideological transformation of the French union movement, matching the decline of the French Communist Party (PCF) and the notion of the united working class. In 2000, a leading CGT official explicitly linked the abandonment of central CGT bargaining targets to its dissociation from the PCF. The termination of CGT centralist communist orientation caused a revitalization of its original syndicalist roots (Groux and Mouriaux 1992) rather than a rise of equally centralized, neo-Keynesian, and neocorporatist policy orientations. Finally, the predominance of company-level bargaining also reflects the occupational origins of French union officials. Most French union leaders emerged from the largest French enterprises, such as, for example, the national railway company Société Nationale des Chemins de Fer Français (SNCF), in the case of CGT leader Thibault. The lack of union presence in most French small and medium-size companies also explains why the unions rely so much on the state, as indicated by the union claims in favor of the thirty-five-hour working-week laws or the SMIC.[10]

Against the background of these peculiarities of French collective bargaining, it is not very surprising that the European bargaining coordination approaches of the EMF and the Doorn group did not raise widespread interest among French unionists (Dufour and Hege 1999). Furthermore, the CFDT did not perceive the EMU as a threat, in contrast to the Doorn unions (Trogrlic 1999). Nevertheless, it would be wrong to argue that the

Euro-idealistic CFDT orientation reflects only ideological choices (Gobin 1997). Because French interest rates were constantly held above those of Germany to offset the exchange risk of holding a hypothetically weaker currency, the introduction of the euro diminished, at least initially, the competitive pressures on French industrial relations (Usher 2001). The fact that the negative French perception of European wage-coordination targets weakened over time reflected the growing microeconomic competitive pressures due to transnational company restructurings and mergers. Thus, for instance, the general secretary of the CFDT metalworker branch supported the EMF collective bargaining coordination approach as far back as 1999—but not as an answer to the macroeconomic pressures that the Doorn unions associated with the euro (Bonnand 1999). In contrast to them, he perceived it as an effective tool against the relocation of businesses to other EU countries because international firm structures, supply chains, imports, and exports are framed by regional trading blocks, such as the EU.

The introduction of the thirty-five-hour working week in France was the key commitment in Lionel Jospin's socialist electoral manifesto of 1997. Accordingly, the working-time reduction was first and foremost represented as a domestic policy objective. The French discussion was not related to particular European aspects, although the preceding successful implementation of the thirty-five-hour working week in German manufacturing evidently favored the implementation of Jospin's promise. Nonetheless, the French government was also concerned about the implications of the working-time reduction for French international competitiveness. Therefore, it tried to motivate the Italian center-left government to introduce simultaneously the thirty-five-hour working week (Usher 2001). This transalpine coordination attempt failed (Ravaioli and Agostinelli 1998), but the French government nevertheless went ahead. This suggests that the French government was confident that the introduction of the thirty-five-hour working week would not be undercut by a competitive wage-bargaining policy of its neighbors and major trading partners. Correspondingly, the French government and parliament observed the coordinated bargaining approach of the Benelux and German unions with much sympathy (Ministère de l'Emploi et de Solidarité 1999; Assemblée Nationale 2000).

The Commissariat Général du Plan and the French Labor Ministry commissioned several studies on the prospects for a European coordination of collective bargaining (Maurice 1999; Ministère des Affaires Sociales 2001, 2003a).[11] The Labor Ministry organized, in cooperation with its German counterpart, a Franco-German meeting on the subject in Lyon, where union officials from both countries and invited experts could explain their views. This exchange calmed the French fears that the Doorn process would lead to a fragmentation of the European social model reflecting the different industrial relations systems (Freyssinet 1999). After the French parliament recognized the necessity of a European coordination of wage bargaining in its report on social dumping in the EU (Assemblée Nationale 2000), the French trade unions perceived the Doorn approach even more positively. The French union confederations stopped rejecting the idea of European targets and in December 2000 supported the adoption of the ETUC wage-bargaining coordination benchmark. This change mirrored not only the strong presence of Euro-Keynesian approaches in the Jospin government (Maurice 2001) but also an increasing fragmentation and transnationalization of French companies (Hancké 2002) that made it increasingly difficult to obtain meaningful bargaining results at the company level, even in company strongholds. As a result, the French unions acknowledged the merits of the ETUC target in the union press (Ardondel 1999; Force Ouvrière 2000; Juquel and Metz 2001; Thiéry and Bass 2001).

Nevertheless, it is not very likely that the French unions will become wage pattern setters in the future. French wage development will continue to depend on the pattern-setting role of the government (Barrat, Yakubovich, and Maurice 2002). Even though the center-right parties that governed France after 2002 triggered several contentious attempts to deregulate the French labor and social security law (Pernot 2005), no leading French politician, including the new president Nicolas Sarkozy, questioned the statutory national minimum wage. As a result, national minimum wages continued to increase, however at a slower pace than that experienced under the preceding socialist government of Prime Minister Lionel Jospin.

The Italian Case

Since 2003, average and collectively agreed-on wages in Italy have grown more or less in line with the ETUC benchmark, mostly because of low productivity growth (Keune 2005, 2006). Moreover, until 2002 the negotiated wage increases even failed to compensate for the rise in inflation (ETUC 2002b). The substantial gap between the negotiated and the average wage increases mirrors the bargaining structure that was introduced by the 1993 social pact. The pact introduced a two-tiered system that linked wage growth in national agreements to the projected inflation rate while payments for productivity growth became an exclusive issue for company-level bargaining.

Although some observers incorrectly argued that the inflation target of the 1993 social pact would set an insuperable ceiling for national collective bargaining, no subsequent national collective bargaining agreement has produced increases that went beyond the projected inflation rate (Megale, D'Aloia, and Birindelli 2003).[12] This also applies in the pattern-setting metal industry, in which the left-wing union confederation, CGIL, supported a separate bargaining platform in 2003, drawn up by its metalworkers' branch (FIOM), that went slightly beyond the wage-moderation policy benchmarks of the Italian social pact of 1993. The FIOM even went on strike to get wage increases above the inflation rate, but without much success because the metalworkers' branches of the smaller Catholic CISL and the moderate UIL union confederations signed a separate national agreement that contained wages increases at the level of the inflation rate.

This reflects not only the moderate policies of the two smaller unions but also their dedication to decentralized collective bargaining. Whereas the CGIL is still influenced by its historical attachment to the notion of a united working class and therefore favors all-encompassing national agreements, the two smaller unions are much more influenced by Anglo-Saxon concepts of business unionism and favor company-level agreements. Given the huge regional productivity differentials that characterize Italian firms, company-level bargaining might even generate better bargaining results, at least in northern Italy where unemployment is very low, union membership is greater, and productivity is very high. In contrast, southern Italian workers did not benefit from the decentralization of collective bargaining at all because there were hardly any company-level agreements in the south.

Since 2003, however, Italian wages have been developing in line with the ETUC benchmark, due to company-level wage rises and low productivity increases. However, this trend was influenced neither by Italian social pacts nor by union European wage-bargaining targets. Local negotiations almost never took macroeconomic indicators into consideration. This applies also to the ETUC and EMF benchmarks because the Italian unions did not publicize these either.[13] European comparisons started to influence the Italian wage setting in another way, however. After the introduction of the euro, in some sectors Italian employees started to compare their wages with the wage levels in other eurozone countries. The autonomous COBAS unions and the Refounded Italian Communist party (PRC), which did not support the 1993 social pact, claimed that Italian wages should equal average eurozone wages. In sectors such as education, in which both the COBAS and PRC exercise considerable influence, the three established union confederations embraced this claim, too. In the public sector, for instance, in 2001 all education unions successfully fought for considerable wage increases that brought the Italian wage level up closer to the euro-zone average.

Europe also played a crucial role in legitimating the income policy benchmarks of the 1993 social pact (Ferrera and Gualmini 1999). Its reference to the EMU was a useful tool to justify seemingly necessary but unpopular national wage policy changes (Dyson and Featherstone 1996; Mania and Sateriale 2002). In turn, the reluctance of many Italian unions to adopt EMF and the Doorn bargaining coordination benchmarks reveals the crucial impact of national considerations despite the outspoken Euro-federalist discourse of the Italian unions (Ciampani 2000; Pernot 2001).

In view of the introduction of the euro, the Italian metalworkers' unions suggested a campaign for a genuine EU framework agreement for the whole metal sector. In so doing, they went far beyond the EMF coordination approach of national collective bargaining, but the proposition of the Italian unions did not become EMF policy. The majority of EMF trade unions could not understand why the Italians preferred a Euro-federalist solution and not the EMF benchmarking approach, which would respect national diversity provided that the total value of an agreement was in line with the benchmark. However, a close reading of the historical and political background to the Italian approach reveals that its content is less Euro-federalist than it appears.

Like the ETUC benchmark, the Italian Euro-federalist approach was also formulated by union-related academics. Aris Accornero, a renowned Italian industrial relations expert, proposed in June 1998 a gradual development of European framework agreements as a response to the creation of the euro. However, unlike the Doorn unions, Accornero saw the creation of the euro as beneficial, not as a threat. He analyzed it as an epochal change that would lead to European political union, similar to the transformation process of the German customs union to the German Reich in the nineteenth century. Accornero's EU collective bargaining approach was also inspired by historical comparisons because he projected the historical development of national bargaining in Italy to the EU level. Accornero advised the unions to seek a Europeanization of collective bargaining following the step-by-step pattern that led, in Italy, to the making of the national collective bargaining agreements. The unions should, therefore, seek first European framework agreements that basically restate the norms and provisions that already exist in most national agreements (Accornero 1998).

Accornero's vision of European framework agreements mirrors the logic of the EU social-dialog agreements, which seek to establish at least some social rights at the EU level. He proposes a trade-off between a small number of contractual norms and a greater geographical scope. However, neither Accornero nor the federal CGIL, CISL, and UIL union leaders questioned the 1993 social pact. The only alternative to company-level bargaining that was widely discussed was territorial multi-employer bargaining at the regional or local industrial district level.

With the electoral victory of Silvio Berlusconi's right-wing coalition in May 2001, however, the political context of Italian industrial relations changed fundamentally. Both the Italian employers' organization Confindustria and the government lost their interest in neocorporatist arrangements and started to implement labor law and welfare state reforms without the consent of labor. Although the government and the employers continued to consult the unions, the latter lost much of their influence (Mania and Sateriale 2002). This led to a massive increase in industrial action, including several general strikes, but also to an increasing polarization of the Italian unions between the two moderate union confederations, the CISL and UIL, and the left-wing CGIL. This increase in industrial and intra-union conflicts effectively put an end to the Italian social pacts of the 1990s, although all three union confederations preferred these social pacts to the social conflicts experienced under the Berlusconi government.

Although the new leader of the CGIL, Guglielmo Epifani, admitted that the pacts failed to secure an equal distribution of productivity gains between capital and labor (Epifani 2003), he also stated that this shortcoming did not outweigh the strengths of the pacts, such as the mandatory recognition of the RSU union bodies in Italian companies. Nevertheless, during the second Berlusconi government, the CGIL not only supported the aggressive wage-bargaining claims of its metal industry affiliate FIOM, but also showed more interest in European bargaining coordination (*Quaderni Rassegna Sindacale* 2002). In June 2002, FIOM decided to discontinue the use of the target inflation rate as a point of reference in its bargaining policy. Giorgio Cremaschi, the national FIOM official in charge of collective bargaining, not only justified this step with the end of social concert given the anti-union policies of the Berlusconi government, but also linked it to the Frankfurt declaration of the EMF.[14] However, the electoral victory of the center-left coalition of Romano Prodi in 2006 led to a revival of social pacts rather than a strengthening of the European bargaining coordination attempts of FIOM-CGIL.

Comparing the German, French, and Italian Cases

We next assess the impact of the ETUC and EMF benchmarks at the national level in Germany, France, and Italy. Studying the national bargaining policies of labor proves to be a difficult task: the more we analyze the wage-bargaining policy of a national union, the more we realizes that most unions do not have a single consistent bargaining policy. These ambiguities reflect not only the different political and regional interests that exist within national unions but also the organizational division of tasks within each single union organization. On the one hand, union experts play a significant role in specifying the available distributive margins and determining the wage claims of the union. On the other hand, other officials carry out the wage negotiations in practice, without referring much to academic expertise. Moreover, these functional divisions often correspond to different political orientations, especially within the German unions. Whereas Euro-Keynesian thinkers control the union think tanks, the union negotiators generally pursue a rather pragmatic approach.[15] It is therefore not surprising that our review of the German, French, and Italian wage-bargaining policies reveals ambiguous results concerning the impact of European targets on national wage bargaining.

All wage-bargaining experts from German, French, and Italian unions that we interviewed supported the ETUC bargaining targets. This suggests that we can indeed observe the creation of a European conceptual framework for wage-bargaining coordination (Traxler and Mermet 2003). Incidentally, the ETUC targets even caused French CGT experts to question the CGT bargaining policy (Juquel and Metz 2001). On the other hand, however, the pattern-setting German 2000–2001 bargaining round and the Italian bargaining agreements for the metal industry in 2001 and 2003 clearly demonstrate the limits of the European benchmarks. In fact, in all these cases, the unions signed agreements that were at odds with the ETUC and EMF benchmarks. This suggests that it would be a mistake to overrate the practical impact of the European benchmarks, but it would be equally wrong simply to dismiss the EMF and Doorn coordination attempts, as suggested by Bob Hancké and David Soskice (2003). They argue that both the EMF and the Doorn coordination attempts failed for the same reason: "the most important proponents of coordination to prevent wage competition were the German unions, since it was difficult for Germany to retaliate against small countries which sought to undercut German unit-labor-cost developments. Unions in the other member states, however, wanted to retain their freedom because they wanted to be able to undercut German costs" (Hancké and Soskice 2003, 153).

However, an analysis of wage trends between 2000 and 2003 shows that Hancké and Soskice are wrong. German wage agreements were undercutting Dutch and Belgian trends, and not vice versa (ETUC 2002b; Keune 2005). A comparative analysis of wage trends between 1969 and 2003 in the Austrian and German metal industries also concludes that "the wage pattern setting union of the large country is not necessarily compelled to pay for cooperation of their counterparts in the small countries by conceding them somewhat lower wage increases" (Traxler et al. 2007). This suggests that the success of a European coordination of wage bargaining depends first and foremost on the ability of the unions in large anchor countries, such as Germany, to meet the EU target and thus to set in train corresponding bargaining patterns for its neighboring countries.

Our review of wage-bargaining policies in Germany, France, and Italy also demonstrates that awareness of the European benchmarks in national debates is not just dependent on the unions; the impact of the benchmarks also reflects the political support for Euro-Keynesian policies. Therefore, it is hardly a coincidence that the German compliance with the European wage targets coincides with the tenure of Oskar Lafontaine as Finance Minister. In France, political interest in the benchmarks was even instrumental in overcoming the initial reluctance of the French unions toward them. In turn, the prevalence of the Italian 1993 social pact and the lack of Euro-Keynesian thinking in Italian center-left politics also explain why interest in the European benchmarks remained rather limited in Italy.

In conclusion, our review of recent German, French, and Italian wage trends reveals both the potential force and the limitations of the Doorn, EMF, and ETUC targets. On the one hand, the experts of the different national unions managed to agree, for the first time ever, on a joint European benchmark to assess their bargaining policies. On the other hand, the impact of these benchmarks remained limited because they did not produce very encouraging results. It seems that the unions regularly fell back into competition bargaining patterns if they were confronted with strong pressures from both their government and employers' organizations. This does not mean that the vision of a coordinated European wage-bargaining policy is useless, but it emphasizes that European trade unions need to mobilize more people to support their bargaining coordination policies than just the European experts of the different national unions.

Bargaining Coordination, Technocracy, and Euro-Democratization

European wage-bargaining coordination is a voluntary enterprise, dependent on the cooperation of the national unions involved. The European trade union federations, such as the ETUC and the EMF, cannot enforce the targets. However, it would be wrong to dismiss the European coordination approaches as an altruistic enterprise that is only supported by naïve moral claims to union internationalism and European solidarity. The unions seem to be increasingly aware of the costs of noncooperation that result from a competitive race between different national bargaining systems (Maurice 2001). Because the *individual* collective action dilemma has not precluded the rise of (local) unions (Crouch 1982), it is just as likely that the *collective* collective action dilemma characterizing the Doorn, EMF, and ETUC wage-coordination approaches can be overcome if national unions realize that they are mutually dependent on one another. After all, there would be no need for a European coordination of wage bargaining if there were no threat of transnational competition.

However, the preceding review of the wage-bargaining policies of organized labor is not a goal in itself. The analysis of the tensions between national competition and European coordination in this policy area was made to assess the role of the unions in the EU-polity formation process. This points toward the concluding question: Are the unions of the Doorn group, the EMF, and the ETUC simply emulating the technocratic benchmarking patterns that mask European governance? If yes, does this explain why national unions have, at times, neglected the European wage-bargaining benchmarks?

If we look at the technical approach (Traxler and Mermet 2003) that directs the European labor wage-coordination policy, then the answer to the first question is yes. The technical language spoken in the union European collective bargaining committees effectively excludes many national and local unionists from these policy debates. Moreover, the quantitative European wage-coordination targets mirror in their form the convergence criteria idea of the Maastricht Treaty, which does not leave much space for political discussions. Certainly, the content of the European wage-coordination benchmarks questions many of the neoliberal assumptions that guide the macroeconomic policy making of the Commission and the ECB. However, it is equally true that target setting is a typical instrument of technocratic policy making (Lascoumes and Le Gales 2007).

As previously stated, academics played a crucial role in the European bargaining coordination policy of labor. The Observatoire Social Européen (OSE), the Hans-Böckler-Foundation of the DGB, and the ETUI of the ETUC contributed much to the rise of the Doorn, EMF, and ETUC approach. In 1994, Busch (1994) suggested Euro-Keynesian wage recommendations that linked the national (sectoral) real wage to productivity development. Subsequently, Noé (1998) also argued that the labor market actors in the eurozone must abide by a macroeconomic criterion of wage determination because with wages set either too high or too low there would be chaos in euroland. The Doorn, EMF, and ETUC benchmarks match the proposals of Klaus Busch and Claus Noé, which incidentally were commissioned by the Hans-Böckler-Foundation and the ETUI, respectively. In addition, the benchmarks also mirror the European social snake scheme that was proposed in 1989 by Belgian social security experts. That scheme was designed to upgrade social provisions by stipulating objectives for the various member states lagging behind (Dispersyn et al. 1991). This technical approach proved to be attractive for the union experts because the social snake idea shows that coordination is possible even though there are no harmonized European standards. However, the technical approach of the European bargaining coordination policy of organized labor made it difficult to politicize this strategy. Anne-Catherine Wagner's (2004) participant observation of the debates in the ETUC wage-bargaining committee largely confirms this point in a rather accidental way, namely, by portraying the ETUC wage-bargaining target as a typical tool of apolitical EU governance. Although Thorsten Schulten (2003) emphasizes that the ETUC target questions the neoliberal approach that dominates the economic EU integration process, the supporters of the ETUC wage-coordination target should realize that this message is not understood by everybody.

The ETUC chose its technical European bargaining benchmark not only because it was in need of a tool to coordinate collective bargaining at the EU level. It also adopted the benchmark to make a responsible contribution to the macroeconomic dialog established by the European Council meeting in June 1999 in Cologne. The macroeconomic dialog is a confidence-building exercise involving the coordination of monetary and budgetary policy and wage developments. Those participating in the technical and political groups of the dialog include the Council, the Commission, the social partners, and the ECB. The autonomy of the parties is fully respected, and the discussions are confidential. The process is not binding, no formal conclusions are drawn, and each party is responsible for reporting back to its own constituency. The ETUC saw the Cologne dialog as a way of building a consensual European strategy because the European trade union movement supported the adoption of the Maastricht Treaty and has made an important contribution to a positive policy mix (Putzhammer 1999). After the first political-level meeting of the macroeconomic dialog, held in the second half of 1999, the ETUC reported that active discussions were taking place within the union movement on framework formulas for coordinated collective wage bargaining based on compensation for inflation plus productivity. However, the other participants in the macroeconomic dialog, and especially the ECB, did not show any interest in coordinating their activities with the European unions (Schroeder and Weinert 2003).

To conclude, the European wage-coordination benchmark effectively emulated the technical benchmarking or open method of coordination approach that is typical for EU governance and its Euro-speak (Gobin 2005).[16] This reflects the objective difficulties of formulating precise political objectives at the EU level because of the continuing national differences and practices. Thus, the benchmarking approach seems sensible in that it combines the setting of EU-level targets with the formal recognition of national diversities. The European trade unions also chose the benchmarking approach because it fits into the dominant language of the European institutions and, therefore, facilitates communication between the union experts and the European institutions.

The Doorn, EMF, and ETUC benchmarks could be effective without "being perfect in terms of coherence, coverage and inclusion" (Traxler and Mermet 2003, 245). However, as long as organized labor has not proven its capacity to have an EU-wide effect on other macroeconomic variables, such as price stability, it is not likely that the benchmarks can effectively set consistent European wages patterns. Only when a critical mass of unions not only agree on common objectives but also collectively campaign for their implementation will the other wage policy actors, such as the European governments, employers' organizations, and the ECB, develop any interest in a European coordination of collective bargaining. Only in this case can we expect a successful European bargaining coordination policy because politics plays a decisive role in national wage-bargaining coordination, too. Hence, the development of a coordinated European bargaining policy will not be an inevitable outcome of Euro-Keynesian expertise, however rational it may be. An idea must become a material force to become influential. Likewise, mobilization theory and social movement research suggest that mobilizations are more successful the clearer and the more morally persuasive their objectives are.[17] From this perspective, and given that the union grassroots have not been involved in the formulation and implementation of the European bargaining coordination policy, it is not surprising that the benchmarks have not had a major impact on national bargaining.

Nevertheless, there are no fundamental reasons why the European bargaining coordination policy should not become more inclusive in the future. On the one hand, the emerging campaign for a coordinated European minimum wage policy suggests that the Euro-Keynesian union experts have realized the importance of moral claims and arguments (ETUC 2006; Schulten, Bispinck, and Schäfer 2006). On the other hand, European trade unions are increasingly aware that the unions should Europeanize not only their objectives but also their actions (Sauerborn 2001). Finally, the European bargaining coordination attempts on the part of labor could gain in authority if the European trade union federations not only relied on the national union experts but also involved the unions' EWC members in their bargaining coordination policies. Although collective bargaining remains a sectoral-level issue in most EU countries, the EWCs could play an important role in spreading the European bargaining targets beyond the small circles of the national EU experts. In fact, the EWC secretary of the French multinational Pechiney wondered why the EMF does not simply produce a European EMF bulletin for all its EWC delegates. In fact, this could represent a first step in the direction of a truly European trade union.

This leads us to the next part of this book, which analyzes the Europeanization attempts of organized labor at the company level by examining two transnational company mergers.

PART THREE
Responses by Labor to Transnational Company Mergers

The European Regulation of Transnational
Company Mergers

G iven the institutional framework of EU competition policy, it is reasonable to think that organized labor cannot influence the regulation of cross-border mergers. Yet unions have increasingly been trying to influence EU competition policy. Their activities, however, have differed considerably. Whereas organized labor politicized the ABB Alstom merger case, labor adopted a strategy in the Alcan-Pechiney-Algroup (APA) merger case that did not challenge the technocratic merger control policy of the European Commission. The adoption of these conflicting strategies is surprising because the same German and French unions played a decisive role in both merger cases. The following chapters analyze the contradictory strategies adopted by labor in these two parallel cases in order to identify the mechanisms that explain the divergent strategies. First, however, it is necessary to determine the wider context of EU merger control policy. What are the implications of mergers for corporate governance and labor relations? How does the Commission regulate company mergers, and what are the roles played by other social, economic, and political actors in its competition policy?

The (Strong) EU Politics of Merger Control

Transnational Mergers: Implications for Management and Labor

Mergers and acquisitions usually reflect the following motivations. First and foremost, corporations merge to increase their efficiency by taking advantage of economies of scale and by realizing synergy effects. This frequently implies a reduction of the combined workforce. Second, companies may merge to secure their position in a market. Third, companies may merge to seek to acquire a dominant position in the market.[1] Finally, the executives of multinational corporations often have a personal interest in company mergers because their personal income, prestige, and power usually depend on the size of their corporation (Möschel 2000; Chaterlety 2002).

The new merger wave has also been a product of some specific developments of the 1990s, such as the geographic expansion of the capital and product markets as a result of the establishment of the European single market and EMU.[2] Mergers were also facilitated by low interest rates, booming stock markets, and the deregulation of the telecommunications, media, energy, transport, and finance sectors. The merger wave also reflects a change in management philosophy. Up to the 1980s, many companies tried to diversify their activities and, thus, also their risks. Today's management philosophy favors instead a concentration on core activities. Consequently, companies sell their secondary sectors and try to become the best in class in their core businesses.

Until recently, multinational firms reproduced ethnocentric home-country-centered or polycentric host-country-centered governance structures, but almost no firm created genuine global or geocentric structures (Perlmutter 1965). Correspondingly, labor relations in multinationals reflected either the system in the corporation's country of origin or the system in its host country (Ferner and Quintanilla 1998; Geary and Roche 2001). Therefore, many scholars described the whole concept of the global corporation as a myth (Ruigrok and Van Tulder 1995; Hirst and Thompson 1996).[3] Recent cross-border mergers, however, have departed from these underlying national legacies. The takeover of Mannesmann by Vodafone, for instance, blurred the boundaries between continental and Anglo-Saxon corporate governance (Höpner and Jackson 2003). Likewise, the EU recently adopted a new EU takeover directive to create a truly integrated EU capital market.[4]

Transnational mergers typically entail three consequences for labor (Edwards 1999): (1) collective dismissals, (2) a divide-and-rule policy on the part of central management with regard to workers' representatives from different countries, and (3) enduring divergences between national management-labor relations systems. However, cross-border mergers also create new transnational dimensions in both labor-labor and management-labor relations, challenging the privileged relations between management and unions from the company's country of origin.

Competition Policy: A Paradigm Case
of Regulatory Policy Making

Since the Treaty of Rome in 1957, competition policy has been one of the core EU policies considered necessary for the creation of the common market (Majone 1994a, 1994b). EU competition policy differs from other policy fields in that it developed almost in tandem with national antitrust policies (McGowan 2000). European and national antitrust authorities reinforced one another and finally prevailed over the Schumpeterian traditions that remained dominant in many European states until the late 1980s.[5] The sovereignty of the EU in the area of competition policy is recognized even by the United States, as in the case of the EU rejection of the acquisition of Honeywell by General Electric (GE). Correspondingly, Vivien Schmidt (2006) describes the EU as a regional state—a state that would differ considerably from the democratic nation-state, but a state nevertheless.

According to the dominant logic of EU regulatory policy making, neither elected politicians nor pressure groups should interfere with the regulation and control of company mergers by the Commission. The officials from its Directorate-General (DG) for Competition are advised by an exclusive community that is composed of the Advisory Committee of Member States and competition lawyers, economists and experts from the directly affected companies, and other reasonably concerned third parties (McGowan 2000). Nevertheless, the Commission is free to choose whose ideas and proposals to adopt. Finally, the College of Commissioners adopts the decision of its DG for Competition on whether, or under which conditions, to allow European mergers and acquisitions.

In more than 90 percent of the notified merger cases, the Commission accepts the proposed merger during the primary examination phase, which lasts only 1 month. The more problematical merger cases are subject to a 4-month intensive examination that normally leads to approval of the proposed concentration, conditional on the cessation of some business activities. Formal prohibitions of company mergers are very rare, although they often generate headlines in the business press, as in the Honeywell-GE case.

The Commission has, thus, acquired a high degree of autonomy in its competition policy. It autonomously specifies and executes the merger control regulations of the Council and enjoys extensive investigation, decision, and fining powers. The Commission assumes all executive and substantial legislative functions, but it also acts as an investigator, prosecutor, and judge. It decides whether or not, or under which conditions, to allow transnational company mergers. The strong position of the Commission relies on two EC Treaty articles (Articles 81 and 82 TEC), although the EC Treaty does not explicitly refer to merger control. The Council has further reinforced the discretionary powers of the Commission through several Council regulations.

In contrast, neither national parliaments nor the European Parliament have any powers in the field of competition policy. The Council adopts competition policy legislation by a qualified majority without having to take note of any parliament vote; and the Commission can use its extensive executive and regulatory powers in the absence of any parliamentary control. As with EU monetary policy, EU competition policy making is completely insulated from the citizens that are affected by the decisions of the EU and from the directly elected parliamentarians.

This extraordinary concentration of power in the hands of unelected officials challenges any notion of democracy. Moreover, it also questions predemocratic notions about the separation of powers as formulated by Baron de Montesquieu back in 1748. The competition policy of the Commission is subject to review by the Courts, but access to the EU Courts is very restricted.[6] Natural and legal persons can challenge a decision of an EU institution only if the decision is either directly addressed to that person or is of direct and individual concern to that person (see Article 230 TEC).

It follows that EU competition policy is a paradigm case of the technocratic model of decision making, not because its actors are all technocrats but, rather, because the notion of political debate and conflict is absent from this policy field. In this respect, the decision-making process in the competition policy area also differs from the so-called comitology procedure in other policy areas (Article 202 TEC), according to which European decision-making powers are delegated to committees composed of national and European technocrats and representatives of interest groups. Although this procedure is also questionable from a democratic viewpoint (Craig and de Búrca 2003), the committees at least recognize the existence of social and political conflicts and try to come to decisions that are acceptable to a large number of concerned constituencies (Joerges and Vos 1999; Joerges and Falke 2000). In contrast to the procedures in the field of EU competition policy, European comitology is, at least, a deliberative process in which the logic of market integration has to be made compatible with the social and political concerns and interests in member states (Joerges 2001).

Nevertheless, despite the technocratic and allegedly apolitical logic of EU competition policy, the political sensitivity of Commission merger policy must be kept in mind. This is not very surprising, given that merger control has become—together with monetary policy—one of the most important fields of public intervention in the economy. In the past, the Commission paid attention to political pressures from member states and multinational corporations (McGowan 2000), although the Commission officials involved always emphatically denied this (Rakovsi 2002; Monti 2002). We must keep in mind that it is politicians who make the final decisions, namely, the members of the College of Commissioners. Moreover, the institutional framework of the EU competition policy fundamentally depends on the prevalence of the free-market doctrine, which is also a very political ideology. Hence, the Commission view that the only criterion for merger control is the effect of an operation on competition reflects, above all, its political will, although it assumes the contrary.

It is not very likely, however, that the Commission will ever acknowledge that noncompetition factors play a role in its merger control policy. The Commission justifies its authority in terms of the effectiveness of its policy in accordance with the principle of an open market economy with free competition, not in terms of its democratic origin. At one stage, the EU commissioner in charge of competition even claimed that any appraisal of political factors would undermine the efficient reasoning of the Commission (Monti 2002). Although it is known that political factors influence EU competition policy, in the event of the Commission wishing to support the creation of a European monopoly, it would legitimate its creation with technical rather than political arguments. It would simply deny that a monopoly was being created by enlarging the definition of the relevant product market (Van Bael and Bellis 1994). In 2000, for instance, the Commission approved the politically desired oligopolistic European Aeronautic Defence and Space Company (EADS) merger of the three leading European civil and military aircraft manufacturers by emphasizing the strength of a competitor company from the United States.

The Role of Organized Labor in European Union Competition Policy

The Commission assesses only the competition effects of a concentration (Rakovsi 2002). Additional concerns, such as its implications for labor, are excluded from the frame of reference that guides EU competition policy.[7] Therefore, we would expect labor to have no role whatsoever in EU competition policy (Mestmäcker 1991; Scharpf 1999; Streeck 1998c; Bieling and Steinhilber 2000). Marxist and neoliberal authors share the view that the institutional framework of the EU does not leave significant space for agency, given the neoconstitutional constraints of disciplinary neoliberalism in Europe (Gill 1998). Nevertheless, such conclusions often tend to be too static because they underestimate the role of alternative, although dormant, repertoires of a specific empirical political setting (Crouch 2005). Even EU competition policy is not free from internal contradictions, which might in turn generate institutional change.

Notwithstanding the underlying free-market paradigm, Article 18 of the EU Merger Regulation refers directly to the rights of labor in the EU merger control procedure. The article entitles recognized employee representatives of firms that are involved in a merger case, upon application, to be heard by the Commission. Even though the Court of First Instance stated in 1995 in its *Comité Central d'Entreprise de la Société Générale des Grandes Sources and others v Commission* (Perrier) judgment that the Merger Regulation gives primacy to the establishment of a system of free competition, it also emphasized in the same judgment that the Commission may reconcile its

> assessment of whether a concentration is compatible with the common market, with the taking into consideration of the social effects of that operation if they are liable to affect adversely the social objectives referred to in Article 2 of the Treaty. The Commission may therefore have to ascertain whether the concentration is liable to have consequences, even if only indirectly, for the position of the employees in the undertaking in question, such as to affect the level or conditions of employment in the Community or a substantial part of it.[8]

In addition, the thirteenth recital in the Preamble to the Merger Regulation states that the Commission must place its appraisal within the general framework of the attainment of the fundamental objectives of the EC Treaty, including that of strengthening economic and social cohesion. In 1997, the Amsterdam Treaty further reinforced the social obligations of the EU.[9]

The practical and legal implications of the EU Treaty social obligations remain, however, very limited because the Court stated in the Perrier judgment that employee representatives could legally challenge a merger decision of the Commission only insofar as it affected their rights of representation (Vincenzi and Fairhurst 2002). Hence, no union or works council can bring the Commission to court, even if it adopts a "selective attitude towards obligations deriving from the treaty" (ETUC 2002a; European Parliament 2000). The denial of access to the Court—or *locus standi*—to the employee representatives concerning substantial breaches of law under the Merger Regulation seems to release the Commission from the Treaty social obligations in its application of competition policy. The quoted judgment implies that the employee representatives can defend themselves only against a substantial breach of their procedural right to be heard because only this would, according to the Court, directly concern their interests.

However, in *Schneider Electric SA v Commission*, the Court of First Instance granted, by order of June 6, 2002, for the first time, *locus standi* to a Comité Central d'Entreprise and a EWC in litigation against a merger control decision of the Commission.[10] The Court granted the workers' representatives of Legrand the right to intervene in the proceedings in support of the Commission. The Court argued that the annulment of the Commission decision that prohibited the Schneider-Legrand merger, sought by Schneider S.A., would directly concern Legrand workers' representatives (Pichot 2002).[11] Nevertheless, it is doubtful that the Court would grant *locus standi* to workers' representatives if they were challenging the Commission on the grounds that its merger control decision would breach the EC Treaty social and employment policy obligations. In fact, in this case, the Court would probably argue, first, that dismissals would not follow directly from the merger and, second, that the collective dismissals would not directly affect the rights of the concerned employee representatives.

However, the political implications of the EU Treaty social obligations are significant because the narrow legal interpretation of direct effect is questionable. The denial of *locus standi* to employee representatives does not take into account the fact that an EU merger decision might have a direct effect on employees because one motivation for mergers is the realization of synergy effects and this generally means producing more with fewer employees. Moreover, a denial of *locus standi* to employee representatives effectively frees the Commission from the application of the social obligations of the EU Treaty. Indeed, it is not very likely that the individually and directly concerned parties that actually have *locus standi* (namely, the to-be-merged firms) would ever challenge an EU merger decision on employment-policy grounds.

This legalistic argumentation protects the merger decisions of the Commission only from legal, not from political, challenges. Although the reference in the Merger Regulation to EU social objectives provides only a weak legal instrument, it can be effective in the political sphere. Is the Commission really acting legitimately when it authorizes mergers without evaluating their possible social consequences and, thus, without respecting Article 127(2) of the EC Treaty, according to which "the objective of a high level of employment shall be taken into consideration in the formulation and implementation of Community policies and activities" (Pichot 2002)?

Finally, mergers are subject not only to competition law but also to labor law. The concerned companies must inform and consult their workers' representatives prior to the merger. Hence, although a concentration could violate labor law while meeting the requirements of competition law, the College of European Commissioners approves, prohibits, or conditionally approves concentrations, without considering a possible violation of EU labor law. The Commission DG for Competition has argued that it would be more efficient if national courts controlled the compliance of a merger with labor law (Rakovsi 2002). However, although this procedure arguably increases the efficiency of the Commission merger control policy, it is questionable whether such an ex-post control represents also an efficient procedure for the enforcement of labor law. Indeed, by the time a national court eventually decided on the matter, the merger operation would in any case already be completed, and therefore the possible remedy would be considerably reduced. This explains why many workers' representatives consider that contesting their lack of involvement in merger operations before the courts would be of little use. In the Netherlands, however, a company is formally obliged by competition law to postpone the implementation of a merger for a period of one month if the opinion of its works council is negative. During that period, the works council can go to court to challenge the merger decision (Macaire et al. 2002). In other EU countries, the workers' representatives have to be consulted, according to EU and national labor law, before merger decisions.[12] However, EU Commission and national competition authorities do not delay company mergers, even if the merger violates EU and national labor law.

The director of the DG for Competition claimed that an integration of additional concerns into the merger control procedure, such as the compliance of a merger with labor law, would expose the Commission to serious risks—it would overload the system. The consideration of social issues would also entail the risk of a politicization of the procedure and, thus, destroy confidence in the Commission merger control policy (Rakovsi 2002).

The European Round Table of Industrialists (ERT), the interest organization of the leading European multinational companies, shares this view too. The ERT criticized the inclusion of labor in the European merger control process, stating that there was no need for independent labor representatives because the potential concerns of labor were already addressed by the Commission when assessing the market impact of a proposed transaction. This discourse is obviously tenable only if we counterfactually claim that mergers lead "not only to job preservation, but also to job creation, increased competitiveness and greater prosperity" (European Round Table of Industrialists [ERT] 2002, 4).

Given the dominance of the free-market doctrine and the technocratic institutional framework of the Commission competition policy, it is reasonable to suggest that organized labor has no role in this arcane EU policy field. However, this section also has hinted at some underdeveloped features of EU Merger Regulation that are not consistent with the dominant EC competition policy *référentielle*. First, Article 18 (4) of the Merger Regulation entitles recognized employee representatives to be heard by the Commission. Second, the Preamble to the Merger Regulation emphasizes that the Commission must place its appraisal within the framework of the attainment of the fundamental objectives of the EC Treaty, which include social and employment policy objectives. Hence, it is not surprising that unions have increasingly been trying to influence EU competition policy, although Commission officials have complained that some workers' representatives do not understand that the Commission will ignore their non-competition-oriented arguments (Rakovsi 2002).

The activities of European workers' representatives have differed considerably, although they have tried to break the dominant path of EU competition policy decision making in all cases. Whereas in the ABB Alstom Power case labor emphasized the social objectives of the EC Treaty and politicized the merger, in the APA case the workers' representatives used their right to be heard by the DG of Competition and adopted a strategy that was compatible with the technocratic approach of the EU Commission. The two chapters that follow present the results of an in-depth study of these two cases and explain the adoption of the relevant contradictory union strategies.

CHAPTER NINE

A Euro-Democratization Union Strategy

The ABB Alstom Power Case

On April 10, 2000, about 2,000 workers, mostly from France, Germany, Belgium, and Italy, demonstrated in Brussels to protest against plans by ABB Alstom Power to cut a fifth of its workforce. They were protesting against the Commission for its failure to consult labor before approving the merger between the ABB and Alstom power divisions. This was not the first European labor demonstration, but it was the first time that an EWC, the EMF, and national unions jointly organized such a protest rally (Lemaître 2000). The demonstration did not remain an isolated event, but was the first in a series of several successful transnational mobilizations. Correspondingly, the ABB Alstom case came to be used as a prototype for successful European unionism in labor education seminars (Wagner 2004).

The ABB Alstom Power unionists triggered European collective actions and contributed to the creation of a European public sphere and a politicization of the EU integration process. Thus, the unions followed a Euro-democratization orientation, as defined in the analytical framework presented in chapter 2. This joint action of European, national, and company-level unions and works councils is surprising when compared to other cases. How, then, can we explain transnational collective action and the adoption thereby of a Euro-democratization strategy in the ABB Alstom case?

Toward Supranational Management Structures?

One thesis introduced in chapter 3 is the following: the increasing Europeanization of the economy will force organized labor to cooperate across borders. To assess this thesis, this section discusses the governance structures of ABB Alstom Power compared with the structures of its two mother companies, ABB and Alstom, which were also products of prior company mergers.

ABB—a Trend-Setting, Genuine Multinational

Asea Brown Boveri (ABB) is often presented as a result of one of the most successful company merger cases. In 1988, the Swiss Brown Boveri Corporation (BBC) and the Swedish ASEA announced that the two electro-technical multinationals would merge to reach economies of scale similar to its main competitors, GE and Siemens.

The management also used the merger to restructure and justified this citing the increasing competition that would result from the establishment of the European single market in 1992 (Uyterhoeven 1993).[1] In the 1990s, ABB became a trendsetter in management and globalization debates (Bélanger and Björkman 1999). The press celebrated ABB as the most successful merger case since Royal Dutch linked up with Shell in 1907, and the *Financial Times* ranked the ABB executives, Percy Barnevik and Gördan Lindal, in the top twenty of the world's most respected business leaders (Sklair 2001).[2]

The positive ABB image had three sources (Berggren 1999). First, ABB was a company with genuine global aspirations. Second, the ABB management model was portrayed as a panacea for the big-company disease because it included major cutbacks of intermediate and central management staff. Finally, the ABB matrix structure, which combines local-territorial and global-sectoral dimensions, was praised as the answer to both the persistence of territorial diversity and the increasing transnational integration of business operations. ABB relied on lean headquarters, thirty-four sectoral subdivisions, forty national centers, and more than one thousand daughter companies. Accordingly, Winfried Ruigrok and Rob Van Tulder (1995) suggest that ABB provided local autonomy within the framework of a giant corporation.

However, when we compare the autonomy of former BBC plants with their situation in the ABB matrix structure, it becomes clear that the ABB merger led to a loss of autonomy. The headquarters of multinationals often lacked the capacity to enforce their will against the joint opposition of local management and labor. The central BBC management in Switzerland, for instance, was not able to prevent the BBC Mannheim plant from competing against the Swiss BBC Baden plant with autonomous offers for tenders in third countries. To the anger of the Swiss central management, the German offer often prevailed because the German BBC daughter could count on greater support from its national government than the Swiss mother company could. These conflicts involving export sales were aggravated by a number of other factors, as pointed out by Hugo Uyterhoeven, a Harvard Business School academic and ABB consultant.[3]

It is therefore not surprising that after the 1988 merger the new ABB leadership tried to expand its control over the Mannheim plant. This led to major conflicts with local unionists and managers (Gester 1997), but ABB eventually succeeded in weakening local resistance by dismissals, a fragmentation of its subsidiaries along sectoral lines, and the introduction of centrally devised benchmarking techniques to monitor the performance of the subsidiaries. This implies that the introduction of the ABB matrix structure represents a step on the way to more centralized corporate governance structures, even if this process did not involve an expansion of bureaucratic structures at the headquarters level.

The declining power of the ABB subsidiaries also reflects a change in its client structure. The more power generation and electricity utilities are privatized, the less public authorities influence purchasing decisions to support domestic manufacturers. Accordingly, turbine producers became less dependent on local knowledge to acquire clients and turbines became more standardized across the world (Bray and Lansbury 2001). Therefore, the ABB merger also triggered the Alstom joint venture of two of its major competitors, namely, the French Compagnie Générale d'Electricité (CGE) and the British General Electric Company (GEC).

Alstom—a National Champion with Global Aspirations

The history of Alstom is closely linked to French industrial policy. In 1982, the government nationalized the French Alstom predecessor CGE as part of President Mitterrand's modernization program for French industry. Mitterrand also aimed to create national champions through mergers between similar French firms to enhance their independence, competitiveness, and research and development capacities. In 1985, CGE merged with Thompson and created Alsthom, its subsidiary for the power-generation, railway, and shipbuilding sector. After the successful recapitalization and restructuring of CGE, the center-right government of Jacques Chirac reprivatized it in 1987 (Uterwedde 1999).

In 1988, CGE formed a joint venture with the British GEC, and one year later the two companies merged their power-generation and transport sections. This gave rise to a joint daughter company, GEC-Alsthom, which with its 70,000 employees was only one-third the size of ABB. The French high-speed train, the TGV (train à grande vitesse), was the most famous product of its railway division, and its power-generation section was known for its gas turbines (Björkman 1999). In 1998, GEC-Alsthom was renamed Alstom and was successfully listed on the major stock exchanges, but, unlike the ABB mother companies, CGE (Alcatel)[4] and GEC (Marconi)[5] continued to operate autonomously.

In the 1990s, Alstom split its local subsidiaries along sectoral lines, but it did not copy the ABB matrix structure. Instead, it favored more hierarchical company structures, as was typical of French companies. The Alstom French parent company was also the only one of the eight biggest French multinationals that already had a foreigner on its top board in 1993. As in the Royal Dutch/Shell, Unilever, and ABB cases, this reflects its prior merger activities (Ruigrok and Van Tulder 1995). Although Alstom shared many features of an ethnocentric French multinational, it is also evident that the company aspired to become a genuine multinational.

Merging the ABB and Alstom Governance Structures

In March 1999, Alstom and ABB announced the merger of their power-generation sections. The new identity was called ABB Alstom Power, headquartered in Brussels and held 50–50 by the two partners. With its 54,000 workers in about one hundred countries and its pro-forma turnover of about 9.9 billion euros, it represented, with GE and Siemens, one of the largest multinationals in its business sector. A mere few weeks later, the Commission authorized the merger. The group began to operate on July 1, 1999, but, only nine months later, ABB sold its remaining 50 percent participation to Alstom, which subsequently became the sole owner. Finally, ABB Alstom Power was re-integrated into Alstom and, once again, changed its name and became Alstom Power.

These restructurings are not only complicated to follow, they also entailed negative effects for the concerned EWCs. The creation of the ABB Alstom Power joint venture meant that the existing EWCs in ABB and Alstom were no longer competent to act in the new company. As a result, the workers' representatives had to negotiate a new EWC with the ABB Alstom Power management. These negotiations never materialized, however, because the company was no longer obliged to create an EWC of its own after its re-integration into Alstom.

(ABB) Alstom Power took over not only the apparently better technology of ABB[6] but also its asymmetrical matrix organization structure, although with a reduced territorial-country dimension. This, coupled with the hierarchical corporate culture of the former Alstom managers, led to an additional loss of autonomy for its subsidiaries. According to a local ABB Alstom works councilor from the previously mentioned Mannheim plant, this means that the local management has to ask permission from headquarters for any investments above 50,000 euros. Consequently the Mannheim management, which is responsible for 2,000 employees, would have less autonomy than a local baker. Moreover, it can no longer employ new workers without permission from headquarters. Obviously, the autonomy of the Mannheim plant is continuously declining compared to Uyterhoeven's portrayal of the Mannheim subsidiary within the former BBC group.

The centralization of strategic decision making at the top level of management did not affect the Mannheim plant only. The whole merger process was planned within a period of just three months by only five managers, among them the first CEO of the company, Claude Darmon. The heads of its sectoral business divisions and country departments were not consulted during this process; their function was limited to execution of the centrally made decisions (Hebauf 2002). This is a clear sign of the supranationalization of the company decision-making structures.

The restructuring processes of the last decade have also led to a fragmentation of local company structures. Whereas in the 1970s, for instance, all workers on the huge Alstom site in Belfort belonged to the same company, the Belfort-site personnel are now dispersed over a considerable number of different Alstom core companies, subcontractors, and outsourced service providers. Moreover, new firms have also set up within the Belfort Alstom site. However, whereas in Belfort these restructurings were almost completed before the ABB Alstom merger, the management tried to use the merger to split the remaining multiproduct enterprises in France, as well. Although the fragmentation of a multiproduct enterprise usually does not necessarily signify a deterioration in working conditions, it can entail a much greater economic risk for the workforce because the performance of the enterprise depends on the success of only a single product. Furthermore, the fragmentation of an enterprise hampers collective action. This provides another explanation for the strong resistance of the French unions against the restructuring plans of management.

The fragmentation of integrated local company subsidiaries into many small single product units have had different effects in different labor relations systems. In the countries where collective bargaining took place at the company level, the unions lost a lot of their negotiation power. In France and Switzerland, the fragmentation of a company eventually led to an erosion of collective wage bargaining. In Germany, however, it did not directly affect wage bargaining because this takes place at a regional level between IG Metall and the metal industry employer organization. Moreover, the postmerger 1988–1989 wave of strikes by the Mannheim workers against the restructuring plans persuaded ABB to sign an agreement that adapted German codetermination to the ABB matrix structure. The agreement establishes business-area-specific committees of the local works council and stipulates that the employees on a common site elect a joint local works council, even if they belong to different ABB companies (Gester 1997). This pioneering arrangement continues to exist as a result of the contract on works council organization signed on January 24, 2001, and a corresponding amendment to the German codetermination law in 2001 that was also inspired by the ABB case (Hebauf 2002).

We can observe a centralization of the strategic decision-making structures within the companies involved in this merger case. However, the assessment of the recent corporate history of the companies also highlights the fact that this centralization process is accompanied by a parallel decentralization, or even fragmentation, of company structures. Although the centralization of the decision-making structures represents an incentive for a transnationalization of union activities, the parallel fragmentation of firm structures suggests that transnational union action could also become increasingly difficult.

Transnational Premerger Union Activities

Before we examine the activities of labor in the two companies involved in the ABB Alstom Power case, we provide an overview of the preceding company-level transnational union activities. This historical perspective introduces an additional comparative dimension that is necessary for assessing the explanatory power of another thesis introduced in chapter 3, namely, that the EU integration process leads to interactions that may favor a Europeanization of social movements and unions.

Between 1966 and 1977, sectoral international union federations established world company councils (WCCs) for over sixty multinational companies (Etty 1978). The declared aim of this campaign was the setting up of multinational free collective bargaining according to the voluntarist Anglo-Saxon model (Levinson 1972). This campaign represented an important change in the history of international unionism, implying a major shift in the focus of the free international union federations from Cold War politics to economics.

The growing importance of multinationals also motivated communist French and Italian unions to establish European shop-steward committees (Pernot 2001). These councils involved not only communist unionists but also local workers' representatives from other unions that criticized the bureaucratic approaches of their national and international union organizations. In contrast to the WCCs, these European shop-steward committees usually refused transnational collective bargaining and emphasized, instead, cross-border information exchanges and a transnational coordination of local industrial action. As a result, in several companies, two rival international union councils existed side by side. These reflected two overlapping cleavages: one political, anticommunism versus a united left cleavage, and one structural, top-down versus bottom-up unionism cleavage (Busch 1983). Among these, the union activities following the Dunlop-Pirelli merger in 1971 are perhaps the best example of these conflicting orientations of international unionism (Busch 1983; Miller 1978; Moore 1978; Brumlop 2002).

Despite some successes, for instance in the AZKO case, most of these early initiatives came to nothing.[7] On the one hand, the executives of multinationals frequently did not want to meet workers' representatives at the international level and nothing forced them to do so. On the other hand, political rivalries and the persistence of national exit options frequently put an end to these voluntary cross-border union councils and committees (Etty 1978). Nevertheless, the campaign by labor in favor of WCCs highlighted the need for transnational workers' councils at the company level (Rehfeldt 2000).

After the social protocol of the Maastricht Treaty abolished the national veto in some policy areas, the EU adopted in 1994 the European Works Council (EWC) directive. The EWC directive turned out to be a catalyst for the reemergence of transnational labor relations in the 1990s. For the first time, executives of multinationals were obliged to meet workers' representatives at a European level. By the end of the 1990s, over 630 EWC agreements had been signed (Lecher et al. 2001), indeed, a far greater number than the 65 WCCs of the 1970s.

ABB Transnational Labor Relations

On January 1, 1970, the Swiss BBC centralized the managerial control of some operations that were formerly highly decentralized. This motivated the International Metalworkers' Federation (IMF) to request a meeting with the BBC management (Northrup and Rowan 1979). On September 4, 1970, a delegation composed of IMF officials, BBC works councilors, and union officials met the management, but there is no evidence of any subsequent meetings despite the fact that the IMF reported that there was agreement to meet yearly and, when important problems arose, to renew contacts.

Years later, in 1987, the BBC-ASEA merger again stimulated unions to coordinate their activities within the IMF. Shortly after the announcement of the merger, Swedish, German, and Swiss union officials met in Stockholm and then in Mannheim. In January 1988, they established a WCC (Rüb 2002). Moreover, two larger conferences were held in March 1988 in Mannheim and in August 1988 in Berne. The latter conference was again organized by the IMF and not by the EU-oriented EMF.[8] It brought together seventy IMF-affiliated unionists from ABB plants in twenty countries. This meeting did not include all ABB unions, however; it excluded communist unions, such as the French CGT, and white-collar unions (Hammarström 1994). Although the Berne conference urged ABB to respect labor rights and achievements, the Mannheim IG Metall newsletter acknowledged that it would be difficult to prevent an ABB policy of playing off one production site against the other (Gester 1997). These exchanges continued to take place, however, and eventually contributed to a better mutual understanding. Although nationalistic voices against the Swiss and the Swedish sites were quite common in Mannheim shortly after the merger, they disappeared after the Mannheimers realized that the sites in the other countries had lost at least as many jobs as the German ones.

Between 1990 and 1994, the ABB WCC held a meeting every year to exchange information and to engage in a dialog with management. The ABB workers' representatives also tried to establish international segmental committees to deal with issues specific to ABB divisions, namely, power generation, transmission, and transport (Rüb 2002), but the ABB management did not wish to enter into negotiations with international union secretariats (Bray and Lansbury 2001). Finally, it was the EWC directive that forced management in September 1996 to sign a voluntary EWC agreement and recognize the EMF as a contractual partner. Subsequently, the EU level became the prevailing locus of transnational union cooperation, although the IMF still organized ABB conferences (Bierbaum et al. 2001).

In recent years, the EWC has become a significant instance of employee involvement, despite the lack of codetermination rights. The German ABB unionist, Adolf Schmitt, for instance, argued that his presence on the EWC eventually turned out to be more important than his presence on the group works council (GWC) and the supervisory board of ABB Deutschland AG. The more ABB centralized its decision making at its global headquarters, the more the German management lost its discretionary power and the more the formal German codetermination rights became de facto redundant. Correspondingly, Schmitt discusses important issues with the competent central management at the supranational level rather than with the weak national management in Mannheim. However, we must take into account that this is a very recent development that occurred after Schmitt's experiences in the ABB Alstom Power merger case (Hebauf 2002).

Alstom Transnational Labor Relations

In the Alstom case, major company restructurings motivated national unions to develop transnational contacts among the employee representatives from different countries. In 1986, the joint venture between the Alstom mother company CGE (Alcatel) and ITT entailed major company restructurings and 35,000 job losses. In this context, several unions also created a CGE WCC within the IMF. However, this WCC met only twice, in 1986 and 1987 (Rüb 2002). Nonetheless, the transnational union cooperation among different European sites reemerged during a subsequent wave of dismissals in 1996.

On May 22, 1996 many rank-and-file CGE (Alcatel) unionists had their first transnational experiences as they joined a European demonstration in Paris against a massive collective dismissal plan. Although Alstom was not directly concerned by the restructuring plans, many Alstom unionists also joined the demonstration to support their CGE (Alcatel) colleagues because they still belonged, at least partly, to the same mother company. An ad hoc network that included several IMF-affiliated unions from Belgium, France, Germany, Italy, and Spain and the postcommunist French CGT organized this pioneering demonstration. In contrast to the preceding WCC, the Alcatel demonstration for the first time gathered unionists from divergent ideological traditions. According to a French CFDT unionist, this resulted from the centralization of the Alcatel decision-making structures in supranational business divisions that would make joint union activities inevitable (Escande 1996). Days after the Alcatel demonstration, Alstom signed a voluntary EWC agreement that established an EWC according to Article 13 of the EWC directive.

The first action of the Alstom EWC was the adoption of a joint declaration in December 1998 after the flotation of Alstom on the stock exchange in June 1998. The EWC met only once a year, but its select committee met more frequently, four or five times a year. Its five members collaborated in an open-minded way, despite their very diverse national union cultures. The leading French EWC representative spoke English, Spanish, German, and Russian, and the leading German EWC representative was proficient in English; as a result, the EWC members communicated well with one another. The joint EWC activities also led to better cooperation between French unions at the national level.

This section has shown that the CGE-ITT (Alcatel) joint venture of 1986 and the BBC-ASEA merger of 1987 had already motivated unions to seek transnational union cooperation. These attempts led in both cases to the creation of WCCs within the IMF, but these WCCs functioned for only two and six years, respectively. The short-lived existence of the WCCs reflected their voluntary character, the exclusion of all non-IMF-affiliated communist and white-collar unions from them, and a reluctant attitude on the part of the management toward them.

The 1994 EWC directive, the end of Cold War divisions in the labor movement, and the increasing centralization of decision making in multinational companies reinforced transnational union cooperation in Europe. Since 1996, both Alstom and ABB unionists from different countries, professional categories, and ideological traditions have worked with one another on a regular basis within their EWC. Although this finding confirms Turner's (1996) expectations, the existence of EWCs as such represents by no means a guarantee of a successful Europeanization of labor. Therefore, the sections that follow thoroughly trace the activities of labor in the ABB Alstom Power case to identify further mechanisms that favor transnational union cooperation and the adoption of a corresponding Euro-democratization strategy.

The ABB Alstom Merger Union Activities

First Reactions of Organized Labor after the Merger Announcement

On March 23, 1999, Alstom and ABB announced the merger of their power-generation sectors to create ABB Alstom Power. Both the ABB and the Alstom EWCs learned about the merger project via the press. Alstom informed its EWC only after the approval of the merger project by the Commission at an EWC meeting in Frankfurt on June 10, 1999. Hence, the Alstom EWC insisted that it had not been consulted in good time by either the management or the Commission. The same fate befell the ABB EWC, which was not consulted before the merger decisions either (Hebauf 2002).

The Alstom EWC feared that these restructurings would lead to collective dismissals across Europe and wrote two letters: one to Pierre Bilger, the chairman and CEO of Alstom and one to Romano Prodi, the president of the Commission. In the first letter, Bilger was urged to meet the select committee of the EWC and to recognize the responsibility of the Alstom EWC for the power sector, at least until the new company had established its own EWC. In the second letter, the EWC questioned the Commission's authorization of the merger because it had not consulted the workers' representatives and considered aspects other than those of competition policy. These letters were translated into German, French, English, and Spanish and sent—together with a statement from the Alstom EWC—to workers' representatives on different European Alstom sites for distribution to the workforce.

Prodi responded that the Commissioner in charge of competition policy was not available at the moment but would be willing to meet an EWC delegation later, but Alstom management agreed to meet with the EWC select committee. However, at a subsequent meeting in July 1999 the head of the Alstom human resources department declared that he no longer possessed the competence to say anything about the Alstom Power sector because it now belonged to the new ABB Alstom entity. Stating this, he pointed to the fact that the EWC directive failed to regulate the functioning of EWCs in 50–50 mergers (European Parliament 2001). This behavior encouraged the subsequent protest movement because nobody likes to be told that, first, it is too early to discuss the merger because it has not taken place and, then, it is too late to discuss it because it has already taken place.

In turn, the German ABB European works councilors managed to direct the attention of the IG Metall union headquarters to the ABB Alstom case. Because multinationals frequently ignored the consultation rights of their EWCs during company mergers, the central committee of IG Metall commissioned a study to examine the scope of action of the union in the ABB Alstom merger process. IG Metall engaged a consultancy firm, INFO Institut (Institute for Organizational Development and Corporate Politics), which had already advised the ABB works council in the past. The institute survey of employee attitudes, which included most German ABB and Alstom sites, revealed that the management information policy concerning the merger was close to zero and that the employees feared negative consequences for their sites and careers.

The study also indicated that the German ABB and Alstom employees were ready to envisage industrial action and to unite themselves with workers from other countries and production sites.[9] The interviews conducted for the present study support this view: IG Metall unionist, Wolfgang Alles, from the Mannheim plant concluded from his experience with previous ABB company restructurings that the more multinational corporations increase their penetrating power due to transnational organization structures, the more unions must construct alternative structures and perspectives on this level. Likewise, a CFDT delegate from the Alstom Belfort plant stated, "if we are not organized in the new enterprise before there are problems, it will be too late." Given these observations, IG Metall decided to organize, in November 1999, an international union seminar about the ABB Alstom Power merger in Mannheim.

The Mannheim Seminar: Developing a Common Strategy

The Mannheim seminar gathered together approximately forty individuals, namely, the members of the two EWCs, the general secretary of the EMF, national works councilors, and unionists and experts from eleven West and East European countries and from twenty unions, including representatives from the previously excluded communist and white-collar unions.[10] Compared with the failure to unite all unions during the previous ABB merger in 1988 (Hammarström 1994), the mere fact that such an encompassing meeting was possible already represented progress. Only some years earlier, a meeting involving, for instance, both the French CGT and the Polish Solidarnosc union would have been unimaginable. The ABB Alstom Power management was also invited to the Mannheim meeting, but it did not attend. On the contrary, it tried, although without much success, to preempt the Mannheim meeting by organizing a meeting with European workers' representatives just a week before to negotiate a new ABB Alstom Power EWC agreement.

The encompassing nature of the Mannheim meeting reflects, especially, the existence of EWCs in the two companies. The EWCs provided a framework within which enterprise-level workers' representatives from all European countries could get to know one another, notwithstanding the different backgrounds of their organizations. The Mannheim meeting also profited from the pragmatic approach of EWC members who believed that they "could build up something in Europe only from below, starting from the realities of our workplaces." This statement, made by the CGT EWC delegate, Francine Blanche, indicates that the ideological conflicts in international union politics diminished remarkably after the end of the Cold War and with the growing effects of economic and political Europeanization processes (Abbott 2001). While the WCCs only included unions that were affiliated to the IMF, the 1994 EWC directive empowered the CGT to send delegates to any EWC where it represented a sufficient share of the company workforce. Moreover, it is also important to note that in the 1990s the CGT cut its ties with the French Communist Party (PCF), which also facilitated the affiliation of the CGT to the ETUC, EMF, and the IMF after 1999.[11]

Furthermore, the ambiguous information and consultation rights of the EWCs in 50–50 mergers and the organizer's ability to work in a transnational context contributed to the success of the ABB Alstom seminar. Moreover, a grant from the European Commission DG for Employment covered the costs for simultaneous translation, accommodation, and travel expenses for all seminar participants.

The seminar participants inferred from the reports of the workers' representatives from the different countries and a joint preliminary study by Alstom's French work council's consultancy firm, Alpha Consulting, and the German works council consultancy, INFO Institut, that the management was planning a restructuring that would threaten between 10,000 and 12,000 of the 58,000 jobs in all countries and in all business sectors. Moreover, the participants' conclusion that the restructurings hit more or less all ABB Alstom Power sites proportionally triggered a certain feeling of common interest. Incidentally, for the federal training department of IG Metall this learning process was a central motivation to support the Mannheim seminar. Eventually, the seminar led to the unanimous adoption of a joint Mannheim declaration on November 24, 1999, drafted by active seminar participants only some hours before. The declaration demanded a stop to any plant closure and dismissals plans, and demanded immediate consultation with the national and international employee representatives. Furthermore, the declaration envisaged a joint European day of action, although several unions had initially strong reservations about joint European demonstrations.

There was indeed a certain lack of confidence vis-à-vis the representatives of other countries, according to Richard Croucher, the expert representing the British ABB Alstom unions. The working groups that discussed the Mannheim declaration proposal had been national. Nobody wanted to be the only one on the barricades, and the British delegates in particular feared that the continental unions would push them into an industrial conflict against their will. The Italian, Spanish, and Portuguese unions supported in principle the idea of a European demonstration in Brussels, but emphasized its significant practical problems, namely, huge travel costs. Initially, only the German, French, and Belgian unions supported the idea of a European demonstration on a working day in Brussels. Nevertheless, the reservations about the adoption of the Mannheim declaration could be addressed because the meeting was transparent and no pressure was put on anybody. Finally, even if the British and Scandinavian delegations remained skeptical regarding the idea of the European demonstration, they did not veto the Mannheim declaration because the declaration allowed them to organize a European day of action at the local level according to their national laws and practices.

At the Mannheim meeting, the labor representatives also agreed to create three working groups: one to negotiate a new EWC agreement (this group was composed of the EWC Special Negotiation Body (SNB) that united national works councilors and IG Metall official, Thilo Kämmerer, as EMF trade union coordinator) (EMF 2000); one to create an information exchange network; and one to prepare the European day of action. However, the SNB working group was the only one that actually functioned. As a result, the information network project was neglected and the European day of action became an issue at the margins of the SNB meetings and a meeting at the European Parliament.

Politicizing the Conflict—the European Parliament

Because the answer of Commission President Prodi to the previously mentioned letter from the Alstom EWC did not satisfy the EWC, its secretary contacted French MEPs of the Confederal Group of the European United Left/Nordic Green Left parliamentary group, asking them for advice. After discussing the issue with other MEPs from the Socialist Group and the Group of the Greens in the European Parliament, they advised them to write a letter to all groups in the Parliament emphasizing that the EWCs had not been consulted by either the Commission or the management before the ABB Alstom merger decision even though it might lead to between 10,000 and 12,000 dismissals. On January 19, 2000, a delegation of twenty-five ABB Alstom Power unionists from six countries was received in the Parliament by a delegation of social-democratic, green, and left-wing MEPs. This meeting was very successful, and it put the ABB Alstom merger case on the Parliament agenda.

On February 17, 2000, the European Parliament adopted a resolution "On restructuring of European industry, with special attention for the closure of Goodyear in Italy and the problems of ABB Alstom." This resolution emphasized that labor had not been informed either before or after the merger and that the Commission, when authorizing the ABB Alstom merger, had not evaluated its social consequences, thus not respecting Article 127(2) of the EC Treaty, according to which the objective of a high level of employment should be taken into consideration in the implementation of European policies and activities (European Parliament 2000). Thus, the Parliament urged the Commission:

- not to authorize mergers, if the companies concerned do not respect European social legislation, mainly on worker representative information and consultation;
- to undertake without delay an evaluation of the directive on collective dismissal and propose effective sanctions; and
- to speed up its reexamination of the EWC directive, in order to strengthen the consultation rights of EWCs.

This resolution triggered a debate about collective dismissals and worker consultation in the Parliament between its free-market and its social-Europe wing. Finally, the social-Europe wing prevailed and Erkki Liikanen, the Commissioner for Enterprise, admitted that, in the two cases debated by the Parliament, the companies may have exploited ambiguities in the legislation. Therefore, he urged that the following Council presidency, held by France, should give top priority to the drafting of a new directive on worker information and consultation. Likewise, Anna Diamantopoulou, the Commissioner for Employment and Social Affairs, concluded the day before in a meeting with a European Alstom EWC delegation that in her opinion the EWC directive had been violated in the ABB Alstom Power case.[12] She promised to write to the French Minister of Employment on the matter. Moreover, Diamantopoulou wrote to Commissioner Mario Monti urging him not to authorize mergers when companies failed to comply with European social legislation.

These debates also influenced company policy because the press covered the initiatives of the ABB Alstom EWC and French and EU politicians lobbied the management. Although it did not abandon its redundancy (lay-off) plans, it adjusted its strategy in response to the politicization of the merger case.

Negotiating a New European Works Council Agreement

Possibly because the ABB Alstom Power management feared an eventual condemnation by the courts for infringing EWC rights as in the Renault-Vilvoorde case, it suddenly pushed for a rapid negotiation of a new EWC agreement for the new company. Because ABB Alstom Power had its new headquarters in Brussels, an SNB composed of labor representatives was set up in accordance with the Belgian transposition of the EWC directive.[13]

At the first SNB meeting, the CEO of ABB Alstom asked the workers'

Table 9.1. Announced job cuts at ABB Alstom Power, February 29, 2000

	Announced number of job cuts	Percentage of workforce
Belgium	−227	−47
Czech Republic	−237	−14
France	−1,500	−19
Germany	−1,361	−23
Italy	−230	−24
Norway	−104	−32
Poland	−385	−14
Portugal	−84	−24
Spain	−20	−3
Sweden	−479	−15
Switzerland	−219	−6
United Kingdom	−549	−9
Total Europe	**−5,431**	**−16**
China	−650	−51
India	−1,655	−36
Rest of the world	−2,264	
Total	**−10,000**	**−19**

Source: "Bericht an das besondere Verhandlungsgremium," Brussels, 29 February 2000.

representatives whether they would agree to consider the SNB as a provisional EWC. Most workers' representatives reacted positively. Many EWCs believed that this step on the part of the management was a good sign for future labor-management relations. However, these hopes were rapidly dashed as, immediately after the workers' representatives' positive reaction, the CEO presented a restructuring plan that included the closure of some plants as well as a reduction of the ABB Alstom Power workforce worldwide by 19 percent (table 9.1). Obviously, Darmon recognized the SNB as a provisional EWC just in order to comply formally with the letter of the EWC directive.

Most of the workers' representatives were shocked by this declaration. They had not been expecting it because the management had treated them cordially. The workers had been invited to a first-class hotel and offered excellent meals. The workers also felt that they were important because the CEO personally had attended the meeting. However, CEO Claude Darmon had already said at the presentation of the company results in February 2000 that he would not be satisfied with a profit margin of 3–4 percent and had promised the company shareholders a major restructuring program to reduce costs by 30 percent in three years and to increase profit margins to 7–8 percent.

Political Reactions to the Collective Dismissal Plan

The announcement of the huge collective dismissal plan provoked not only an immediate reaction on the part of the unions, but also protests from politicians representing the locations where the company was based, especially in France. Despite their different political backgrounds, on March 7, 2000, local members of parliament (MPs) and the mayors of the three major French ABB Alstom sites, namely, a left-wing republican mayor from Belfort, a communist mayor from La Courneuve, and a conservative mayor from Lys-Les-Lannoy, attended a round table discussion in Belfort with unionists. On the following day, the ABB Alstom case came up for mention in the French parliament. The two MPs from Belfort, a member of the republican Mouvement des Citoyens and a member of the Socialist Party, urged the government to denounce the company restructuring plan and to defend employment and French production capacities by all means, including the use of the bargaining power of the state as a major client. But, whereas the socialist MP was above all concerned about the negative impact of the Commission policy on the legitimacy of the EU, the republican MP made sarcastic comments, along the lines of the Euro-skepticism of her party: "The CEO of the multinational ABB Alstom Power announced on 29 February in Brussels the closure of 10 production sites throughout the world and further restructurings in 14 additional locations. This plan will lead to the suppression of 10,000 jobs, among them 5,431 in Europe—Is this the Citizen's Europe and the Social Europe you are talking about?"[14]

The fear that the Commission policy could reinforce anti-EU sentiments also explains the remarkable speech of the president of the European Parliament, Nicole Fontaine, a co-founder of the right-wing French Union for a Popular Movement (UMP) party, at the European Council meeting in Lisbon in March 2000, in which she questioned the merger control policy of the Commission:

> Given the public outrage to which such issues can give rise in Europe, Parliament is asking you to take the necessary measures to introduce balanced rules on company mergers within the European Union. The way in which some mergers have taken place since the establishment of the single market—sometimes as an adverse side effect of that development—is turning a lot of people against the whole process of European integration.[15]

Hence, the ABB Alstom workers' representatives managed to politicize the EU company merger policy even before their European demonstration in Brussels. In France, the workers' representatives even succeeded in convincing the mayors from the concerned municipalities to cover the travel costs of local ABB Alstom workers to facilitate their participation in the demonstration in Brussels. Hence, the mayors' supportive words during the round table discussion were followed by concrete action. The politicization of the merger succeeded, mainly because labor targeted politicians at all levels simultaneously, from the local municipality to the European Parliament.

The Brussels Demonstration

The announcement of the ABB Alstom Power dismissal plan obviously reinforced the determination of the workers' representatives to organize a European action day. At the end of the SNB meeting on February 29, 2000, a coordination group was set up that included a German IG Metall official, a Belgian CSC Métal official, and an EMF official, as well as the former Alstom EWC secretary and CGT delegate, Blanche. On March 13, 2001, the group met in Brussels, in the EMF office, and set the date for the day of action. In turn, on March 17, 2000, the EMF informed its affiliates about plans to organize a day of action against the ABB Alstom Power dismissal plans. However, the relevant letter from the EMF general secretary was written in a very cautious way. It emphasized that some national unions—rather than the EMF itself—would stand behind these plans. The general secretary of the EMF committed himself only to organizing a press conference in Brussels and writing to the CEO of ABB Alstom Power urging him to receive a European workers' delegation after the planned demonstration. Nevertheless, the EMF would politically (but not financially) support the action day, provided that its members would not contest this decision before March 24, 2000. This means that not until seventeen days before the event did it become clear whether the EMF would support the European demonstration.

Several IG Metall unionists, who were used to the meticulous preparation of collective action, doubted that it would be possible to organize a European demonstration at such short notice. On March 23, 2000, the German ABB Alstom Power GWC became aware that the EMF information about the planned action had not reached everybody and that the Italian workers' representatives had received incorrect information about the day of action from the Italian ABB Alstom Power human resources department. Therefore, the administrator of the German GWC retranslated the EMF letter into English and sent it via e-mail to works councilors across Europe. Incidentally, this retranslation emphasized much more clearly than the original letter that the EMF supported the demonstration.

Eventually, the EMF also supported the demonstration because no affiliate expressed any objections, and on March 24, 2000, the IG Metall headquarters instructed its local union officials to actively support the demonstration in Brussels. Meanwhile, local German and French labor representatives mobilized for the Brussels demonstration, and it soon became clear that the demonstration would not be a failure. The French unions predicted that they would have 1,000 participants, the Germans 300, and the Belgians 350, and the management agreed to meet an EMF delegation after the demonstration.

In the meantime, on April 5, 2000, the EMF general secretary cited the planned ABB Alstom Power demonstration as an example for the Europeanization of union action in his speech at the congress of the CGT metalworkers' federation. The demonstration of some national unions became the first official EMF demonstration in Brussels. Finally, on April 7, 2000, even Emilio Gabaglio, the ETUC general secretary, phoned the Alstom CGT delegate Blanche and asked her whether he could also deliver a speech at the demonstration.

Despite its rather symbolic character, the support of the demonstration by the ETUC and the EMF leaders was important. It provided the demonstration with a European legitimacy that facilitated collaboration among unions with different national and ideological roots. At the same time, the efforts of EMF and ETUC leaders to become involved in the demonstration suggests not only that they expected it to be a success but also that they had an interest in a greater visibility of EU-level unionism.

Nevertheless, several organizational problems, such as the police authorization for the demonstration, the actual route, and the meeting place for the arriving buses, were resolved only at the last minute. The EMF fax with the relevant information (meeting places, demonstration route, etc.) did not arrive until the morning of Friday, April 7, 2000, at the national headquarters of its affiliated unions. This was too late to reach, for instance, all works councilors and unionists at the German ABB Alstom Power sites. Nevertheless, only the Dortmund and the Nurnberg workers canceled their participation, whereas the buses from Butzbach, Neumark, and Mannheim started their journey to Brussels without clear indications. Many unionists wrongly assumed that the EMF would take care of practical questions. This misunderstanding was discovered only some days before the actual demonstration but still early enough for the local Belgian unions to get a last-minute authorization from the police for the demonstration.

On April 10, 2000, almost two thousand workers participated in the European demonstration. Most of them came from France, Germany, Belgium, and Italy, but some were also from Portugal and Switzerland. The demonstration was a success for the participants, the union delegates, the

ETUC, and the EMF. With this demonstration, workers from different production sites and countries highlighted the fact that they had not only the same problems but also the same goals. The speeches and banners of the ABB Alstom Power unionists underlined the importance of this transnational mobilization and called for a continuation of the movement.

The remarkable differences in the mobilization capacity of the unions reflected not only different repertoires of collective action but also different sets of resources, provided by different national political opportunities that unions could exploit (Tarrow 1994). If we compare, for instance, the internal resources of the unions, we may not have expected the poor French unions to be capable of mobilizing twice as many protesters as the wealthy IG Metall. However, if we consider also their external resources, this result is less surprising. Whereas IG Metall mobilized no external resources, the French unions urged the mayors of Belfort, La Courneuve, and Lys-Les-Lannoy to cover the travel costs of the workers from their cities. This displays not only greater political support for the ABB Alstom Power workers in France but also much greater sensitivity on the part of the French media toward these issues.[16]

Notwithstanding the fact that the management refused to start negotiations about the restructuring plan at the European level, the demonstration was perceived as a success by the participating unionists. According to the CFDT works councilor, the demonstration exemplified the making of European unionism (Heller 2000). Likewise, Kämmerer, the IG Metall official, emphasized that many German unionists were happy that a joint European demonstration was possible, something that had not been the case at the time of the preceding ABB (ASEA-BBC) merger. This increased considerably the self-confidence of many local workers' representatives. It might also explain why the pictures of the Brussels demonstration were left for a long time on almost every works council notice board in Germany.

The Beginning of the End?

The Brussels demonstration was a success for the workers, the ETUC, and the EMF, as well as the press, but nobody organized an immediate follow-up at the EU level. To explain the pause in EU-level union action in this case, we now examine the activities of key workers' representatives at the different levels.

At the EU level, the EMF failed to provide any follow-up, despite the personal involvement of its general secretary as the leader of the union delegation that met with central management after the demonstration on April 10, 2000. Certainly, after this meeting the EMF general secretary wrote a letter to the CEO, Darmon, in which he requested EU-level negotiations on the restructuring plans, but as the May 10 deadline set by the EMF letter expired without effect, no other EMF action followed, due to its limited resources.[17] This does not preclude sporadic EMF interventions, especially in highly visible cases, but EU-level union action depends above all on the initiative of national labor representatives.

Meanwhile, on March 31, 2000, ABB Alstom Power was incorporated into Alstom and thus became again a subsidiary of Alstom, called Alstom Power. As a result, the ABB Alstom workers' representatives lost their most important forum for EU-level union coordination, the SNB, because Alstom Power was no longer obliged to have its own EWC. Consequently, the management dissolved the SNB and delayed the incorporation of the Alstom Power delegates into the Alstom EWC. Only more than one year later were labor representatives from ABB Alstom Power included in the Alstom EWC, on the occasion of its annual general meeting of March 5, 2001 in London.

This loss of the Alstom Power workers' European forum effectively stymied transnational union cooperation and prevented a European coordination of the various national and local postmerger social plan negotiations. Moreover, because the restructuring plans had to be implemented in accordance with national laws, the unions had to concentrate their activities on the national level. Accordingly, the labor representatives who initiated the European demonstration were completely absorbed in difficult social plan negotiations or engrossed in the war of attrition that frequently characterizes labor relations in the case of collective dismissals.

It seems that the Alstom management, especially in France, adopted a rather adversarial approach.[18] In turn, union coordination virtually ceased to function, even at the national level, because the labor representatives at the different French production sites were not able to agree on a joint strategy. Although initially all French workers' representatives from all unions and production sites continued to work together, this cooperation came to an end in December 2000. Eventually, the Belfort CFDT section accepted the restructuring and stopped delaying the corresponding social plan (Peillon 2000), whereas all the CGT, all the FO, and the Parisian CFDT section continued to contest the restructuring by all means, including industrial, political, and legal action.

Although an employer is not obliged to negotiate a social plan with its labor representatives, under French law a company can only make use of collective dismissals if such a plan is economically justified and if it has consulted its works council beforehand. However, on April 27 and May 12, 2000, hundreds of workers successfully prevented the management from starting the consultation procedure by occupying the offices of the works council. By doing this, the workers successfully delayed the collective dismissals, at least for some months. In December 2000, however, the works council of the biggest Alstom plant in Belfort accepted a social plan in which Alstom committed itself to find new jobs for its dismissed workers in other firms in the region, at a wage level that would equal between 75 and 80 percent of the previous wage. In turn, the unions and works councils from the other plants continued to challenge the antisocial social plan by all means. Moreover, with the help of a union-related consultancy firm, the CGT also developed alternative business plans that were used in discussions with public authorities to demonstrate the lack of economic justification for the dismissal plan. The adoption of these two divergent union strategies mirrors two features of French industrial relations: the independence of local union representatives due to the absence of strong national union organizations[19] and the French union pluralism, which implies an ongoing electoral competition between the unions for works council seats.[20] As a result, the personal relationship between the two French EWC members, Jean-Marie Heller and Francine Blanche, worsened, and this obviously negatively affected European trade union cooperation, even if the German unions remained neutral regarding these French conflicts.

In Germany, all local Alstom Power works councils delegated the social plan negotiations to the national GWC, with one exception. This coordinated approach prevented the closure of all endangered production sites, except in Nurnberg where labor representatives wrongly thought that they would get a better deal if they negotiated on their own. Conversely, management also benefited from the central negotiation because it led to a settlement in a comparatively short time. This settlement reflected not only cooperation between local representatives within the GWC but also the support by Kämmerer, the IG Metall official, who directly participated in the national GWC negotiations. He played the role of moderator between divergent local interests, which favored nationwide coordination among the various production sites.[21]

Nevertheless, the union resistance to the restructuring plan was fairly effective. By April 2001, only 2,960 of the announced 5,400 job cuts had taken place in Europe. In particular, in Germany and France the unions succeeded in reducing or postponing job cuts and preventing the closure of threatened production sites, such as Lys-Les-Lannoy (France), Butzbach (West Germany), and Neumark (East Germany). This relative success owed much to a combination of union mobilization and an elaboration of alternative business plans in collaboration with union-related consultancy firms (Altmeyer 2001a, 2001b). Regardless of their comparable results, the French and the German restructuring processes were quite different because German law assigns codetermination rights to the works councils in the case of collective dismissals. Whereas the German GWC had agreed in September 2000 on a national reconciliation of interest agreement with management, the French unions had to use all means at their disposal, including industrial action and disruptions of meetings with management, to delay the consultation procedure and, thus, to prevent the execution of the restructuring plan. Until September 2001, the French unions were quite effective because only 234 job cuts out of the 1,000 announced occurred. In the United Kingdom, however, where the workforce had almost no consultation rights and where the union resistance was weaker, the number of jobs shed was three times greater than the five hundred originally planned.

The 2000 European ABB Alstom Power demonstration did not prevent the restructuring plan, and the management refused to negotiate about it at the European level. During the following implementation phase of the company restructurings at the national and local levels, there was no explicit European coordination of the local union activities. Nevertheless, the European ABB Alstom Power demonstration was a great success in the eyes of all interviewed unionists. Although none of the unionists interviewed believed that the demonstration would directly affect the management, they conceived it as an effective tool to manifest their discontent and indignation, as emphasized by Monique Besançon, an ordinary worker from one of the Belfort plants: "We must go to Brussels! Even if it does not change anything, we must show that we are here." Moreover, the Brussels demonstration also increased the self-confidence of the participating unionists, as demonstrated by subsequent successful mobilizations and social plan negotiations in France and Germany. In addition, the various placards that were used by workers during these protests not only targeted management but also highlighted the need for political initiatives against the uncontrolled power of multinationals and to promote a social EU in general. For all these reasons, it is not so surprising that on June 2, 2003, the Alstom EWC agreed to organize another European demonstration in Paris to protest against a renewed attempt on the part of the company to dismiss more than five thousand workers (Sauviat 2003).

A New Beginning! How European Collective Action Secured the Survival of Alstom

The June 2003 demonstration by the Alstom EWC was a success. It had even a much more significant effect than the workers' representatives themselves initially expected. Alstom would not have survived its debt crisis in August 2003 if its workers' representatives had failed to politicize the case. The Commission DG for Competition would hardly have agreed to rescue Alstom if they had not feared the public outcry and labor protests that would have followed the bankruptcy of Alstom and the subsequent losses of almost 100,000 jobs.

The June 2003 demonstration, which took place at the Alstom Paris headquarters, was even more European than the demonstration of April 2000 in Brussels. In actual fact, the Alstom EWC mobilized 2,200 Alstom workers from sixteen countries[22] and twenty-five unions. Francine Blanche and Albrecht Kotitschke, the IG Metall unionist who had become the new Alstom EWC secretary, concluded that the Paris demonstration was an unqualified success (Kotitschke 2003). The revival of transnational cooperation resulted in part from a one-week seminar of the Alstom EWC held in Barcelona in autumn 2002, hosted by the Spanish unions and prepared by EWC consultants from the French Alpha Consulting and the German INFO Institut. On this occasion, the Alstom unionists and works councilors eventually found a stress-free space in which to discuss and overcome the unspoken tensions between the different Alstom unions that had become apparent during the implementation of the 2000–2001 company restructurings.

How was it possible that Alstom, which in 2000 predicted a return on investment of 7–8 percent, posted in March 2003 an annual loss of 1.3 billion euros and an accumulated debt of 4.9 billion euros? This question definitely goes beyond the scope of this chapter. Nevertheless, it seems that Alstom was not a victim of "management errors" as suggested by Sarkozy (2006, 55) but, rather, a casualty of a deliberate strategy on the part of its major shareholders, namely, its mother companies, Alcatel and Marconi, and their agent, CEO Bilger.[23] According to *Le Figaro*, the problems began in 1998 when the two companies floated Alstom on the Paris stock exchange. Alstom paid extremely high dividends of 1.2 billion euros to inflate the value of its shares, which dramatically reduced the reserves of Alstom (A.Se. 2003). In June 2001, however, Alcatel and Marconi sold all their Alstom shares at a high profit before the debt crisis became public and before the shares lost 95 percent of their value. Hence, it is not surprising that in March 2003 the Alstom management was accused of fraudulent accounting and CEO, Bilger, had to resign (Braud 2003a, 2003b).[24]

In August 2003, French President Jacques Chirac agreed to acquire Alstom shares—half of a planned 600 million–euro capital increase rescue package—because the banks had been reluctant to assist Alstom. This decision seems to have represented a victory for Francis Mer, finance minister and former steel industrialist, and Nicole Fontaine,[25] the minister for Industry and former president of the European Parliament, over the neo-liberal factions in the government. Because French law does not provide protection for creditors in the way that the corresponding Chapter 11 rules in the United States do, Mer saw no other option but to partially re-nationalize Alstom, even though right-wing governments are usually in-clined to privatize, especially in the present neoliberal climate (Harvey 2005; Graham and Arnold 2003). Incidentally, the same politician, Chirac, who privatized the mother company of Alstom, CGE, at the outset in 1987, also wanted the partial renationalization of Alstom. Hence, economic pol-icy also mirrors changing power constellations; this renders economic pol-icy making susceptible to being politicized and even reversed, whenever this is deemed to be a political necessity.

However, on September 18, 2003 the Commission was still ready to force Alstom into bankruptcy in order to preserve the credibility of its competi-tion policy. It banned the Alstom rescue plan that included its partial re-nationalization, because that would represent forbidden "state aid" (Monti 2007a). This decision outraged not only the Alstom employees but also the wider public, especially in France, where the many commentators feared a social and industrial Waterloo (UG 2003; Blanche 2003). The German government did not support the Commission decision either, although the Munich-based multinational, Siemens, would have largely profited from the bankruptcy of its main competitor. The direct intervention of the French president in Berlin and the lobbying of German politicians by the German Alstom workers paid off. Chancellor Gerhard Schröder recog-nized that Alstom also employed 11,000 German workers and joined Chirac in urging the Commission to review its judgment.[26] On September 22, 2003, the Commission approved a short-term rescue package (Braud 2003a; Betts and Dombey 2003), despite a neoliberal campaign against state aid (*Financial Times* 2003a, 2003b).

In spring 2004, it became clear that the initial package did not provide enough time to solve the Alstom crisis. After a cabinet reshuffle that fol-lowed a defeat of the UMP in the French regional elections, Sarkozy be-came finance, economy and industry minister and decided to get involved in the Alstom case. Whereas Blanche (2007) and Chevènement (2007) as-sert that Sarkozy (2006) is exaggerating his role as a heroic Alstom rescuer, his account of the Alstom negotiation between the DG Competition and the French government is nevertheless of great interest. He is directly at-tacking the Commission "technocrats" (Sarkozy 2006, 54–58). Whereas Monti (2007a) denies that the DG Competition "had decided that the company should be 'punished,' that it had been helped too much and that it could only survive for a few months" (Sarkozy 2006, 57), it is certain that the Commission had to be pressured to accept the final Alstom rescue package. Finally, the Commission accepted a 20 percent (700 million euros) participation of the French state (Sarkozy 2006), that is a higher share than the 600 million euro package that was initially rejected by the Commission. Instead, however, Alstom had to sell 10 percent (1.6 billion euros) of its activities to its competitors as a remedy for the distortion of the market allegedly created by the French state aid (Chevènement 2007; Monti 2007a).

The Alstom labor representatives did not call for state aid, but for a reference shareholder that would be interested in developing Alstom in partnership with the workforce (Blanche 2007). Accordingly, the CGT did not contest the sale of shares of the French state to the construction conglomerate Bouygues in April 2006, after the successful recapitalization of the firm. Incidentally, the sale price of two billion euros entails a huge profit of 1.3 billion euros for the French state which fundamentally questions the use of any notion of state aid in the Alstom case.

In the negotiations with the Commission in 2003, the Alstom workers also ably exploited the internal contradictions of EU competition policy: "The Commission risks the disappearance of Alstom, if it bans the participation of the state in its capital. The Commission claims to act in the name of respect for competition. However, if Alstom disappeared, Siemens would remain the only European company occupying this market. Will there be competition if Brussels is creating a monopoly with its decision?" (Blanche 2003, translated by the author).

This argument is surprising, considering Sarkozy's hostile attitude towards the Commission and Blanche's initial refusal to adapt to the language of the Commission competition policy. Does this change represent a mere tactical concession to fit into the Commission policy framework? Although Blanche denounced the Commission for its initial rejection of the Alstom rescue package, she also correctly predicted that partial state ownership would not guarantee that the company would act in the general and the workers' interests. Although state aid would be indispensable, Blanche also understood that the survival of Alstom would eventually depend on the actual policies of its management. Therefore, the Alstom EWC engaged a consultancy firm to work out alternatives to the proposed restructuring plans and urged the management to accept the participation of the unions as stakeholders of the enterprise (Blanche 2003). This represents a remarkable development when we recall the CGT legacy as a communist organization that rejected any sort of codetermination in the past (Groux and Mouriaux 1992). It is also noteworthy that the CGT elected

Blanche at its forty-seventh congress in March 2003 to its federal executive, where she became the head of the CGT EWC department.

On October 7, 2003, on the occasion of an extraordinary meeting of its EWC, the new Alstom CEO, Patrick Kron, confirmed that the restructuring plans announced in March 2003 would not be engraved in marble and that the alternative propositions put forward by the EWC consultancy firms could open up new perspectives (L.B. 2003) However, after some initial concessions, such as a rather generous social plan for Germany that banned collective dismissals until summer 2007, the Alstom management recurrently broke their promises and tried to sack workers wherever and whenever they did not encounter strong local, national, and European resistance. Four years later, the French CGT delegate Blanche was still pleased with the interventions of labor at all levels that contributed to the survival of Alstom, but she also had to acknowledge that the post-rescue plan restructurings led to the loss of 11,500 jobs world-wide. Therefore, Blanche (2007) concluded, workers and local communities must continue to fight for a bigger say in corporate and EU decision making.

Conclusion

This chapter underlines how in Europe a cross-border unionism is emerging, not only among the committed EWC members but also at the level of the rank and file. The unionists did not accept the collective dismissal plans and targeted the central headquarters that designed these plans in the first place. They also marched for a social Europe and against the Commission because they felt that they had no voice in its competition policy. In so doing, the Alstom Power workers highlighted the need for better EU workers' rights and for an integration of social concerns in EU competition policy.

Although it is not easy to measure the impact of the European actions of the ABB Alstom workers, it is notable that they reinforced the position of unions as an actor within EU competition policy. As a direct result of the ABB Alstom Power case, the European Parliament adopted a relevant resolution (2000) and the ETUC drafted its first merger policy manual for EWCs (ETUC 2001b). This represents an improvement if we bear in mind that, only two years earlier, the German company-merger guidelines for works councilors completely ignored the European dimension (*Die Mitbestimmung* 1999). The ABB Alstom case also turned the debate about the conflicting relations between employment and competition law on its head. Whereas in 1999 a European Court of Justice judgment triggered an interesting debate about the extent to which labor law is sheltered from competition law (Bruun and Hellsten 2001; Vousden 2000), the European Parliament (2000) resolution and the ETUC (2002a) criticized the exclusive focus of the Commission on competition and recalled the social obligations of the EC Treaty, including Article 127 (2) TEC.

The legal debate about the relationship between EU social and labor law, on the one hand, and EU competition law, on the other, goes beyond the scope of this chapter. Nevertheless, it is evident that the EU social, employment, and competition objectives increasingly conflict with one another. This implies that the Commission must find a balance among the conflicting objectives in carrying out its competition policy; however, the need to reconcile conflicting interests questions the technocratic legitimacy of Commission decision making because the reconciliation of conflicting interests requires political and not technocratic choices (Ferron 2002). Precisely for that reason, the DG for Competition still rejects the integration of additional concerns in its merger control policy (Rakovsi 2002). In contrast, Diamantopoulou, commissioner for Employment and Social affairs, declared that the Commission could not remain silent given the massive increase in collective dismissals (Zecchini 2001). On May 10, 2001, she announced a package of initiatives to help companies and workers to adapt successfully to change. It included a commitment to balance EU competition policy in order to mitigate the negative social consequences of mergers.[27] The new Merger Regulation, however, indicates that notionally free-market concerns still prevail over social concerns.[28]

The ABB Alstom Power case had a more discernible impact on the debate over the European consultation rights of labor representatives and on French industrial policy (Béthoux, Brouté, and Didry 2006). On the one hand, the Alstom case provided politicians and union officials with concrete arguments in favor of the improvement of these rights, for example in the debates about the introduction and implementation of the EU information and consultation directive. On the other hand, the Alstom case became a central issue in the French presidential elections of 2007. The sixteen-page-long manifesto of Sarkozy used Alstom as a paradigm case for his industrial policy: "The example of Alstom shows that it is possible and effective to fight for our industry" (2007). Precisely because Sarkozy is an opportunist rather than a friend of labor, the Alstom case shows that political mobilizations do influence policy makers if their election depends on popular support.

The Alstom case is even influencing the development of EU constitutional law. European free marketers tried to elevate the undistorted, free market to a core objective of the EU through the introduction of a new

Article I-3-2 in the Treaty establishing a Constitution for Europe (TCE) (Généreux 2005). This attempt, however, has failed so far precisely because Sarkozy convinced the European Council in June 2007—mentioning his Alstom experiences—not to include any reference to "free and undistorted" competition in the EU objectives section of the Reform Treaty that is poised to replace the rejected TCE, as noted by an irritated Mario Monti (2007b).

Nevertheless, the Alstom Power workers were essentially interested in the impact of their actions at the company level, although the EWC displayed an exceptional sensitivity to the political dimensions of the case. It has been shown that the European demonstrations led to a reduction of the planned collective dismissals. The management only agreed to consider the alternatives to collective dismissals after collective action created the space in which the union-related consultancy firms could operate. The engagement of union-related consultancy firms by the Alstom EWC required the prior adoption of a Euro-democratization strategy by labor. The consultants accepted the logic of the market, but they gave it an alternative meaning. This was only possible because the transnational collective actions of labor enlarged the scope for the alternative options (Béthoux, Brouté, and Didry 2006). Even if the Alstom EWC subsequently developed an argument that was meant to fit into the antitrust discourse of the Commission, it prevailed only due to the prior politicization of the Alstom case. The Commission would hardly have agreed to rescue Alstom from bankruptcy if the unions had failed to voice their concerns forcefully beforehand.

CHAPTER TEN

A Euro-Technocratization Union Strategy

The Alcan-Pechiney-Algroup Case

On August 11, 1999, the Canadian Alcan, the French Pechiney, and the Swiss Algroup announced a joint merger project to create the world's largest aluminum company, called APA.[1] The company executives expected that the postmerger cost savings would increase profits by US$600 million. This program included a 5 percent reduction in the combined 91,000 APA workforces. Seventy-five percent of the expected profit growth would result from labor cost reductions. This represents a high share; labor costs in the industry do not usually represent more than 8 percent of total production costs.

As in the ABB Alstom case, labor leaders from Alcan, Pechiney, and Algroup immediately started to cooperate with one another.[2] They convened a working group within the EMF, aimed for negotiations with APA executives, and lobbied the European Commission. In contrast to the ABB Alstom case, however, APA unionists adapted their policy to fit into the framework of the Commission merger control procedure. Because the Commission antitrust requirements led in April 2000 to the abandonment the Alcan-Pechiney leg of the APA project, many unionists thought that they had achieved a victory. This suggests that labor had successfully adopted a Euro-technocratization strategy, but the failure of labor to prevent the subsequent takeover of Pechiney by Alcan in 2003 also suggests that the prospects of this strategy are limited. This chapter analyzes, first, the characteristics of the APA corporations and the logic of their merger project; then the activities of labor are examined in detail. As in the ABB Alstom case, the focus is on the EMF, the EWCs, and the German IG Metall and French CFDT and CGT metalworkers' unions.

Toward Supranational Management Structures?

Like turbine production, aluminum production is a very capital-intensive process that is not easy to master from the technical point of view. Aluminum smelting also requires a lot of energy and creates pollution. Moreover, the aluminum industry has always been subject to cyclical swings, given the relative rigidity of the aluminum supply as opposed to its demand (Bélanger, Edwards, and Wright 1999). This reflects the industry client structure; the car industry is the greatest consumer of aluminum. This has often led to overproduction crises but also to attempts by the corporations to govern the market by means of cartels, tariffs, long-term contracts with clients, the vertical integration of the whole product chain within the same firm, and, finally, cross-national company mergers.

Cartels, Oligopolies, and the Regulation of the Aluminum Market

Aluminum corporations have regularly created cartels. In 1901, the Swiss industry leader AIAG (which became Alusuisse/Algroup) increased production, which flooded the market, and then urged other firms to join the Aluminium-Association cartel. The cartel collapsed in 1918 when the new industry leader, Alcoa, used its monopoly in the United States and its U.S. government protection to attack the European market (Cowen 2000). While the major Alcoa shareholder, Andrew Mellon, was secretary of the U.S. Treasury (1921–1932), the government actively protected the Alcoa monopoly against attempts by European aluminum corporations to enter the U.S. market.

In 1926, the corporations settled their trade conflict with a new cartel agreement that was institutionalized in 1931 with the creation of the Alliance Aluminium Compagnie in Basle. Even though Alcoa was not a member of this trust, given U.S. antitrust legislation, it joined it through its Canadian sister company, Alcan, with which Alcoa shared its major shareholders (Cowen 2000). The cartel was very successful. It kept prices high despite the Great Depression. Moreover, the control over patents made it almost impossible for outsiders to enter the industry. Even after the patents on the smelting processes ended, the increasing returns to scale represented an enormous advantage for the established firms.

After 1945, the cartel was finally challenged when the U.S. government sold its own aluminum plants that had been created during Word War II, and, in 1951, a court obliged the Alcoa stockholders to dispose of their holdings in either Alcan or Alcoa. Nevertheless, the leading corporations managed to control the market until the economic crisis of the 1970s (Organisation for Economic Cooperation and Development [OECD] 1983).

Ethnocentric Multinationals

The aluminum corporations belong to the first multinationals. Similar to the oil companies, aluminum firms had to locate themselves where the ores they wished to mine were. They also selected particular sites for their smelting plants, namely, places where cheap electricity was available. However, the corporations usually created their overseas subsidiaries in the zones of influence of their home country.

During the GATT trade liberalization negotiations in the late 1960s, the French government defended the 12 percent tariff on aluminum imports. In 1968, however, the EEC removed the intra-European tariffs on aluminum products. Subsequently, Alcan and Alcoa created subsidiaries in the EEC and challenged the European aluminum firms. In turn, Pechiney and Alusuisse also acquired notable subsidiaries in the United States. Nevertheless, the aluminum corporations effectively remained ethnocentric firms with a strong home-country orientation.

The headquarters of aluminum corporations were able to control the daughter companies long before the invention of computer-based audit techniques. The vertical integration of aluminum corporations enabled the headquarters to manipulate intracorporation transfer pricing and, thus, to avoid tax payments.[3] In the 1970s, for instance, Alusuisse transferred earnings from its mines in Australia and its smelting plant in Iceland to Switzerland. It forced its Australian subsidiary to sell the alumina at a low price to the mother company, which, in turn, sold it for a 30 percent higher price to its Icelandic daughter company. As a result, neither subsidiary was profitable and, therefore, not liable to Australian or Icelandic taxation.[4] The reverse practice of Pechiney—it used transfer pricing to avoid French taxes—was an argument used in favor of the nationalization of French multinationals in 1981.[5]

The production of aluminum represents only a minor activity of aluminum corporations. They increasingly concentrate on value-creating activities further down the production chain. These new activities were integrated into firms through acquisitions. This focus was reinforced by a change in the ownership structures of the firm that obliged the European firms to find alternatives to their traditional providers of capital, namely, the Swiss banks and the French state, respectively. The companies turned to international capital markets in which investors were much less keen to accept long-term-oriented policies and profits below the average capital market profitability. In the 1990s, Alcan introduced a new accounting metric, economic value added (EVA), that is calculated by subtracting a capital charge from net operating profit after taxes. This would allow the measurement of real profitability, namely, the difference between the return on capital and the cost of using that capital over the same period. Consequently, every Alcan operation that fails to be EVA-positive, albeit profitable, risks being punished. This means that an Alcan subsidiary must produce higher returns than the capital markets (Amernic and Craig 2001).

In the 1990s, shareholder value replaced the industrialist paradigm of the engineers that had run the industry before investors, such as Martin Ebner,[6] took over. This led to much higher profit expectations of about 15 percent and radical cost-reduction programs (Rodier 1999). Pechiney, for example, adopted in 1996 a plan that included the loss of 5,100 jobs, that is, 15 percent of its workforce. Similar programs also took place in other multinationals, and this further increased competition.

The Alcan-Pechiney-Algroup Merger Project

On August 11, 1999, the Alcan, Pechiney, and Algroup executives praised APA as the new world industry leader[7] and assured shareholders that the APA merger would significantly enhance shareholder value. However, the antecedents of the APA merger project precede its official announcement by three years.

In 1996, Sergio Marchionne, a former CEO of a Canadian packing company acquired by Algroup, became the first non-Swiss CEO of the Alusuisse Lonza Group, or Algroup. Since then, he had been trying to merge Algroup with a powerful partner. In 1998, he announced a merger project with the German VIAG group, a company with activities in various sectors, including packing and aluminum, but this project failed in March 1999 (Eberwein, Tholen, and Schuster, 2001). At the same time, the CEO of Alcan contacted his Pechiney counterpart and proposed a merger of the two groups, but Pechiney initially declined this offer, because such a merger would have been "too unequal" (Rodier 1999, 22), until the failed Algroup-VIAG merger unblocked the situation. Then Pechiney agreed to the APA merger, which would prevent any of the three groups from having too much weight in the merged entity (Wright 2000).

The APA merger project profoundly undermined the ethnocentric nature of the corporations involved. Although Pechiney was definitely a French multinational for Jean Gandois, its chairman and CEO between

1986 and 1994 (Karlin and Lainé 1994), his successor claimed that APA would be neither Canadian, nor French, nor Swiss (Rodier 1999). Precisely for that reason, the APA merger would be a demonstration of the willingness of firms to transcend boundaries.[8] Alcan was also poised to shed its Canadian identity, as a Canadian newspaper emphasized, but just because power within the merged company would be leaving Canada did not mean that it would be going anywhere specific (Amernic and Craig 2001).

After the merger announcement in August 1999, much of the future of APA remained unclear, including the specific sites that would be most affected by postmerger restructurings (Alcan-Pechiney-Algroup [APA] 1999). Correspondingly, the actual APA organization was subject to enduring negotiations and rivalries. The APA companies established over ninety joint working groups to negotiate the design of the new company. Finally, the APA executives agreed to guarantee a proportional distribution of key management positions, but nationality ceased to be a factor in the selection process.[9] Hence, the announcement of the APA merger project fundamentally departed from the ethnocentric character of the three multinationals, implying a shift to a more geocentric type of multinational corporation.

Transnational Premerger Union Activities

Alcan Transnational Labor Relations

Since 1943, the United Steelworkers of America (USWA) has been representing Alcan workers in the United States and Canada (Harrod 1972). In the 1970s, it supported the creation of an aluminum industry working group within the IMF. This group organized several conferences to discuss structural change and occupational health hazards. However, the IMF hardly ever focused on union action, except in the case of the successful campaign against the lockout of USWA workers by the Ravenswood Aluminum Corporation (International Metalworkers' Federation [IMF] 1993; Juravich and Bronfenbrenner 1999).

Until recently, local Alcan unionists also ignored the global dimension of their industry (Wright and Edwards 1998). This is not surprising, given the stable division of the aluminum market up to the 1980s. But after a major collapse in the world-market aluminum price in 1990, the situation changed dramatically. Subsequent company restructurings and threats of plant closures disciplined Alcan unions not only in the United Kingdom but also in Québec (Bélanger, Edwards, and Wright 1999; Maschino, Boivin, and Laflamme 2001). The impact of global competition on Alcan labor relations, however, was still mitigated by the long-term nature of investments, local mobilizations and labor laws, and the greater impact of energy costs compared to labor costs (Bélanger and Dumas 1998; Bélanger, Edwards, and Wright 1999; Bélanger 2001).

The increased global competition did not lead to the transnationalization of Alcan unions, apart from the legally required creation of an EWC. In 1996, the Alcan management sponsored the establishment of an EWC under Article 13 of the EWC directive. But only the management of Alcan Deutschland, the largest Alcan branch in the EU, and the German GWC signed the EWC agreement, although in September 1993 the EMF organized a meeting of Alcan unionists in Brussels (EMF 1995). As a result, the Alcan EWC never functioned well because neither its leadership nor its composition was stable. During the APA merger discussions, in fact, the Alcan EWC changed its president twice.

Pechiney Transnational Labor Relations

In 1973, the IMF tried to establish a Pechiney WCC, but Pechiney stated that international labor negotiations would be unthinkable given the extreme differences between national union movements and the strong politicization of some unions (Beaud, Danjou, and David, 1975). The Pechiney management rejected not only international agreements but also any dialog with labor at the holding level. Capital-labor discussions took place exclusively at the subsidiary, plant, and workshop levels.[10] This situation changed with the adoption of the Auroux labor laws by the socialist government in 1982. This reform obliged all holding companies to establish GWCs.[11] This development facilitated the subsequent establishment of EWCs, especially in the Pechiney case (Rehfeldt 1998).

In 1989, Pechiney set up an informal European Information Commission, the first EWC in history. This initiative reflected the desire of the French government, which had nationalized Pechiney in 1981, and European and French unions to establish a precedent for the adoption of a EWC directive. In 1992, the commission was institutionalized through a French collective bargaining agreement. Initially, the CGT Pechiney branch hesitated about endorsing the agreement because Europe would be constructing itself against the workers (Verdier 2000). However, months later, the CGT signed the EWC agreement, like the EMF and all other French unions.

The lack of enthusiasm on the part of the CGT does not merely mirror Euro-skepticism. It also reflects organizational concerns. The CGT, which held the majority in the French *comité de groupe* (GWC),[12] feared EU-level affairs because most non-French unions did not cooperate with the CGT until it became an ETUC member. Accordingly, the EWC elected a CFDT delegate as its secretary who could take advantage of the resources that Pechiney allocated to the EWC secretariat.

In 1997, the unions renegotiated the EWC agreement with the management to meet the standards of the EWC directive. Although eighteen of the thirty-three workers' representatives on the Pechiney European Information Commission were not French, the 1997 negotiation group was entirely composed of French unionists. However, the EMF had been associated with the negotiations. The EWC was useful for unionists from countries with fewer consultation rights, such as the United Kingdom, in the case of collective dismissals. Yet, the EWC never organized any transnational action, although the Pechiney restructuring program in the late 1990s led to major collective dismissals. After its privatization, Pechiney adopted an adversarial stance despite the increasing number of strikes that this implied.[13]

Algroup Transnational Labor Relations

Apart from the participation of Swiss Metal and Watchmakers' Union (SMUV) representatives in the IMF aluminum working group, there is no evidence of transnational labor activities prior to the creation of the Algroup EWC in 1996 when the management took the initiative to conclude a voluntary EWC agreement in accordance with Article 13 of the EWC directive.[14]

The Algroup management proposed an EWC agreement that did not foresee any union involvement, but the Algroup national works councils and the EMF rejected the proposal. Eventually, Algroup and workers' representatives from ten countries concluded an agreement that went beyond the requirements of the EWC directive. The workers' representatives succeeded, in particular, in securing the access of three full-time union officials to all plenary and select-committee EWC meetings at the expense of the management. They also made sure that the EWC agreement included Swiss and British delegates, even though the original EWC directive did not cover these countries.

The EWC included three members from Germany, Switzerland, and the United Kingdom,[15] and a single member from France, Italy, the Netherlands, Iceland, Spain, Ireland, and Austria. Within the EWC, the German, Swiss, and British representatives played a leading role. The select committee of the EWC included its president, a German representative who was also the full-time president of the German GWC; its vice-president, a

British shop steward; and a Swiss company-level workers' representative. The three external union officials also came from the German IG Metall, the British Graphical, Paper and Media Union (GPMU, now part of Amicus), and the Swiss SMUV (now part of Unia). Between 1996 and 1999, the EWC met five times. Although most EWC members recognized that the EWC was far from being an organized EU-level actor, they argued that the direct contacts between EWC delegates made it more difficult for management to play one production site off against another. Communication among the EWC members represented a problem (Miller, Tully, and Fitzgerald, 2000); this was due, however, not to language problems or national divergences but to an asymmetrical distribution of work and influence among its president, its select committee, and its ordinary members. Therefore, the EWC asked the management to provide resources to prepare a training program for the EWC (Eberwein, Tholen, and Schuster 2001). In June 1999, it was agreed that the British GPMU would design a training package to put to the management at the meeting in September 1999, but the APA merger dramatically changed the priorities of the EWC, and the training issue was taken off the agenda.

Until 1999, the EWC did not organize any activity that went beyond its meetings. Nonetheless, the German president and the British vice-president in 1999 had already envisaged an increasing role for the EWC in the future, namely, in the field of negotiations on collective redundancies (Eberwein, Tholen, and Schuster, 2001). This mirrors a major learning process within the EWC, but this process was limited to a small number of active EWC delegates and did not concern the unionist at local production sites. Local unionists did not attach much importance to the EWC, and the Algroup EWC never drafted any declaration for local distribution, in contrast to the Alstom EWC—not even in the case of the planned VIAG-Algroup merger when Algroup also failed to inform the EWC. The CEO of Algroup always managed to appease the EWC before it envisaged any public activities. He formally apologized at the subsequent EWC meeting for having failed to consult the EWC about the VIAG-Algroup project, answered personally all questions from EWC members, and promised to improve the company consultation policy.

The Alcan-Pechiney-Algroup Merger Union Activities

The First Reactions of Labor

The Algroup management informed the select committee of its EWC via a telephone conference one day before the APA merger announcement;

the secretary of the Pechiney EWC heard about the merger project after its official announcement. Nonetheless, Pechiney EWC secretary and French CFDT union delegate, Lucien Fesser, acknowledged that the Pechiney management formally respected the EWC directive because it announced only a project and not an accomplished fact.

The Pechiney executives were indeed very concerned about formally respecting EWC consultation rights. During its discussions with the Alcan and the Algroup executives in July and August 1999, the Pechiney executives did not commit themselves to a merger before giving notice to its EWC. The Pechiney management emphasized that this consultation would only be a formality with no effects on the merger, "but a necessity nonetheless, without which no merger agreement could be signed" (Wright 2000, 46). Although EU labor law required that all three companies consult their EWCs before the merger decision, only Pechiney would have faced severe punishment if it had infringed the consultation rights of labor. According to French law, the nonconsultation of labor representatives could even constitute a *délit d'entrave,* that is, a crime punishable by imprisonment.

The company executives decided to split the APA merger into two distinct transactions. Whereas the Alcan and Algroup executives signed a merger agreement on August 11, 1999, the signature of the corresponding Alcan-Pechiney merger agreement was postponed until September 15, 1999. Due to this postponement, Pechiney could respect its consultation obligations without having to inform its labor representatives beforehand. Likewise, the Pechiney president and CEO consulted only the major board-level shareholder representatives, such as Etienne Davignon,[16] and not the whole company board before formally requiring the approval of the APA merger project at the board meeting of September 15, 1999.[17]

The APA merger plan worried most EWC representatives, but some unions publicized their fears much more than others. The merger plan, and the corresponding disappearance of national flagship companies, generated front-page articles in the Swiss and the French union press (Chauvel 1999). In contrast, the German IG Metall monthly devoted only a few critical lines to the APA merger in its regional Baden-Württemberg supplement.

Immediately after the merger announcement, the EWC leaders from the three companies requested extraordinary EWC meetings. By agreeing to hold these meetings, the APA executives not only acted in accordance with EU law, but also sought to prevent any conflict during the merger process. The EWC leaders also supported the idea of organizing a joint meeting within EMF. It was agreed that a group of three EWC members and one union official per company should discuss (1) the consequences of the merger for employees, plant locations, and products of the three firms; (2) the consultation process between management and labor, and among labor representatives in the three firms; and (3) the content of a new APA EWC agreement.

Incidentally, the union experts and leaders of the three EWCs communicated in German, including the French CFDT EWC secretary, because of his Alsatian origins. However, the CGT Pechiney EWC delegate and the British and Italian EWC representatives of Alcan were not approached by the Swiss union official who was coordinating the EMF coordination attempts. Apparently, he assumed that the EWC leaders of the three companies would consult their fellow EWC members themselves; however, as it turned out later, this assumption was only partially correct. Nonetheless, the CGT also emphasized the need for transnational union solidarity. The CGT delegate on the Pechiney company board, a computer operator at its Rhenalu plant in Neuf-Brisach (Alsace), announced that the CGT would contact the Swiss and the Canadian unions to facilitate a joint union reaction (Labbé 1999).

The leaders of the APA EWCs and the French, the German, and the Swiss unions agreed to cooperate. However, on August 19, 1999, they postponed the agreed-on EMF meeting to await the results of the three extraordinary EWC meetings and of an IMF aluminum working group meeting, which had by chance already been scheduled before the APA merger for September 27–28, 1999, in Geneva. On this occasion, the European APA labor representatives hoped to discuss the APA case with USWA delegates from the United States and Canada.

The Algroup European Works Council Meeting

The APA corporations had already announced a workforce reduction of 5 percent. Hence, EWC members were most interested in knowing which plants would be most affected by it. However, they not only sought information to further local interests, but also hoped to use the EWC as a tool to foster a coordinated response from labor.

The Algroup EWC members arrived well prepared for the extraordinary EWC meeting near Rotterdam on August 26, 1999. In addition to the official invitation issued on August 11, 1999, all EWC members received a preparatory document that had been drafted by the Algroup SMUV union official, Alfred Eger. It contained a questionnaire and a catalog of requests to be addressed to the management, including the involvement of union officials in any new APA EWC. The questionnaire sought information for each Algroup plant such as union membership levels, production capacities, and planned investments.

At the EWC meeting, the management was confronted with a coordinated set of requests. In turn, the EWC was not pleased to learn that major job cuts would occur in Germany, France, and Britain. The EWC urged Algroup CEO Marchionne, who was also designated APA director in charge of human resources, to guarantee a wide-ranging involvement of the EWCs during the whole merger process. The Algroup EWC proposed the conclusion of a European employment pact (*Beschäftigungspakt*) between management and labor in the three APA companies. The president of the Algroup EWC acknowledged that it might not be possible to prevent plant closures, but, precisely for that reason, he stressed the importance of an employment pact. This pact should include transnational requalification schemes to increase workforce mobility across national borders. This would be of specific interest for the Upper Rhine Valley area, including the French Alsace; the German Baden-Württemberg; and Northern Switzerland, where all three APA corporations run operations in the same business areas. Eventually, the pact could also regulate the social issues that were on the agenda anyway, such as incentive systems, part-time work schemes for elderly workers, and the introduction of new working time models.

In the eyes of the Algroup EWC, the adoption of such a transnational job security agreement represented an important trust-building measure, to prevent intracompany conflicts. The Algroup EWC was aware of different national practices and existing animosities among the national unions, but these difficulties would not preclude a European employment pact. Seeking solutions through job security arrangements obviously matched the repertoire of all major Algroup unions.

Although Marchionne did not exclude a transnational agreement, he called for a more realistic approach. While supporting social partnership, he emphasized that the ultimate objective of the merger process was an improvement in the competitive position of the company. At the end of the meeting Marchionne agreed to a proposal to establish a joint management-labor APA working group. Marchionne promised that he would talk to the Alcan and Pechiney CEOs, and the labor representatives said that they would contact the EWC of the two other APA firms.

Eger informed the Alcan and Pechiney EWC leaders about the Algroup EWC meeting and urged them to support the following requests: (1) the conclusion of a transnational job security agreement, (2) the creation of a joint working group to monitor the merger and to negotiate agreements on job security and a new EWC, (3) the convocation of a joint plenary session of all three EWCs, and (4) the creation of a world works council.

The Pechiney EWC Meeting

Despite the rather limited information that the management made available at the European and French works councils meetings in September 1999, the Pechiney EWC quickly acquired a good overview of the locations, products, and potentially redundant activities of APA in Europe, as a result of a study produced by the union-related consultancy firm, Groupe Alpha.[18] Because Pechiney was not in very good shape, the EWC hoped that the merger could contribute to its revitalization. However, the EWC was also very worried that APA would concentrate its future investments in Asian low-wage countries.

The Pechiney unions also endorsed the idea of a joint response of all APA EWCs, but the reports from the French GWC and the EWC meeting did not include references to the most ambitious Algroup EWC request, namely, to seek a European APA employment pact. In turn, the Pechiney unions forwarded the Alpha EWC consultancy report to the Alcan and Algroup EWCs and suggested that it serve as a background paper for the necessary joint meeting of the select committees of the three EWCs.

The Alcan EWC Meeting

Although the Alcan management did not specify the job losses that would result from the APA merger, the EWC was satisfied with the information the management provided during their meeting on September 8, 1999. The Alcan EWC labor representatives also discussed the reports from the earlier EWC meetings held by Algroup and Pechiney and agreed to join the working group of the three EWCs in the framework of the EMF. One of its first tasks was to be the identification of the overcapacities within the three companies. These facts and figures should then lead a joint European strategy. Only at this point should the three EWCs envisage a plenary meeting of all EWCs. The Alcan EWC also agreed to the opening of transnational negotiations about a European APA employment pact. In addition, the Alcan EWC emphasized that labor should demand the establishment of one or more European APA companies in order to preserve existing board-level codetermination rights. This would also strengthen the European subsidiaries relative to the APA headquarters. In turn, the Alcan management emphasized its interest in a cooperative management of the merger process in a way that would avoid unrest at the local plant level.

In sum, the Algroup and Alcan EWCs explicitly endorsed European negotiations about an APA job security agreement, in contrast to the Pechiney EWC. This difference reflected not only different experiences with job security agreements, but also divergent understandings of the role of works councils. According to the German model, which was dominant in Algroup and Alcan, a works council tries to negotiate agreements to limit the social consequences of company restructurings. In France, however, works councils are only consultation forums because the negotiation of agreements is a union prerogative. Nonetheless, the EWC labor leaders from all APA firms agreed to cooperate in the framework of the EMF. This represents a considerable achievement, especially when compared to the breakdown of transatlantic union coordination within the IMF.

Toward Transnational Union Cooperation?

In September 1999, three local USWA unionists from the Alcan Bécancour and Arvida plants in Quebec visited the French Pechiney unions in Hessenheim. At this meeting, the Canadian delegates, who were affiliated with the USWA, and French CFDT, CGT, CFE-CGC, and FO unionists signed a statement in which they affirmed their determination to pool their efforts in preventing the announced 4,500 job cuts and in reorienting the APA merger project in the interest of the workers.

However, only some days later, USWA officials boycotted the IMF aluminum working group meeting because it would be premature to discuss the APA merger case. On September 22, 1999, the IMF secretariat distributed a provisional agenda for its aluminum working group meeting on September 27–28, 1999, in Geneva. It suggested discussing a code of conduct for the merger process as well as the prospect of a WWC for APA. However, these topical issues did not please the USWA headquarters. Deprived of the participation of its leading American affiliate, the IMF eventually had no choice but to cancel the meeting.

Transatlantic union cooperation arguably faces more resistance than intra-European cross-border cooperation. The rather nationalistic rhetoric of the USWA in its campaign in 2001 and 2002 in favor of a protective 40 percent tariff on steel imports further supports this observation.[19] Nonetheless, U.S. unions, including the USWA, have asked for international solidarity (Juravich and Bronfenbrenner 1999) and have supported international causes on other occasions (Greven 2003; Harrod and O'Brien

2002). However, transnational cooperation and protectionism are not necessarily mutually exclusive, as demonstrated by the successful USWA lobbying to exempt Canada from the protective U.S. steel tariffs (McBrearty 2002).

Hence, although regional networks, such as U.S.-Canadian or European labor structures, seem to provide a better frame for cross-border cooperation than the IMF, it would be a mistake to explain this in terms of a lack of material resources in the IMF. A comparison of EMF and IMF budgets indicates that the IMF has much more money at its disposal than its European counterpart. The Europeanization of the APA unionists reflects primarily the existence of EU structures, such as the EWC and the Commission, and the regio-centric, rather than internationalist, consciousness of many unionists. Likewise, a German Alcan union official emphasized that European cooperation would be the only feasible way to contain the influence of U.S. APA managers. Conversely, precisely this Eurocentrism irritated the French CGT delegate and Pechiney EWC member, Claude Verdier (2000), who was much more at ease with the concepts of national and international, rather than European, solidarity.

The European Metalworkers' Federation Alcan-Pechiney-Algroup Working Group

Following the cancellation of the IMF meeting, the EMF invited the select committees of the three APA EWCs to an ad hoc meeting on October 22, 1999 in Brussels. This meeting was about adopting a joint strategy vis-à-vis the APA corporations and the Commission. However, in contrast to the Mannheim seminar in the ABB Alstom case, the EMF did not cover the travel costs of the delegates because it could not obtain Commission funds. Moreover, the EMF could provide only simultaneous translation in French and German, and consecutive translation in English. Nonetheless, these limited resources did not represent an obstacle because the APA corporations reimbursed the travel expenses of their EWC representatives.

In anticipation of the EMF meeting in Brussels, the EMF EWC coordinators met the representatives of the three consultancy firms that had been engaged by the French Pechiney and the German Alcan and Algroup works councils. At this meeting, it was agreed that they should identify the overlapping activities of the APA firms and the potential consequences of their merger.[20] Incidentally, the first Groupe Alpha study had revealed that the expected postmerger restructuring program threatened more than the announced 4,500 jobs.

Moreover, on October 11, 1999, the Commission declared that the merger notification of the three APA companies was insufficient and required additional information. It invited third parties to address the Commission within a period of ten days. This notice triggered the IG Metall official, Bertold Baur, to suggest to the EMF general secretary that he should immediately contact the Commission and highlight this issue in the subsequent EMF meeting on October 22, 1999.

The German works councils from the APA companies met on October 15, 1999 to discuss a joint strategy, in anticipation of the mentioned EMF meeting. In addition, on October 18, 1999, Swiss and German unionists attended the extraordinary general meeting of Algroup shareholders in Zurich, distributed leaflets, and urged the executives to seek a conciliation of shareholder and stakeholder interests to the advantage of both sides. However, although the joint statement of the German Algroup, Alcan, and Pechiney GWCs explicitly called for the creation of a joint EMF committee, only the Algroup workers' representatives emphasized the need for a joint transnational job security agreement. Equally, the French Pechiney GWC met again on October 20, 1999, but the minutes of the meeting listed only the likely negative consequences of the merger for Pechiney, without referring to any union strategy to counter them.[21] Nevertheless, the CFDT delegates distributed several newspaper articles and documents to Alcan and Algroup labor representatives.

The EMF meeting of October 22, 1999, was reasonably productive. The APA labor representatives agreed:

1. to commission a study on the consequences of the APA merger from the union-related consultancy firms mentioned previously. Each firm was to be in charge of one company, and Groupe Alpha was to coordinate the project.[22]
2. to establish a working group composed of two unionists per company (the group of six) in charge of drafting a new EWC agreement which was to be based on prior experience without endorsing one of the existing EWC agreements.
3. to write a joint letter to the EU Commissioner in charge of competition policy, requesting a meeting to discuss the grave concerns about the APA merger.
4. to write a joint letter to all APA CEOs, requesting a joint plenary meeting of all three EWCs.
5. to mandate the group of six to negotiate with managements a transnational job security agreement that would guarantee employment and the survival of all APA plants.

6. to write a joint leaflet about the results of the EMF meeting for distribution in the locations of the APA corporations in Europe.[23]

At the Brussels meeting, the diverse tasks had been distributed among the participants at the EMF seminar. Whereas the EMF secretariat drafted the letter to the Commission, the Pechiney EWC secretary, Fesser, prepared the letter to the CEOs of the three corporations. The Algroup IG Metall official, Baur, was charged with coordinating the group of six.[24]

The participants at the EMF meeting thus agreed on the following two lines of action: first, direct negotiations with the APA managements about a new EWC and a transnational job security agreement; and second, direct involvement in the merger control decision-making process of the Commission. However, neither of the two activities was backed up by a mobilization of the labor rank and file.

The APA labor leaders did not try to mobilize the APA workforce, despite the contrary decision by the Brussels EMF meeting. Nobody prepared a joint EMF-EWC leaflet to be distributed among the entire APA workforce. The Alcan IG Metall official, Detlev Kiel, only drafted a succinct letter for APA EWC representatives. Neither the EMF nor the APA labor leaders politicized the APA merger case in the public sphere. This reflects, according to Fesser, the frustration with the useless engagement of politicians in past restructuring processes. The Pechiney EWC concluded that politics would not change the behaviors of multinationals. Given the vital role of political action in the Alstom case, the lack of political agency in the APA case is remarkable.

Although Alstom unionists did not convey any romantic views about the role of political mobilizations either, they recognized the benefit of making their disagreements with the management and the EU institutions public. Conversely, the APA unionists and their consultancy firms accepted the dominant logic, according to which the merger must lead to redundancies. As a result, labor was mainly interested in mitigating the consequences of the merger.

Moreover, the managements tried to avoid any alienation of their EWCs to prevent a politicization of the APA merger in view of the antitrust process of the Commission. Therefore, some labor leaders thought that they could reach an agreement with management without having to trigger collective action process. From this point of view, collective action could even have had a counterproductive effect, as noted by a German Alcan unionist; it could destroy the grounds for an exchange: if unions refrained from contesting the merger, APA workers might receive some job security guarantees.

Negotiating Transnational Agreements?

The joint EWC-EMF letter to the APA executives, which was drafted by Fesser, did not mention transnational negotiations. Instead, it urged managements to convoke an extraordinary plenary meeting of all APA EWCs to obtain additional information about the measures to secure employment and to guarantee the functioning of national and European works councils. Arguably, the idea of transnational negotiations remained under the surface because the CGT section at Pechiney stated that it would not confer a negotiation mandate on the EMF group of six.

The Pechiney EWC secretary Fesser, however, did not inform the EMF about the objection from the CGT. After all, the Pechiney management had frequently discussed its restructuring plans with the EWC select committee in the past, which then guided the implementation of the plans at the local level (Lévy 2002). Likewise, the CGT branches of other firms also called for European negotiations about restructuring plans, despite the ambiguous status of such EU-level negotiations. However, it seems that the more the prospects of European negotiations deteriorate, the more unionists fall back into their established national patterns, recalling that, strictly speaking, there is no place for European negotiations. Hence, the lack of a legal framework for EU-level negotiations does not entirely explain the reluctance of the CGT unionists, although they explicitly invoked this argument (Verdier 2000). Indeed, European agreement would hinge on equally shaky legal grounds in Germany, but, as long as the German unions felt wholly involved in European negotiation, the status of an agreement was never a major issue.

Because the CGT Pechiney branch feared that it could be bypassed at the EU level, it told the EMF on December 7, 1999, that any transfer of negotiation powers to the EMF working group would require the consent of the national unions. This intervention reflects not only legal and organizational but also substantial personal concerns of the CGT delegate. These are linked to the tensions between the full-time union officials with a specific expert knowledge in EU labor relations (the union experts) and the EWC and union delegates who represent specific local sites (the union activists). Although these tensions also exist at the national level, they are definitely more evident in the context of EU-level politics (Wagner 2005).

The CGT delegate Verdier justified his opposition to a negotiation mandate to the group of six with the lack of rank-and-file involvement in such negotiations. He also emphasized the less specialized background and the fewer resources of the Pechiney unionists compared with other members of the group of six. Whereas the Algroup union representative was a labor lawyer and full-time official of the IG Metall central EWC department, the union delegates from Pechiney were workers who were just allowed some time off from their regular factory work to carry out their union duties. The Pechiney unionists would be much more vulnerable to pressures from the management than the sheltered IG Metall official, who did not have any employment relationship with the APA companies. French union delegates could lose their jobs if the company decided to outsource the unit in which they were formally employed. If this happened, the representative affected would be forced to resign from the works council and also lose his union mandates that protected him against unjustified dismissal. Therefore, the CGT representative, Verdier, urged the involvement of as many unionists as possible in negotiations with the management in order to diminish the pressure on a particular person.

In sum, transnational negotiations do not depend only on formal authorization procedures but also on union perspectives of such negotiations. In the next section, we explore the bargaining strategies of labor and the willingness of the management to enter into discussions with the EMF and the EWCs.

European Management-Labor Negotiations

In November 1999, IG Metall had been informed, off the record, that the APA executives had empowered the Algroup human resources director, Leo Houle, to resume negotiations about a new EWC agreement. These negotiations would start well before the conclusion of the APA merger. The APA executives apparently rejected the other requests that the EMF had made, namely, the joint plenary session of all EWCs, the establishment of a WWC, a European supervisory board, and job-security and plant-location guarantees. At this point, IG Metall official, Baur, suggested on November 15, 1999, that labor should not accept separate negotiations about a new EWC agreement but should insist on keeping the whole package of requests together.

However, on December 3, 1999 at an IG Metall meeting of works councilors from the German APA plants, Baur had to learn that it would be difficult to achieve the agreed-on goals, given the reluctance of local Alcan labor representatives to engage in collective action. Nobody criticized Baur's call for a more dynamic union policy, but, equally, nobody actively supported it either. Baur also learned that Alcan Deutschland had rejected the request to cofinance the study regarding the consequences of the merger. In doing so, the management correctly anticipated that the German works' council would not challenge this decision. In turn, Alcan Europe invited the economic committee of the German works council to an exclusive briefing in London about its postmerger human resources strategy and promised an additional EWC meeting in the third week of January 2000, to be attended by the Pechiney CEO.

Even though the IG Metall APA working group discussed Baur's idea of a token strike, or joint worker assemblies in all European APA plants, he finally concluded that the workforce could not be mobilized easily. Because several APA works councils were not yet sufficiently prepared for a conflict, Baur convinced the EMF to postpone its second APA working group meeting from December 13 to January 14, 2000. Baur then informed his colleagues that the APA executives had not yet replied to the EMF-EWC letter of October 29, 1999 and suggested supplying as much information as possible to the workforces so that they might be prepared for necessary action. However, the European APA unionists never adopted any concrete proposal for collective action. In some sites, there is no evidence of even simple information dissemination; however, there is evidence of local uncoordinated strikes in some Pechiney plants.

In mid-December 1999, Alcan Europe, Pechiney, and Algroup finally replied to the EMF letter of October 29, 1999. The human resources directors of the three companies agreed to meet the EWC leaders to discuss the mechanisms for establishing a future EWC. However, whereas the Alcan and Pechiney human resources directors did not recognize the EMF, the Algroup human resources director stated that it would be useful to meet the EMF in the first quarter of 2000. This is no coincidence. Whereas unions officials always had access to the Algroup EWC, the Alcan and Pechiney EWC agreements did not provide for the presence of full-time union officials. These different human resources strategies led to conflicts between the APA firms because each human resources director argued that the strategy of his company was the best (Lévy 2002). Nevertheless, all APA companies agreed to resume negotiations about a new APA EWC in order to avoid the tricky procedure of establishing a new EWC in accordance with French law. In turn, Baur wrote to the Algroup human resources director that the EMF APA group would certainly like to meet the APA executives and also to discuss the job protection agreement.

On January 14, 2000, the leaders of the three APA EWCs and the union officials concerned met again in Brussels. This meeting revealed growing tensions between and within the EWCs. Italian Alcan EWC members protested that there would be no democracy inside the Alcan EWC. Nevertheless, the meeting decided to restate the six requests to be addressed to the management and urged the EMF to write a second letter to the three CEOs, clearly restating the original EMF requests. Nevertheless, the conflicting interpretations of the role of the group of six endured. The Algroup EWC and IG Metall understood it as a group that would conduct negotiations with managements. In contrast, the Pechiney EWC emphasized that the group should prepare a project, which then must be ratified by the EWCs in accordance with French labor law. After the French CGT sent an additional fax to the EMF on January 20, 2000, these different interpretations became very evident. In this fax, the CGT urged the EMF to clarify this issue by the next EMF APA meeting, which had been scheduled for February 1, 2000 in Luxembourg.

Shortly before January 14, 2000, the human resources directors of Alcan, Pechiney, and Algroup invited the EWC leaders to a meeting on January 27, 2000, at the Zurich airport to discuss the possible procedure for creating a new APA EWC. The national German Alcan human resources director informed the IG Metall official, Kiel, that no union officials would be admitted to that meeting; however, at the Brussels meeting of January 14, 2000, the EMF and the APA EWC delegates rejected this condition. On the contrary, the EWC leaders confirmed their participation at the Zurich meeting together with an EMF coordinator for each company (EMF 2000). In the Pechiney case, the EWC secretary also assumed the coordinator function for the EMF; therefore, the second Pechiney seat was allocated to CGT delegate, Verdier. In contrast, the EMF maintained that the EMF coordinators and IG Metall officials Baur (Algroup) and Kiel (Alcan) should meet the managements rather than the respective deputy EWC presidents. Finally, the managements had to accept the participation of Baur, whereas Kiel did not attend the meeting.

However, on entering the conference room, the five EMF APA delegates were surprised by the presence of additional Algroup and Alcan EWC members. Evidently, these EWC members had accepted the invitation from their management, even though it was decided at the Brussels meeting that they would not attend. Although this did not create immediate conflict, it undermined the trust relations among the labor representatives. Nevertheless, labor managed to speak with one voice. IG Metall official, Baur, and the Pechiney EWC representatives embraced a joint position, even in regards to the group of six. Baur emphasized that the workers' side would have to form a prenegotiation team that would be identical with the labor delegation at the Zurich meeting, but he also stressed that an additional plenary meeting would have to be convened to assess the results of the negotiations. Fesser stated that the group of six would be competent to resume prenegotiations, and Verdier urged managements to accept the autonomous decisions of workers' representatives.

The Zurich meeting did not produce any material results because the managements did not have a joint position concerning, for instance, the negotiation of a new EWC agreement. For that reason, they emphasized that the discussions did not represent negotiations but only a brainstorming. However, the Zurich meeting produced some procedural results because the managements agreed to meet with the labor representatives again. The Pechiney human resources director proposed meetings every 3–4 weeks to resolve remaining problems. The managements also agreed to cover the travel and accommodation costs of their EWC members to facilitate their participation at the planned EMF meeting in Luxembourg. Finally, the managements invited the labor representatives to a second meeting on February 24, 2000, in Frankfurt.

It is worth noting that the EMF did not threaten the managements with collective action. Instead, Baur mentioned a meeting of the EMF with Monti of the European Commission and proposed a deal that guaranteed open information about the EMF discussions with the Commission in exchange for an open information policy on the part of the managements. Hence, Baur tried to transform EMF involvement in the antitrust procedure into a power resource vis-à-vis the managements. Although EMF access to Commissioner Monti impressed the managements, Baur's top-down approach irritated the Pechiney EWC.

The EMF meeting on February 1 in Luxembourg failed to solve this confidence crisis, and the EMF group of six never met again. The planned meeting with the APA managements on February 24 never took place because the Pechiney EWC recalled its two members of the group of six on February 18, 2000. The CGT Pechiney EWC delegate explained the failure of the EMF group of six in the following way:

> Should one negotiate at the EU level? Negotiate in the name of whom? In the name of a supranational body that is out of reach of the trade unions and the workers? Negotiate with what objective? With the objective of trading one company site against another, rather in one country than in another? Oppose the European countries against the rest of the world, while the merger covers 49 countries on three continents? What a huge gap between this and what we stand for! (Verdier 2000, 7; translation by the author)

Thus, the EMF had to cancel the planned February 24, 2000, meeting with the managements. In turn, the Pechiney EWC proposed a special negotiation body to negotiate a new EWC agreement in accordance with French law. This outcome represented a big disappointment for the EMF and IG Metall, which tried to negotiate an EU-level agreement, similar to the parallel Ford-Visteon case.[25] After the Commission blocked the APA merger project, however, the EMF, IG Metall, CFDT, and the CGT evaluated the APA case again more positively.

Influencing the European Commission Competition Policy

The APA merger control procedure started on September 20, 1999, when the Commission received notification of the two mergers by which Alcan would like to acquire control of Pechiney and Algroup. On September 24, the Commission declared that the notifications submitted were incomplete. On October 6, the companies submitted the missing information and the Commission started the initial examination phase of its procedure. On November 10, the Commission decided that the Alcan-Algroup and the Alcan-Pechiney legs of the APA merger would raise serious doubts concerning their compatibility with the single market. Therefore, it initiated a detailed appraisal of the merger to be completed within a supplementary period of four months. During this second phase of its merger control process, the Commission consulted the Advisory Committee of Member States and sufficiently interested third parties.

At their first meeting in Brussels on October 22, the EMF and EWC representatives chose to contact the Commissioner in charge of competition policy. However, the main concern of APA workers, namely, the negative employment consequences of the merger, was not mentioned in the letter that the EMF general secretary, Reinhard Kuhlmann, wrote to Commissioner Monti. The EMF assumed that even massive dismissals would not prevent the Commission from approving the APA merger. Whereas Kuhlmann identified some positive aspects of the merger, he emphasized that APA would acquire a dominant position in some product markets. Kuhlmann explicitly asked to be heard in the course of the Commission APA merger control procedure and requested a meeting with concerned officials. Hence, the EMF framed its objections to the merger in a language that was compatible with the dominant views of the Commission merger task force. Kuhlmann's letter to Commissioner Monti proved to be effective. An informal meeting between the two took place following the decision by the Commission to study the APA case in more detail, but on January 14, 2000, the EMF still did not know the date of the APA merger hearing, not to mention any other information about the Commission APA proceedings. For this reason, the EMF was not able to foresee that the APA hearing would clash with the Luxembourg meeting of its APA working group.

The role of organized labor in the APA merger has to be seen in a wider context. As already stated, the Commission DG for Competition must consult recognized employee representatives of merging undertakings if they have requested to be heard. However, the Commission did not consult any employee representatives before the Total-Fina-Elf (January 21) and the APA merger (February 1) hearings. In the first place, this reflects a failure of unions to act because labor representatives were generally not aware that they had to summit an explicit request to be heard by the Commission. Moreover, the Commission and the firms involved usually showed no interest in encouraging the participation of labor in the antitrust procedure. Furthermore, some companies, such as ABB and Alstom, avoided consulting their EWC representatives prior to the authorization of the merger by the Commission, and this effectively circumvented the right of the employee representatives to be heard by the Commission. The recognition of the EMF as an interested party in the APA case therefore constituted a step forward for labor.

On January 21, 2000, the Commission DG for Competition invited the EMF to its joint Alcan-Pechiney and Alcan-Algroup merger hearings scheduled for January 31 and February 1 2000. Notwithstanding the lateness of the Commission invitation, the EMF secretariat did not forward it at once to the APA EWC leaders and union experts. The EMF secretariat lost an additional two days before it urged Baur to name two representatives to represent the Algroup and Alcan workforces at the hearing. Because Baur chose to participate in the parallel EMF APA working group meeting in Luxembourg, he proposed Eger, the Swiss union official, for Algroup and Kiel, the IG Metall official, for Alcan, but the EMF secretariat failed to reach Eger, and it did not provide Kiel with essential practical information about the merger hearing. As a result, the Algroup workforce was not represented at all and Kiel, the IG Metall Alcan official, was unable to speak at the hearing. Instead, the Pechiney EWC representatives managed to participate at the hearing and made use of the whole period that the Commission had assigned to the EMF.

Nevertheless, Fesser, the Pechiney EWC secretary, was also surprised about the handling of the preparation of the APA hearing by the EMF secretariat. He even suspected that the EMF secretariat had intentionally asked him to participate at the Commission hearing to prevent his participation at the parallel EMF APA meeting in Luxemburg. Fesser eventually decided to participate at the EMF meeting; Xavier Guiglini from the EWC consultancy firm, Groupe Alpha, and Patrick Reinbold, CFDT EWC member from the Pechiney Rhenalu plant, went to the APA hearing.

This account reveals major flaws, even if we exclude any negative intentions on the part of the understaffed EMF secretariat. At the origin of the situation, which triggered reciprocal suspicions among the APA workers' representatives, were the late invitation and the even later distribution of the preparatory documents by the Commission. The very short time frame of the Commission merger control procedure caused crucial difficulties for the employee representatives because bottom-up consultation processes within democratic employee organizations are necessarily more time-consuming than the top-down processes within managerial hierarchies (General, Municipal, Boilermakers and Allied Trade Union [GMB] 2002, 5). Indeed, it is impossible to imagine how unionists from different countries and companies, who had met one another for the first time three months earlier, could prepare for a Commission hearing in a coordinated way when the Commission did not e-mail the relevant hearing documentation—that is, its very detailed and technical statement of objections—until after office hours on the Friday before the Monday morning meeting of January 31.[26] Because the Commission DG for Competition is certainly not an understaffed organization, it is likely that the distribution of the statement-of-objections documents was delayed on purpose.

In addition to the EMF, the local section of IG Metall in Nurnberg requested that it be heard by the Commission because Pechiney had announced, simultaneously with the APA merger, the closure of its Cebal aerosol plant in Nurnberg for competition policy reasons. This approach was coordinated neither with the EMF nor the IG Metall headquarters but, instead, with the Pechiney EWC. The request was successful, and the president of the Cebal works council, Günter Fröba, who is also a member of the Pechiney EWC, also participated at the APA hearing.

The workers' representatives at the APA hearing had not met one another before the Commission hearing. The coordination between the French EWC representatives from Pechiney and Kiel, the IG Metall official, failed because of the short preparation time and mutual suspicions. Yet it would be wrong to characterize the conflict between Kiel and the French Pechiney EWC representatives as a national conflict. The growing conflicts among the APA workers' representatives reflected different company loyalties and established EWC trust relations. Correspondingly, Fröba, the president of the Cebal works council and Pechiney EWC member, cooperated with the French Pechiney unions rather than with the IG Metall officials, Baur and Kiel. At the hearing, these tensions within labor remained under the surface because only Pechiney EWC representatives spoke at it.

In its initial investigation, the Commission came to the conclusion that the two notified APA mergers would be incompatible with the single market (Giotakos 2000), but the Commission gave the representatives of the undertakings to be merged, their clients and competitors, and the union representatives the opportunity of being heard on that matter. The hearing focused not only on the overall impact of the merger but also on the competition problems in each product market with the intention of identifying remedies that would permit an endorsement of the merger. Whereas the managements tried to dismiss the reservations of the Commission, APA clients and competitors emphasized their worries with regard to the merger. In contrast, the labor representatives neither fully endorsed nor disagreed with the Commission reservations.

The Pechiney EWC delegates did not back all of the objections of the Commission against the APA merger because the EWC representatives had no interest in damaging APA. The labor representatives urged, like the managements, a wider definition of the can and aerosol markets via the inclusion of tinplate cans because such a wider definition would possibly also have allowed the Pechiney Cebal plant to remain part of APA. Conversely, however, the only available intervention that could prevent the APA merger was precisely the Commission antitrust control procedure. Because Guiglini and Reinbold expected the merger to lead to massive collective dismissals, especially in either the Alcan Norf or the Pechiney Rhenalu rolling plant, they backed the concerns of the Commission concerning this part of the merger operation. They focused on the Alcan-VAW (Vereinigte Aluminium-Werke) joint venture in Norf, Germany, and not on the French Pechiney Rhenalu plant when they emphasized the problems that would result from the merger.

Günter Fröba, from the German works council of the Pechiney Cebal plant in Nurnberg, also intervened at the APA hearing. Pechiney had announced the closure of its Nurnberg plant to demonstrate its compliance with the Commission antitrust policy because this closure would substantially reduce the APA share in the aluminum aerosol can market. In doing so, Pechiney obviously wanted to send a positive sign to the Commission, but at the hearing Fröba suggested that the management had instructed local customer relations employees to shift clients from Cebal Nurnberg to other Pechiney plants. This interested the Commission very much, and a Commission official continued to question Fröba in a confidential private discussion. Furthermore, a major Cebal client further supported Fröba's testimony. Obviously, the APA management representatives were

not pleased about Fröba's intervention. Given that the Pechiney management had rejected any rethinking of the closure of the Cebal plant, Fröba
had nothing to lose, in contrast to the other workers' representatives. Incidentally, because of the announced Cebal closure, the Pechiney EWC was
the first to realize that the APA merger could raise EU competition policy
problems.

Finally, the Commission concluded that the Alcan-Pechiney merger
would create a dominant position in the markets for beverage can body
stock, aerosol cans, can sheet, and aluminum cartridges. On March 14,
2000, it conditionally approved the Alcan-Alusuisse merger, as a separate
merger, whereas Alcan and Pechiney withdrew their merger notification.
With this withdrawal, the three APA companies were trying to gain additional time to find remedies that would eventually assuage the concerns
of the Commission regarding the Alcan-Pechiney merger. Although APA
proposed solutions for almost all product markets, the companies failed
"to sever their link with VAW—their immediate competitor in the flat
rolled product markets—by disposing of their 50 percent participation
in the Norf joint venture" (Giotakos 2000, 11). Because Alcan was un-
willing to sell its shares of the Norf plant, Pechiney abandoned the APA
project.

Obviously, the APA labor representatives were pleased with this outcome. The approved integration of Algroup into Alcan set off fewer synergy effects and, therefore, fewer collective dismissals than those planned
in the APA merger project. Moreover, Houle, the Algroup human resources director was able to convince Alcan to accept the presence of a German, British, and Swiss union official as experts in the new Alcan EWC and
to sign a corresponding explanatory note to the Alcan EWC agreement.
Finally, the election by the new Alcan EWC of Ulrike Kraus, Algroup EWC
and IG Metall member, as its new president also secured union influence
in the new Alcan.

Changing Conclusions: From the Alcan-Pechiney-Algroup Merger to the Alcan-Pechiney Takeover

The Commission rejection of the APA merger suggests that labor successfully adopted a Euro-technocratization strategy in this case. Due to the
confidentiality of Commission debates, it is not easy to measure the impact
of labor on the Commission decision-making process. However, it is evident that the contribution of labor supported the negative assessment by
the Commission. The Commission later acknowledged the involvement of

employee representatives because they were able to add empirical substance to its appraisal. This conclusion is also confirmed by the more open-minded attitude of the Commission DG for Competition about the role of unions in its competition policy. Although the director of the DG for Competition still refuses to consider social and employment aspects, he has explicitly recognized that the information provided by unions can offset the information deficits of the Commission: "But often the workers, who know their terrain perfectly, can contribute to fill the information gap between the notifying companies and the Commission, and help the latter to evaluate the case with a better understanding of it, including matters of competition." (Rakovsi 2002, 21; translated by the author)

Nevertheless, in 2003 the positive assessment of the APA case by labor turned out to be premature. In summer 2003, Alcan launched a successful takeover bid against Pechiney. Once more, the labor representatives from Alcan and Pechiney tried to influence the Commission. Once more, the EWC of the two companies mandated the EMF to act. And once more, the EMF requested that it be involved in the merger control procedure of the Commission. However, on September 29, 2003, the Commission cleared the Alcan takeover bid for Pechiney without entering into the second phase of its examination procedure and without hearing any third parties, including the EMF. Although the review of the Commission highlighted serious concerns in a number of markets, Alcan was able to address these concerns by offering to divest itself of a number of businesses (European Commission 2003a).

The situation in the 2003 Alcan-Pechiney takeover was entirely different from the APA case. In the first APA merger case, all the APA companies had to accept the disinvestments requirements of the Commission. In contrast, the 2003 takeover of Pechiney allowed Alcan to enforce unilaterally the disinvestment requirements of the Commission against the will of the Pechiney management (Rodier 2003). Hence, the Pechiney and Alcan labor representatives could no longer hope that the disinvestments requirements of the Commission would finally prevent the takeover, in contrast to the first APA merger case.

In the case of disinvestments, the employees' job security interests would theoretically still correspond with the competition policy interests of the Commission. After all, the disinvested plant should be able to continue operating in order to assure continuing competition in this business sector. However, in the Alcan-Pechiney takeover case, the Commission accepted that a financial investor without any experience in the aluminum sector could get hold of the Pechiney Rhenalu plant, despite the opposition of the works council and its union-related consultancy firm (Secafi Alpha

2003). It is, therefore, not very surprising that both the workers' representatives and the management of Pechiney regretted that the APA merger had failed in 2000. Without doubt, it would have allowed a "more balanced and consensual development" than the final Alcan takeover (Secafi Alpha 2003).

This suggests that the prospects of a Euro-technocratization strategy on the part of labor in the field of competition policy are much more limited than we might have thought after the initial blockage of the APA merger. In fact, we must bear in mind that the Commission approves approximately 90 percent of the notified mergers and takeovers without entering into the second phase of its antitrust procedure and, thus, without hearing the employees' representatives (McGowan 2000). Hence, in most merger cases and all takeover cases, a merely Euro-technocratization union strategy does not seem to be very promising, as demonstrated in the final Alcan-Pechiney takeover case. Whereas the Commission DG for Competition neglected the concerns of labor in the Alcan-Pechiney takeover case, it responded to political pressures from governments and labor during the parallel Alstom rescue case in summer 2003. Hence, political power relations seem to be a much more important factor in European competition policy than the Commission is prepared to acknowledge.

It is also worth noting that a comparison of the arguments by the Commission in the 2000 APA merger and 2003 Alcan-Pechiney cases reveals that it changed its assessment, notably regarding the dominant position in the merger of flat rolled and flexible packing aluminum products. These changes cannot be explained if we assume that the Commission always applies the same technocratic yardsticks in its assessments. Hence, they can only result from the consideration of additional concerns that theoretically should not play any role in its competition policy (Secafi Alpha 2003).

In summer 2003, Francis Mer, the French finance and economy minister, also considered the option of politicizing the Alcan-Pechiney takeover case, given its sensitive implications for the French defense and European aircraft industry. Eventually, however, the French government sacrificed Pechiney and challenged the Commission DG for Competition in the parallel Alstom rescue case. The European mobilizations of the Alstom labor representatives had managed to politicize the Alstom case not only in France but, crucially, also in Germany and at the EU level. As a result, France was not as isolated politically at the EU level when it tried to rescue Alstom as it had been in the parallel Pechiney case. This made it more difficult for the Commission to qualify the rescuing of Alstom as a case of economic nationalism. In the absence of any transnational mobilizations in the Alcan-Pechiney case, however, it had been very easy for the Commission to dismiss French resistance to the Pechiney takeover as national protectionism.

This shows the diverging effects of the different union strategies in the two cases. Labor is only likely to affect EU competition policy if it succeeds in politicizing the competition policy in the European public sphere.

CHAPTER ELEVEN

Conclusion

The formation of the European single market and monetary union disadvantaged labor in many ways. Most important, the expansion of markets across national boundaries provided capital with increased options to exit the mid-twentieth-century class compromise that shaped labor relations and welfare states across Western Europe. However, unions had coped with a geographical expansion of capitalist markets before, namely, when governments created national markets during the nineteenth century. Although many local and craft-based unions perceived these national integration processes as a threat, labor eventually established effective national industrial organizations and developed new repertoires of collective action that were capable of shaping nation-building processes.

Today we can witness similar developments in response to the EU integration process. Supranational corporate and EU governance structures not only put national union organizations on the defensive, they also triggered new forms of transnational union action. This supports the conclusion that neither diverse national identities nor the establishment of an integrated European market nor the formation of supranational EU governance structures preclude European collective action. On the contrary, our analysis shows that transnational collective action by labor is triggered not only by unions that politicize the supranational reorganization of firms and the increasing cross-mobility of workers but also by the contradictions internal to the EU integration process.

By enabling collective action, unions empower otherwise isolated individuals to engage with governments, EU institutions, and firms. Labor thereby performs a function essential to democracy. Likewise, union membership and collective bargaining remain significantly and positively associated with higher levels of political activism and electoral participation across Europe (D'Art and Turner 2007). However, although unions contribute to a democratization of the EU, they also adopt technocratic (rather than democratic) and national (rather than European) strategies in response to the EU integration process. Focusing on what unions actually do rather than on what their conference resolutions say, we have therefore assessed the impact of EU integration on two core functions of unions, namely, wage bargaining and job protection following corporate mergers and acquisitions.

Explaining the Strategic Choices of Labor

We have discovered that unionists who belonged to the same national organization and were facing similar constraints adopted very different European strategies in similar cases. Whereas labor oscillated between national and European strategies in the area of wage bargaining, the analyzed local-, national-, and EU-level unions adopted Euro-democratization and Euro-technocratization strategies in our transnational corporate merger cases.

Comparing the Wage-Bargaining Coordination Cases

Part II highlights the pressures that EU economic and monetary integration exerted on national wage-bargaining systems. In response, many national unions adopted a technocratic renationalization strategy in the form of social pacts, and other competitive corporatist arrangements, to gain a competitive advantage for domestic firms over companies from other countries. These arrangements implied substantial wage concessions, but unions hoped that wage restraint would be compensated by employment growth and a consolidation of their institutional role as a key player in labor relations. However, the more unions recognized that such a strategy was generating deflationary downward pressures on wage shares across Europe, the more they were led to seek an alternative.

Because there was no prospect of European wage agreements, given employers' resistance and the lack of an EU income policy, several EU-level union federations adopted a European wage increase benchmark for national union negotiators in order to avert a competitive race to the bottom in wage levels. For the first time, national unions accepted an EU-level evaluation of their national bargaining policies. However, these coordination exercises were carried out by union experts without any rank-and-file involvement. In so doing, labor mimicked the dominant EU mode of governance, however, in its weak form of the so-called open method of coordination. Thus, these wage-bargaining coordination efforts represented, at best, a weak variant of Euro-technocratization that contributed little to the making of a more democratic EU. It does not follow from this that wage-coordination efforts are doomed to failure, but to be a successful tool they would certainly have to be more inclusive.

Whereas the EMF shaped the wage bargaining coordination policy of the ETUC, construction-sector unions adopted a different Europeanization strategy. Instead of adopting EU-level wage bargaining targets as a means to prevent wage competition between workers from different countries, the EFBWW aimed at restoring the national autonomy of collective bargaining. This was a response to the entry into local labor markets of companies that frequently employed migrant workers at wages that undercut the collectively agreed-on wages of the host country. To prevent a race to the bottom in labor standards, the EFBWW did several things. It encouraged the unionization of migrant workers and cooperation among unions from different countries on multinational construction sites. However, the EFBWW also directly requested the EU institutions to oblige firms that employed migrant workers to abide by the labor laws and wage agreements of the host country. For that purpose, the EFBWW required the adoption of the EU posted workers directive in 1996 and, in 2005 and 2006, joined several European demonstrations against the adoption of the initial draft of the EU services directive. Even if these mobilizations had the objective of defending national wage levels against transnational wage competition, the labor campaigns had to target the EU—especially the European Parliament, the only directly elected EU institution—to be successful.[1]

In both the EMF and the EFBWW cases, we can observe a Europeanization of labor activities primarily motivated by local concerns, namely, the protection of local and national wages against the downward pressure of transnational wage competition. It follows that the choice of labor to act primarily at a local, a national, or an EU level is not determined by its aims but rather by its means. Whereas a union always aims to improve the conditions of its local membership, unions learned that the means to achieve this goal are not always located at the local level. Therefore, any analysis of union strategies must assess and compare the opportunities for action at the local, national, and EU levels. Because it was easier for labor to politicize the EU posted workers and services directives than the Europeanization of the goods market and the tight monetary policy of the European Central Bank, the EFBWW campaigns had a stronger Euro-democratization impact than the EMF bargaining coordination attempts.

This observation qualifies the suggestion that "as markets expanded unions had to enlarge their strategic domain to keep workers from being played off against each other" (Martin and Ross 1999, 312). In fact, the world market was created a long time ago without this leading to a global labor movement. Economic Europeanization and globalization do not explain transnational union cooperation. Markets create societies without facilitating association among workers. Or, as Karl Marx observed, the mutual "relations of the producers, within which the social character of their labor affirms itself, take the form of a social relation between the products" (1999 [1887], chap. 1.4). Indeed, the difficulties of revealing the social relations that constitute the market and politicizing them also explains the difficulties of the EMF wage-bargaining coordination strategy. In contrast, the recent liberalization attempts of the increasingly neoliberal European Commission politicized the race to the bottom in wage levels and thus, ironically, triggered effective cases of European collective action by labor.[2]

Comparing the Company Merger Cases

Part III assesses the relation among EU competition policy, transnational company mergers, and labor job-protection policies in two important cases. We have shown that similar transnational corporate mergers triggered very divergent union responses.

In the case of the merger between the power generation divisions of ABB and Alstom, the involved local-, national-, and EU-level unions and works councils pursued a Euro-democratization strategy. They organized a European demonstration, politicized the merger, and contested the post-merger collective dismissal plans of management. This led to fewer job losses, at least in the countries where unions participated in the protests. The protesting ABB Alstom Power unions also convinced the European Parliament to criticize the Commission for its failure to consider the social consequences of the ABB Alstom Power merger in its merger control decision. In August 2003, during the heavy dept crisis of the company, European collective action even helped to secure its survival when unions and EWCs warned the Commission that its bankruptcy would be not only a French but also a European problem. Eventually, the Commission DG for Competition allowed a company rescue package, despite strong neoliberal opposition to this form of French state aid. Hence, even the decisions of one of the most politically isolated, decision-making bodies of the EU can be influenced by transnational labor campaigns.

However, the very same organizations that played a leading role in the ABB Alstom Power case—the EMF and the German and French metalworkers' unions—adopted a Euro-technocratization strategy in the parallel Alcan-Pechiney-Algroup (APA) case. Instead of organizing collective action, the APA unions tried to influence the Commission DG for Competition within its APA merger control procedure. The APA labor leaders did not talk about the likely employment consequences of the APA merger but, instead, tried to stop it using language that was compatible with the Commission free-market concerns. Initially, it seemed as if the technocratic strategy would be successful when the antitrust requirements of the Commission led to the abandonment of the Alcan-Pechiney leg of the APA merger. However, when Alcan launched in summer 2003 an unfriendly takeover bid for Pechiney, the Commission approved it without hesitation. Because Alcan was now in full control of Pechiney, it could satisfy the Commission competition concerns by simply selling off some Pechiney subsidiaries. The Pechiney takeover enraged the French government and unions alike. However, because the APA unions had failed to acquire any experience in European collective action in the preceding APA merger case, labor failed to influence the Alcan-Pechiney takeover decision. This demonstrates the limited utility of the Euro-technocratization strategy for labor. This aside, how can we explain the contrasting strategic choices of labor in these two merger cases?

Actor strategies always reflect the frameworks within which actors are operating. This study also shows that structures constrain, but do not predetermine, the choices of labor. Our quasi-experimental research design allows us to control for many explanations that have been used so far to explain divergent union strategies. Both cases share many features that have been used to explain the variation in EWC and transnational union action in the past (Müller and Hoffmann 2001; Pulignano 2006).

In both cases, unions and EWCs were confronted with a series of mergers that triggered significant collective dismissals in all companies involved. The analyzed companies also operated both in a capital- and technology-intensive manufacturing sector and also shared similar corporate histories. Whereas Pechiney and Alstom were recently privatized ethnocentric French multinationals, Algroup and ABB shared the same Swiss small-country origin and a more geocentric headquarters orientation. All companies also adopted similar shareholder-value-oriented corporate merger strategies. ABB and Algroup even had the very same major shareholder. The governance structures of the involved companies were very similar, too. The European activities of the companies were functionally integrated across national boundaries, and a very small number of central managers took the strategic decisions at the supranational level.

In all companies, there were also similar national and European labor structures, namely, relatively strong European and national unions and works councils. Different national backgrounds and political orientations of the labor representatives cannot explain the adoption of different union strategies either because German IG Metall and French CGT and CFDT unionists played the leading roles in all cases.

However, whereas labor representatives participated in the Commission APA merger control assessment, the Commission approved the ABB Alstom Power merger and the Alcan-Pechiney takeover without including labor in the process. Likewise, the managements adopted adversarial policies toward labor, except in the APA case, in which at least the Algroup management tried to avoid any direct confrontation with labor. Hence, different Commission and management attitudes might explain the Euro-technocratization strategy of labor in the APA case in 2000 to some extent. However, this factor can explain neither the adoption of a Euro-technocratization strategy in the 2003 Alcan-Pechiney takeover case nor the Euro-democratization strategies in the ABB Alstom Power merger and the subsequent Alstom rescue cases. Finally, the fact that labor adopted European strategies in all merger cases also requires further explanation, especially given the importance of national orientations in the area of collective wage bargaining.

Explaining the Europeanization of Organized Labor

All company merger and takeover announcements triggered an immediate transnational reaction. The unions and works councils concerned met one another and tried to seek joint responses. However, in all cases, transnational union cooperation was limited to the core of Western Europe. The timid attempts to develop a transatlantic labor response to the APA merger failed from the outset. This shows again that the existence of a global economy does not necessarily trigger a global union movement.

Instead, the cases expose the importance of statutory supranational institutions, such as the EU or the EWCs, as a catalyst and framework for transnational union action. Whereas a single national affiliate, the USWA, could prevent any discussion of the APA merger project within the IMF, no national union could veto the discussions within the statutory EWCs or the

EMF. Furthermore, the decisive role of the Commission in the area of competition policy left labor no other choice but to Europeanize if they wanted to influence the merger control decisions.

The ABB Alstom case also challenges the notion that EU-wide union co-operation fails because of the competition for local production capacities (Streeck 1998a; Hancké 2000). If economic competition precluded collective action, unions would simply not exist. Although self-interest is an important motivation in capitalist societies, institutional settings and learning processes can lead to the conclusion that these interests can be better satisfied through cooperation, even at a transnational level. These learning processes may have taken place in the ABB Alstom Power case much more easily than in others because most local sites had been more or less equally affected by the company restructuring plan. Moreover, the British unions, which did not participate in the Brussels ABB Alstom Power demonstration in 2000, were not rewarded; instead, the management implemented the largest redundancy plans where it faced the least resistance. The British unions learned from this experience and participated in the 2003 Alstom demonstration in Paris; the German and French ABB Alstom Power unionists had already undergone similar experiences during earlier transnational company restructurings in the 1990s.

There is also a theoretical argument that explains the prospect of transnational union solidarity within multinational corporations. Despite management attempts to present corporate decisions as a result of market pressures, management decisions are always political decisions and not the result of apparently natural market outcomes. Mergers, takeovers, or collective dismissal plans are planned actions of a hierarchical organization, which is the firm. As a result, it is easier to politicize corporate decision making, and thus to create transnational intrafirm union solidarity, than to create union solidarity across the boundaries of the firm, as illustrated in our discussion of the European bargaining coordination attempts of labor in part II. Hence, the central economic driving force that links unions across Europe is not the existence of a European market but the increasingly supranational reorganization of the firm.

Indeed, our cases reveal that the centralization of corporate decision making at a supranational level has played a decisive role in triggering a transnational union response. Correspondingly, in 2001 the level of transnational union action declined again during the decentralized implementation phase of the postmerger restructuring plans according to national laws and practices. And, in turn, transnational union action increased again after the announcement of a new global Alstom collective dismissal plan in 2003 and after the Alcan takeover bid for Pechiney in summer 2003.

The subsidiaries of manufacturing multinationals are no longer relatively independent national offspring of a multinational holding company but are, instead, a link in a functionally integrated transnational production chain. As a result, the subsidiaries of multinationals increasingly cooperate with one another across national boundaries. The headquarters of each multinational tries to support this trend by forging a transnational corporate identity. The cooperation among units of the same company across national boundaries, however, also leads to increased links among workers from different countries that could also promote transnational union solidarity. In fact, the members of the ABB and Alstom EWCs had not only a national identity, for instance as German IG Metall or French CGT unionists, but also transnational identities as workers in the same multinationals.[3] Because national and transnational identities overlapped, the cooperation between ABB and Alstom workers across national and company boundaries can in part be seen as an aggregated outcome of national interfirm and transnational intrafirm identities.

As chapter 9 also shows, Europeanization is facilitated by the fact that many company-level European unionists were able to build on intercultural social skills that they had developed in their previous roles as union or political activists. For example, many ABB Alstom Power union representatives built on their prior experiences either with migrant workers at home or with comrades from other countries within international political activist networks abroad, such as the European marches against unemployment, job insecurity, and social exclusion. Moreover, the European ABB Alstom unionists were also used to adapting to quite different cultures in their dealings with managers, politicians, and workers, who all have divergent social backgrounds. Hence, it would be wrong to assume that the acquisition of intercultural skills is a privilege of academics or the emerging transnational business class. The social capital of European trade union activists is much more compatible with the transnational EU milieu than we would normally assume.

Politics also contributed to the Europeanization of labor in the two merger cases. The regulation of transnational company mergers and takeovers takes place exclusively at the EU level. For this reason, the EWCs and unions had to address the Commission and the European Parliament. The unions also applied pressure on national and local politicians, but this was often done to induce them to lobby the Commission. At the same time, the fact that the Commission controls competition policy effectively precluded the adoption of a renationalization strategy by labor, as emphasized by the initial injunction of the Commission to restore partial state owner-ship of Alstom in September 2003.

Finally, we must recall that the existing European structures of orga-nized labor, namely, the EWCs and the EMF, also played a most important role. The EWC and union activists, who determined the divergent Euro-peanization strategies in the two cases, effectively built their activities on these preexisting cross-border networks. This factor also explains the as-tonishing difference between the approaches of the Alstom and Pechiney CGT EWC delegates. Unions work on those levels for which they consider that they will have the most significant impact. The Pechiney CGT dele-gates preferred the national level because they felt marginalized by the other unions in the Pechiney EWC and the EMF APA working group, whereas the Alstom CGT delegates played a leading role in their EWC. The Alstom CGT delegates even cooperated very well with Polish Solidarnosc unionists, despite their fundamentally opposed political legacies. Who would have thought in the 1980s that these two unions would ever speak to one another?

In short, the Europeanization of labor strategies in the two merger cases is partially a result of the centralization of corporate decision making at a supranational level, the existence of EU-level labor structures, and the dominant role of the European Commission in the area of competition policy. However, the successful Europeanization of labor also depended on unionists perceiving the EU as an effective framework for collective action and not just as a threat.

The Choice between Euro-Technocratization and Euro-Democratization

The repertoire of European collective action is not as predetermined as many scholars think. There is a choice between democratic and techno-cratic actor strategies even at the EU level. The European demonstrations by ABB Alstom Power workers in 2000 and 2003 resulted, above all, from the efforts of a small group of EWC activists who understood how to make practical use of European resources, political links to left-wing members of the European Parliament, and the media. This contradicts the conclusions of Gobin (1997) and Pernot (1998), who argue that the rising access of national unionists to EU politics via EU-level union structures would en-gender a dissemination of a Euro-technocratization policy style, not a rise in European collective action. In contrast, the APA unionists sometimes mentioned the need for the active involvement of the media and even the need to organize collective action, but nobody undertook any action in this direction. This means that the APA unionists believed that the seemingly less demanding and less costly Euro-technocratization approach would be sufficiently effective. It may therefore be fair to say that the APA representatives consciously adopted a Euro-technocratization strategy.

The difference between a Euro-technocratization and a Euro-democratization of labor also reflects the prior experience of the unionists involved in political union action. In the ABB Alstom Power case, the French state is a still major client of the company. Correspondingly, Alstom may be more sensitive to political pressures than the APA aluminum companies. This may explain why the Alstom EWC demonstrated a higher affinity for political action than their Pechiney colleagues. However, the partially state-owned French and European military aircraft industry was equally dependent on Pechiney specialist products. This suggests that the greater political sensitivity of the ABB Alstom labor leaders mirrors above all their larger involvement in social movements and left-wing political parties.

Finally, the ABB Alstom Power demonstrations and the eventual breakdown of the EMF working group in the APA case demonstrate that transnational union cooperation is critically dependent on mutual learning and trust-building (Klebe and Roth 2000) and on intense discussion processes (Kelly 1998) among activists and workers. This points to what is probably the most important difference between the two cases—in the ABB Alstom case, the leading German and French unionists already knew one another from the prior Alstom EWC. Moreover, they also made their European activities public, through leaflets and the press. In contrast, the leading European APA representatives, who did not know one another, failed even to involve all members of the respective EWCs in their European activities. This illustrates that Euro-democratization is difficult but not impossible.

Organized Labor as an Agent of Euro-Democratization

This brings us to our concluding remarks concerning the potential role of labor as an agent of Euro-democratization. The EU integration process has provided a rare opportunity for us to examine the links among nationalism, technocracy, and the democratization of supranational organizations. Many Euro-skeptics have argued that the EU cannot be democratized because national differences prevent the constitution of a European *demos* (people), a European public sphere, and a European civil society. This book approaches Euro-democratization with more diverse analytical lenses. Our studies focus not only on cultural factors but also on socioeconomic factors that might facilitate the making of a transnational EU democracy. In doing so, the book asks whether the tensions resulting from the formation of the European single market and monetary union foster popular mobilizations that might contribute to a more democratic EU, as suggested by Habermas (1996b [1990]).

By assessing the activities of union networks in the areas of collective bargaining and company restructurings at the EU, national, and company levels, we show that in some cases labor is contributing to the making of a more democratic EU through transnational collective action and a politicization of EU policy making. However, the book not only assesses the prospects of a transnational EU democracy, it also offers conclusions about the state of European labor relations. By uncovering the catalysts that facilitated European collective action, our study questions the prevailing view that unions are bound to the nation-state while at the same time business interests act across national boundaries to promote a neoliberal agenda for the EU. The methodologies used in this study allow us to question many deterministic conclusions that have been proposed to explain the success and failure of EU-level collective action. Our findings show that neither diverse national identities nor economic competition nor neoliberal EU-governance structures necessarily preclude European collective action on the part of labor.

The Role of National Identity

Despite its internationalist rhetoric, the labor movement has never been immune to the appeal of nationalistic discourses. Likewise, blue-collar workers tend to vote in greater numbers against EU treaties than do other socioeconomic groups.[4] If this reflected an entrenched attachment to the prematerial value of national identity (Hooghe and Marks 2006), then the prospects of labor engaging in any kind of European collective action would be very bleak indeed. However, if we combine the findings of parts II and III of this book, any kind of culturalist determinism seems to be misplaced. The varied performances of the transnational union networks analyzed in this book do not reflect national cleavages but, rather, diverging economic interests. Although unionists used nationality as an argument in European trade union discourses, they did so only as long as they perceived a congruence between nationality and their economic and social interests. As soon as this congruence disappeared, the unions always pursued socioeconomic rather than national interests.

In the APA case, for example, the local IG Metall unionist from the German Cebal plant cooperated much better with French unionists who belonged to the same multinational than with German IG Metall officials who were linked to either Algroup or Alcan. In turn, the European mobilizations in the ABB Alstom case exemplify both transnational cooperation between unionists who belonged to the same EWC and national cooperation between unionists who belonged to different companies but were united by their national union organization. This shows that successful European collective action does not necessarily depend on a fully integrated European labor movement. It can also result from a combination of transnational (company-level) unionism and national (sectoral or intersectoral) unionism, which can integrate divergent company interests.

The major differences between the wage-bargaining coordination approaches of the European metal and construction workers' federations also confirm the greater salience of sectoral differences relative to national factors. Whereas the EMF has set a European benchmark that aims to guide the wage negotiations of its affiliates, the EFBWW policy fully respects the autonomy of local bargaining. This difference does not mirror an asymmetric influence of national unions in the two European federations but, rather, different types of Europeanization processes in the two sectors. Whereas Europeanization in manufacturing is mediated through the free movement of goods, the Europeanization processes in construction are mediated through the free movement of workers and services. This explains the mobilizations of the EFBWW in favor of the posted workers directive and against the draft services directive. Hence, labor migration, rather than the EMF's wage bargaining benchmarks, may act as the major driving force for a Europeanization of national income policies.

Our analysis suggests that cultural differences are not the main obstacles to transnational collective action. Nationality influences transnational labor action only insofar as it determines the range of activists' networks. The more migrant workers play a significant role in unions and the more transnational networks are constructed, for example, around EWCs and European trade union federations, the more likely is European collective action.

The Role of Economic Competition

Although national identity does not preclude transnational cooperation, the number of successful cases of transnational union action is still relatively small, even within the EU. This suggests that nation-states still provide unions with a practical framework within which to pursue workers' socioeconomic interests. This does not necessarily reflect nationalist attitudes but, rather, the capacity of labor to make deals with governments or national employers' organizations.

In many European countries, unions accepted wage moderation in exchange for other political or socioeconomic goals, such as the provision of a good investment climate for multinationals. By the end of the 1990s, however, the declining share of wages, persistent unemployment, and the threat of social dumping prompted unions to make various European coordination attempts in the area of collective wage bargaining. National manufacturing unions have accepted a European framework within which they have to justify their wage-bargaining policies by comparing them with agreed-on benchmarks. Although these targets have so far failed to set robust European wage-bargaining patterns, this has not led to a cessation but to a new focus of coordination attempts by labor, as exemplified by the calls for a coordinated European minimum wage policy (Schulten, Bispinck, and Schäfer 2006). This shows that economic competition is as much an obstacle to as a trigger of collective union action. After all, unions were founded in response to the commodification of labor power.

This conclusion is also supported by the findings from the ABB Alstom case study. The joint actions of ABB Alstom unionists were possible despite the competition for local production capacities among the various company subsidiaries. Ironically, it could be demonstrated that the more the workforce of a plant participated in transnational union action, the more it was sheltered from the negative effects of the postmerger company restructurings. The same also applies to the APA case but from a reverse angle. In hindsight, Alcan unionists acknowledged that transnational collective action would have been the best response to the APA merger because, despite initial assurances to the contrary by management, the postmerger restructuring also hit their plants.

Nevertheless, the comparison between the chapters on collective bargaining and company mergers also shows that it is easier to politicize supranational management decisions than the modes of operation of a transnational market. Likewise, it is also easier to show the effectiveness of transnational collective action in specific company cases. Although the collective bargaining coordination approach of the European trade union federations did not reach the union rank and file, the ABB Alstom unions managed to involve local unionists in their European activities. This also reflects the technical nature of EMF and ETUC wage-coordination policies, which resembled, arguably too much, the technocratic benchmarking approach of the EU (i.e., the open method of coordination). Hence, despite their unorthodox Euro-Keynesian content, the European wage-bargaining benchmarks of the EMF and the ETUC did not work as a cata-lyst of union mobilizations. However, if the ETUC and EMF wage-bargain-ing benchmarks had been developed not only in conjunction with a few national collective bargaining experts but also with the thousands of Eu-ropean works councilors that exist in Europe, then the European bench-marks would arguably have had a much greater impact.

The Role of Neoliberal European Union Governance Structures

As shown in chapters 4 and 8, the employment and social policy con-cerns of working people are virtually absent from EU monetary and com-petition policies. It has also been shown that the European Parliament has no powers in these policy fields either.

Nevertheless, the unions are not passive victims of the EU integration process but agents that are also capable of politicizing its contradictions. There is, first, the fundamental contradiction between democratic norms and the recognition by the EU that its governance structures are not very democratic.[5] Second, there is also a clear tension between its official purposes, including "a high level of employment and of social protection" (Article 2 TEC), and the adoption of economic policies "in accordance with the principle of an open market economy with free competition" (Article 4 TEC). Our studies show that unions can, at times, exploit these contradictions.

The Alstom case confirms that unions are able to politicize EU compe-tition policy decisions. Although the collective actions of labor have not led to the abandonment of the Commission's technocratic competition policy framework, union pressure effectively contributed to the final en-dorsement of the Alstom rescue package by the Commission, despite the package being at odds with free market ideology. Obviously, the demo-cratic legitimacy of the Commission was so weak and the significance of so-cial and employment issues was so high, that the Commission simply could not afford to force Alstom into bankruptcy.

The role of European mobilization in the Alstom case was exceptional but not unique. European mobilizations of labor occurred in other cases too, as exemplified by the growing number of European demonstrations before crucial European Council and European Parliament sessions, for example, against the adoption of the EU directive on market access to port services in 2003 and the initial draft of the EU services directive in Feb-ruary 2006 (Turnbull 2006).

Overall, our analysis suggests that diverse national backgrounds do not preclude the Europeanization of collective action, neither do the EU governance structures. Our findings also imply that the driving force behind the Europeanization of labor is not the creation of European goods and capital markets but the increasingly frequent supranational reorganizations of firms and the increasing cross-border mobility of workers.

The Prospect of Euro-Democracy

This conclusion not only emphasizes the critical role labor could play in the Euro-democratization process, but also reflects the origins of the EU legitimacy crisis that followed the rejection of the EU constitution in the French and Dutch referendums. The rejection of the EU constitution does not reflect habitual nationalism, as "some of the most stringent criticisms of the EU come from its strongest supporters" (Moravcsik 2006, 238). A Eurobarometer survey revealed that the citizens of the countries where the idea of having an EU constitution was strongest rejected the proposed draft of the EU constitution (European Commission 2006). Many French Euro-federalists rejected it because it would have rendered the pursuit of alternative economic policies unconstitutional (Généreux 2005). In turn, Dutch referendum study data show that a significant part of the Dutch no vote corresponds to fears of social dumping associated with the European single market and monetary union that have been considerably deepened by the enlargement of the EU (Aarts and van der Kolk 2006). French analysts of the vote also concluded that: "the result of the referendum might have been dramatically different if perceived social threats had been lessened and if Europe had not been perceived as [neo] 'liberal' but as 'social'" (Brouard and Tiberj 2006, 267). The era when the EU could simultaneously rely on contrary sources of legitimacy—technocratic market making and democratic policy making—seems to be over.

To solve the current EU legitimacy crisis there is a choice of trajectories. Either we democratize EU governance structures, which would allow the articulation of the citizens' social concerns at the EU level, or "we set aside any democratic participation or deliberation—or any procedural norm— as an absolute standard, and instead seek to design constitutional forms to achieve certain social goods" (Moravcsik 2006, 239). The advocates of the first option should bear in mind that democracy will, like liberty, always remain a utopian aspiration. This implies that the issue is not the constitution of an EU democracy as such but the continuous making of more democratic EU decision-making structures and procedures. In turn, the followers of the second option must be aware that any elitist definition of *social goods* outside of democratic procedures would further marginalize popular concerns and therefore lead to an even greater crisis that might endanger both national democracy and the European integration project.

The contradiction between democratic norms and their absence in practice is not a problem specific to the EU but a recurrent feature of modern governance at the national level. Modern political decision makers hardly ever question democratic principles, but they frequently seek to establish governance structures that allow them to escape democratic accountability. Likewise, governments simultaneously want democratic reforms of the EU and maintenance of the status quo, thus allowing them to bypass public and parliament in many policy areas. The responsiveness of political representatives to citizens and the access of citizens to the decision-making process are always at risk, especially once a set of interests, such as business interests, acquires a dominant position over all the others. Hence, democracy can diminish without any change of its formal constitution, as has been argued with reference to the United Kingdom and the United States. But whereas the threat of a "post-democracy" (Crouch 2004) or "diminished democracy" (Skocpol 2003) does not seem to concern either the U.K. or the U.S. government, EU institutions frequently have to acknowledge the democratic deficit of the EU.[6]

The EU is more sensitive to democratic critiques because it cannot build on the historical legitimacy of an established state. The tensions between democratic norms and undemocratic practice cause more concerns in relation to the EU, not only because it is arguably more difficult to design a transnational democracy but also because the EU is not as deeply ingrained in the mindsets of its citizens. However, the solutions that will be found to resolve the tension between democratic norms and technocratic modes of EU governance will also influence the future of democracy at the national level. If the EU fails to become more democratic, free-market-oriented technocratic efficiency and right-wing nationalism might replace democracy as the principal political paradigms.

There are numerous suggestions for making the EU more responsive to the demands of its citizens, such as the strengthening of social and political fundamental rights and the introduction of a European citizens' initiative and referendum, organized on the same day in all the member states. Eventually, however, Euro-democratization will depend on the adoption of corresponding strategies by the social actors, such as labor, which made active citizenship and egalitarian democracy possible at the national level. The choices made by the unions, however, will not only determine the future role of labor, but will also affect the future development of democracy. When we consider that a small number of well-connected activists were able to politicize the inherent contradictions of the EU integration process and, thus, to trigger major European mobilizations, the prospects for both Euro-democratization and labor are rather encouraging. A generalization of European collective action by labor, however, also requires that EU-level politics be seen not just as a threat but, rather, as a decisive battlefield in the fight for social justice and egalitarian democracy.

Notes

Chapter 1. Introduction

1. See Lepsius (1993a, 1993b); Thibaud (1992); Offe (1998); Grimm (1995); Greven (1998).

2. The adjective *transnational* refers to flows and networks that transcend national boundaries and, therefore, question the autonomy of national systems (Pearsall 1998). In contrast, the term *international* refers to interactions between autonomous national systems.

3. The verb *to nationalize* has different meanings: first, the transfer of a branch of industry from private to state ownership and, second, "make distinctively national: give a national character to: in the 13th and 14th centuries the church designs were further nationalized" (Pearsall 1998, 1233). Here the term *renationalization* is used to refer to its second meaning, as a concept that is opposed to Europeanization.

4. However, access to the union records was only possible due to a time-consuming trust-building process. Generally, I met many unionists several times and acquired, after every meeting, access to additional data. I interviewed eighty-seven European-, national- and enterprise-level union leaders; works councilors; and business consultants. I also attended numerous union meetings and demonstrations. For this purpose, I traveled to Berlin, Düsseldorf, Frankfurt, Stuttgart, Oberursel, Cologne, and Mannheim; to Belfort, Dijon, Paris, Poitiers, Neuf Brisach, Nice, Noisy-le-Grand, and Vélizy; to Prato, Florence, Foligno, Turin, and Rome; and to Amsterdam, Berne, Zürich, Fribourg, Oslo, and Brussels.

Chapter 2. Approaching Euro-Democracy and Its Alternatives

1. The term *supranational* refers to organizations such as the EU or a multinational company that have power over national organizations. Thus, supranational organizations limit not only the autonomy but also the formal authority of national organizations (Leibfried and Pierson 2000).

2. Whereas Schmitter (2000) suggests holding EU-wide referenda on the EU constitution and on other proposals submitted by the European Parliament, others suggest that citizens' initiatives should also be able to initiate a vote from below (Initiative and Referendum Institute Europe 2007; Erne et al. 1995).

3. Nevertheless, Grimm (1999) does not exclude the rise of a European public sphere in the future. He acknowledges that the situation could be different in the event of EU-wide referenda because it would be easier to Europeanize a referendum debate than an entire party system.

4. It is a truism that democratic revolutions frequently arise at moments when people start to believe that their own preferences conflict with the dominant definition of the good as stipulated by their rulers, however enlightened they are.

5. See Diamond and Plattner (1996); O'Donnell, Schmitter, and Whitehead (1986); Linz and Stepan (1996).

6. Ruling elites support democratization processes to contain their effects, as brilliantly illustrated in the novel *The Leopard* by Giuseppe Tomasi di Lampedusa. He portrays how a young Sicilian aristocrat, Tancredi, joins Garibaldi's 1860 insurrection saying to his loyalist father: "Unless we ourselves take a hand now, they'll foist a republic on us. If we want things to stay as they are, things have to change. D'you understand?" (Tomasi di Lampedusa 1998 [1958], 22).

7. See Lipset (1969); Moore (1969); Sinyai (2006); Rueschemeyer, Huber, Stephens, and Stephens (1992); Giugni, McAdam, and Tilly (1998).

8. It should be noted, however, that this is not an irrefutable position. In Poland, for instance, the Solidarnosc union obviously lost its leading political role after the formation of a democratic party system in 1989 (Galin 1994).

9. See Silver (2003); Harrod and O'Brien (2002); Régin and Wolikow (2002); Gumbrell-McCormick (2000); Foster (2000); Moody (1997); Visser (1996).

10. On the contrary, even democratic governments repressed the development of organized labor. In 1791, for example, the French constituent assembly adopted the *loi Le Chapelier,* which prohibited journeymen's organizations until 1884! This law was the reaction of national lawmakers to reports of alarmed employers: "The workers, by an absurd parody of the government, regard their work as their property, the building site as a Republic of which they are jointly the citizens, and believe, as a consequence, that it is for them to name their own bosses, their inspectors and at their discretion arbitrarily to share out work amongst themselves" (Magraw 1992, 24).

11. For instance, the nationwide German printers' union was created in 1866 following a local strike for higher wages organized by the Leipzig printers' union.

Workers from other regions collected money for the strikers and so constituted the nucleus of one of the first national unions in Germany (Schneider 1989).

Chapter 3. Do Unions Have an Interest in Euro-Democratization?

1. Fordism refers to Ford's assembly-line production system. It is characterized by the separation of planning and doing and a deskilled but comparatively well-paid workforce. In the 1970s, however, Japanese corporations set a new paradigm, called postfordism. It is characterized by the replacement of the moving assembly lines by adaptable production platforms, a blurred distinction between planning and doing, just-in-time logistics, and an increasing polarization between a core and a peripheral workforce.

2. For example, the public sector may not only set wage bargaining patterns, but might also require that its suppliers comply with agreed labor standards. Correspondingly, the capacity of organized labor to influence consumers' decisions could represent an additional power resource (Bellemare 2000).

3. The British Labour Party, for instance, receives major contributions from the unions.

4. More workers participated in the European GM strike than in the Renault case. However, the press coverage was very uneven. An Internet search engine found many more articles in the German and the U.S. press than in the U.K. press, in which only the BBC mentioned the European day of action of the GM unions.

5. The right or freedom to strike has already been recognized at the EU level by the Council Regulation No. 2679/98, which protects it against any potential interference derived from the EU rights of establishment or free movement (Veneziani 2006).

6. In the GM case the existence of transnational union grassroots networks was crucial; see www.labournet.de/branchen/auto/gm-opel/index.html.

7. The SPD leadership feared that the Schuman plan would compromise the prospect of German reunification because the Soviet Union would have accepted in the 1950s a reunited, democratic, but also neutral Germany, in line with the Austrian example (Loth 1996).

8. Employers could, for example, apply for subsidies in relation to the introduction of the statutory 35-hour working week only if they concluded a collective agreement with a union. The access of French works councils to paid expertise of their choice is another veiled power resource of French unions (Clavel-Fauquenot and Marignier 2000).

9. See Sassoon's (1997) study on the abandonment of the French government's socialist policy in 1983 and the subsequent moderate policies of European center-left governments.

Chapter 4. Wage Policy and the European Monetary Union

1. It is noteworthy that the Chilean dictator, General Augusto Pinochet, implemented neoliberalism best (Harvey 2005). Supporters of regulatory policy making have even argued that the Chilean experience could serve as a reference for the EU. After all, Pinochet arguably excluded all clientelistic influences on Chilean economic policies (Drago 1998).

2. In the Union Européenne de l'Artisanat et des Petites et Moyennes Entreprises (UEAPME) case, the EU Court of First Instance recognized that the principle of democracy on which the union is founded does not always require the participation of the Parliament but can also be realized through other means—namely, through the neocorporatist European social dialog (Léonard et al., 2007).

3. Dorothea Hahn, "Schöne neue Eurowelt," *Die Tageszeitung,* 18 April 1997, 7.

4. Streeck's use of the term *redistribution* assumes that work has an objective price. Thus, wage settlements, which do not respect this price, have a redistributive effect. However, the term *redistribution* in the field of wage policy is misleading. Wage policies do not have redistributive but, rather, distributive effects because they affect the primary distribution between capital and labor.

Chapter 5. The Rise of National Competitive Corporatism

1. See, for instance, the typology of different forms of wage setting in Western Europe, which distinguishes state-sponsored, interassociational, intra-associational, pattern-bargained, state-imposed, and noncoordinated forms of wage setting (Traxler 2002, 115).

2. This paradox is entrenched in the frequent *erga omnes* extension of collective agreements to an entire sector by the French Ministry of Employment, even if only a minority of unions, representing only a minority of employees, signs them.

3. In contrast to France, the German state rarely extends collective wage agreements to a whole sector, with the prominent exception of the construction industry.

4. The second law on industrial competitiveness, which introduced an *ex ante* labor-cost comparison with Belgium's main trading partners, can in particular be understood as a governmental reaction to the failed social pacts of 1993 and 1996, caused mainly by the opposition of rank-and-file unionists of the socialist Fédération Générale du Travail de Belgique (FGTB) (Pochet 1999a).

5. *The Economist,* August 23, 2003, 21–22.

Chapter 6. European Wage-Bargaining Coordination Networks

1. The total value of an agreement consists of the increase in labor costs caused by both wage rises and other improvements, such as reduced working time.

2. Apparently, this initiative marks one of the first European collective bargaining coordination attempts since the historic call of the Second International in 1889 for May Day strikes in favor of the 8-hour working day, which established May 1 as the workers' day in almost all countries of the world (Sassoon 1995).

3. In Germany, the national orientation of the unions has also been reinforced even more by German unification. The setting up of union structures in East Germany absorbed the resources of many West German unions to the detriment of their EU-level activities.

4. See Council Directives 2000/79/EC, concerning the European Agreement on the Organisation of Working Time of Mobile Workers in Civil Aviation, and 1999/63/EC, concerning the European Agreement on the Organisation of Working Time of Seafarers.

5. Incidentally, in 1999 DGB official Kreimer-de Fries sent an e-mail to other German and European unionists criticizing the European social-dialog bargaining outcome on fixed-term contracts. This e-mail motivated the then ETUC general secretary, Gabaglio, to write a complaint to the DGB executive, which, in turn, tried to penalize the DGB official; see www.labournet.de/solidaritaet/abgeschlossen/dgb.html. Apparently the ETUC general secretary feared that the DGB would oppose the fixed-term contract agreement, despite a DGB promise to support it, if in exchange the ETUC did not seek higher membership fees. Hence, issue linking is not exclusive to decision making in the European Council.

6. The German unions, and especially IG Metall, typically requested wage increases that included a distributive component in addition to the wage-increase component covering inflation and productivity increases.

7. Hence, the decision of the former leader of the Belgian Christian Metalworkers' Union (CSC métal), Bert Thierron, to leave his home country and to become a leading IG Metall official in Germany was very rational. Given the Belgian laws on competitiveness, a strong IG Metall is much more important for Belgian workers than a strong CSC métal.

8. The competitive pressure on wages was much lower in other regions of eastern Germany because the multinational construction firms concentrated their activities in Berlin (Artus, Schmidt, and Sterkel 2000).

9. Directive 96/71/EC of the European Parliament and the Council of December 16, 1996, concerning the posting of workers in the framework of the provision of services. It is also noteworthy that the adoption of the European posted-workers directive has also been facilitated by the adoption of corresponding national laws, such as the German *Entsendegesetz,* which also resulted from corresponding union pressures (Behrens 2002; Davies 1997; Eichhorst 1999, 2000; Kolehmainen 2002).

10. Remarkably, the country-of-origin principle of the draft directive even turns the EC Treaty upside down. While the EC Treaty entitles a service provider to operate in another EU member state "under the same conditions as are imposed by that State on its own nationals" (Article 50 TEC), the draft service directive states that the country-of-origin of a service provider "shall be responsible for supervising the provider and the services provided by him, including services provided by him in another Member State" (Article 16 [2]). By creating different sets of laws for foreign and domestic firms that operate at the very same locations, the country-of-origin principle discriminates against domestic service providers from the EU member states with more stringent labor and consumer protection standards and thus favors social dumping (Höpner and Schäfer 2007).

11. Incidentally, the collectively agreed-on minimum wages for the construction industry are legally binding for all employers and employees regardless of their country of origin, precisely due to the EU posted-workers directive and the corresponding German *Entsendegesetz*. As a result, an unskilled construction worker in 2007 in Berlin was entitled to get at least 10.30 euros per hour, whereas the corresponding minimum wage for skilled workers was 12.40 euros per hour. Moreover, posted workers are also entitled to get additional overtime pay (European Migrant Workers' Union [EMWU] 2007).

12. This case is also relevant because, since June 1999, the EU and Switzerland have signed several bilateral treaties that integrate Switzerland into the European single market. On September 25, 2005, a 56 percent majority of the Swiss people voted, after a very controversial referendum debate, in favor of the opening of the Swiss labor market to workers from new EU member states. This outcome can be explained by the corresponding adoption of accompanying measures that support the implementation of collective wage agreements and sectoral statutory minimum wages in order to prevent the exploitation of posted workers and downward pressures on wages. Incidentally, these accompanying measures have been modeled on the collective labor agreements for the construction industry. See www.admin.ch/ch/f/pore/va/20050925/index.html.

13. See the discussion of the impact of the collective bargaining partnerships that regional IG Metall districts have established with foreign unions in cross-border regions. Although the union officials involved recognized that these exchanges reinforced their international awareness, the effects were said to be, above all, psychological (Marginson, Sisson, and Arrowsmith 2003; Gollbach and Schulten 2000; Gollbach 2000).

14. The metalworkers' unions influence the ETUC directly though the EMF and indirectly through their strong position within national union confederations.

15. Certainly, in many countries the public-service unions became the most important unions, but, even in these countries, the EU and international departments of the union confederations are often dominated by unionists with a background in manufacturing.

Chapter 7. Beyond Competitive Corporatism?

1. The weight for Germany is 31 percent, France 20 percent, Italy 19 percent, and Spain 10 percent. The weight of the remaining eight small states is only 20 percent (Hancké and Soskice 2003).

2. Both Euro-Keynesian economists and SPD politicians published several opinion articles in the press and union-related academic journals that supported this claim (Flassbeck 1997, 1998; Flassbeck and Spiecker 2000; Noé 1998).

3. Incidentally, Streeck acknowledges that this type of social democracy cannot be distinguished "from an activist liberalism which pursues social justice through intervention in the distribution, not of market outcomes, but of the capacities for successful market participation" (1999, 6).

4. However, the negative effects of wage moderation on domestic demand might still outweigh the positive export effects, especially in countries such as Germany (Flassbeck and Spiecker 2000; Maurice 2001).

5. See the transcript of the debate between Streeck and union leaders at the 50 Years DGB Jubilee conference in 1999 (*Gewerkschaftliche Monatshefte* 1999).

6. Although the Alliance guideline stipulated longer-term agreements based on a distributive margin related to productivity growth, unions and employers' associations disagreed on whether this margin should include a compensation for inflation.

7. Meanwhile, however, the French union confederations CGT, CFDT, Force Ouvrière (FO), and Confédération Française des Travailleurs Chrétiens (CFTC) have also joined the Doorn Group (ETUC 2006).

8. France 2. *Mots Croisés,* 30 October 2000.

9. The union density in French metal manufacturing is very low, namely, 5 percent (Dufour and Hege 1999), and the union membership is concentrated in 1 percent of companies, which employ over 500 employees, accounting for 31 percent of the sector's workforce (Usher 2001).

10. Certainly, French unions also frequently signed central agreements with the employer organization MEDEF and the state. However, these negotiations do not represent collective bargaining in the classic sense; they resemble much more the procedures of European social dialog.

11. Notably, from the French Institut de Recherches Économiques et Sociales (IRES) but also from the Brussels-based Observatoire Social Européen (OSE), which has been at the origin of the Doorn process. The OSE is an established EU-level social policy think tank that was originally founded by the Belgian and the Italian Christian trade union confederations, CSC and CISL.

12. In fact, the Italian 1993 social pact permits improvements that go beyond a simple compensation for inflation. National collective agreements could, for instance, lead to a reduction of working time.

13. The Italian trade union press dedicated only very few articles to these European developments.

14. In "Fiom e inflazione," *Il Manifesto,* 2002, 5 July, p. 8. In October 2001, Roberto Maroni, minister of Welfare from the far-right Lega Nord party, pub-

lished a very controversial white paper that favored a deregulation of wage-bargaining structures.

15. This also explains the large difference between the demands of IG Metall, which generally are rather high, and the actual results of bargaining in the German metal industry, which are frequently quite modest.

16. See the European industrial relations dictionary, which explains many relevant terms of Euro-speak: www.eurofound.eu.int/areas/industrialrelations/dictionary/index.htm.

17. See Tarrow (1994); Klandermans, Kriesi, and Tarrow (1988); Kelly (1998).

Chapter 8. The European Regulation of Transnational Company Mergers

1. This motive prompted the establishment of public merger control policies. For a definition of *merger control*, see the European Industrial Relations Dictionary. Available at www.eurofound.europa.eu/areas/industrialrelations/dictionary/.

2. The number of mergers and acquisitions (M&A) worldwide increased between 1990 and 1999 from 9,000 to 25,000 (Möschel 2000). This increase had a strong EU dimension. In 1999, almost 50 percent of the global M&A-related sales and 70 percent of the global M&A-related purchases concerned European firms (Macaire et al. 2002).

3. Accordingly, Streeck argues that EWCs were extensions of the national industrial relations systems in which the company had its headquarters (Streeck 1997).

4. For a definition of *takeover of companies*, see the European Industrial Relations Dictionary. Available at www.eurofound.europa.eu/areas/industrialrelations/dictionary/.

5. Whereas the logic of competition policy mirrors free-market enthusiasm, Schumpeter (1954) claims that technological innovation rather than product market competition accounts for economic progress. Correspondingly, Schumpeter endorses the trustification of the economy because only large-scale trusts and the state have the necessary resources to carry out the uncertain but essential research and development activities. Amazingly, the U.S. antitrust exemption for research consortia of 1984, which engendered a wide rage of cooperative relations between U.S. firms to speed up technological innovations (Block 2007), suggests that anti-competitive Schumpeterian arguments have a much bigger impact in the allegedly uncoordinated U.S. economy than in the coordinated European economies.

6. In 2002, the Court of First Instance annulled three, apparently carelessly prepared, Commission decisions, which weakened its authority to outlaw mergers. Cf. the *Airtour-First Choice* (T-342/99), the *Schneider-Legrand* (T-310/01; T-77/02), and the *Tetra Laval-Sidel* (T-5/02; T-80/02) cases.

7. Article 21 of the Merger Regulation recognizes that company mergers

may touch additional concerns. The Regulation foresees that a member state can impose additional conditions on to-be-merged companies, to protect specific public interests, such as public security or a pluralistic public sphere.

8. Case T-96/92, *Comité Central d'Entreprise de la Société Générale des Grandes Sources and others v Commission*, [1995] ECR, II-01213, para. 28.

9. See Article 2 TEU, as well as Articles 2, 3 (i), and 125–130 TEC (in particular 127(2) TEC).

10. Case T-77/02, *Schneider Electric SA v Commission*, [2002] ECR II-4201.

11. Case COMP/M.2283, *Schneider-Legrand*.

12. In several other countries, such as Ireland, Norway, Germany, Belgium, Spain, and France, labor representatives may also express their views in national merger procedures. In the case of Norway, labor representatives are entitled to express their views to the Ministry of Trade and Industry, which may, in turn, subject a merger to further scrutiny if the merger will have negative social effects (Macaire et al. 2002).

Chapter 9. A Euro-Democratization Union Strategy

1. Incidentally, ASEA and ABB chairmen, Curt Nicolin and Percy Barnevik, belonged to the European Round Table of Industrialists that initially set the agenda for the creation of the European single market (Cowles 1995; Van Apeldoorn 2000).

2. On February 13, 2002, however, the esteem for the two leaders collapsed when the ABB board accused Barnevik and Lindal of having taken "pensions" of 100 million and 54 million euros, respectively, without board approval (Catrina 2003).

3. "First of all, Mannheim has established an impenetrable Siegfried line by hiding behind German corporate, fiscal, and codetermination law. Corporate law made it impossible for Baden to issue orders given the substantial minority holdings in BBC Deutschland. Tax law made transfers of profits prohibitively expensive. Codetermination law required agreement with the Betriebsrat (works council) which defended the local interests tooth and nail. German executives became experts in the use of these defenses. The Swiss, on the other hand, felt that Mannheim was using these devices shamelessly to thumb their noses at Baden." (Uyterhoeven 1993, 190–91).

4. In 1991, the Compagnie Générale d'Electricité (CGE) changed its name to Alcatel-Alsthom and then, effective from September 1, 1998, to Alcatel.

5. In 1999, GEC was renamed Marconi. In 2005, the company changed its name to telent, after Ericsson acquired its telecommunications and international services section.

6. Incidentally, Alstom lost several billions of euros when purchasers of the ABB high-power gas turbines held Alstom liable for serious errors of this supposedly most up-to-date machinery.

7. In 1975, the Council adopted, as an indirect result of the campaign against the closure of four European AZKO plants, the directive (75/129) that

harmonized collective dismissals regulations across the EEC (Fuchs and Marhold 2001).

8. In the early 1990s, the Swiss and Swedish blue-collar unions also joined the EMF, together with their counterparts from other EFTA countries and Central and Eastern Europe (Münch 1994).

9. INFO Institut, ABB Alstom Power, Saarbrücken, November 1999, 4.

10. These included Belgian, British, Czech, French, German, Italian, Portuguese, Spanish, Swedish, Swiss, and Polish unions.

11. The broader participation at the 1999 Mannheim meeting also reflects the amalgamation of the white-collar union Deutsche Angestellten-Gewerkschaft (DAG) with the unions of the DGB. Whereas the DAG unionists did not participate at the IMF meetings in 1987 and 1988 (Hammarström 1994), they went—as new IG Metall members—to the Mannheim seminar in 1999.

12. This meeting was arranged by Stephen Hughes, a British Labour MEP and coordinator of the Socialist Group on the Committee on Employment and Social Affairs.

13. The management also tried to influence the composition of the SNB by rejecting the CGT delegate, Francine Blanche, but this attempt was unsuccessful because the CFDT declined to take a second seat in the SNB. Hence, Blanche (CGT) and Jean-Marie Heller (CFDT) represented the French unions in the SNB. In contrast, the German management cooperated with IG Metall and its representative Kämmerer participated as the only full-time union official at the SNB negotiations.

14. Assemblée Nationale, Compte rendue intégrale, 1er séance du 8 mars 2000, 1598, www.assemblee-nat.fr/cri/leg11/html/20000145.asp#01597; translated by the author.

15. Speech by the president of the European Parliament, Lisbon, 23 March 2000, www.europarl.eu.int/summits/lis-pres_en.htm.

16. Although the French press fully covered the European demonstration, the coverage in other countries was limited to the left-wing or the interested regional media, with the exception of the Belgian newspaper *Le Soir.*

17. The EMF staff consists of only two elected union officials, several advisers, administrators, and some visiting union officials from national member organizations.

18. The management tried to dismiss a leading FO activist at the La Courneuve plant (although without success), and it withdrew the office facilities that it previously accorded to the CGT EWC secretary. In turn, in 2003, a court obliged Alstom to pay almost 100,000 euros to FO and CGT unionists as a compensation for anti-union discrimination.

19. In France, full-time union officials play a minor role at the company level, whereas almost all German GWCs are coordinated by an external union official. In contrast, the French works council experts come from union-related consultancies and do not assume any political leadership role.

20. Although the CFDT held the majority in the works councils in the Belfort plants, the CGT is the biggest union in most of the other French subsidiaries of the company.

21. Initially, Kämmerer played a similar coordination role at the EU level as the EMF coordinator during the EWC negotiations with the management, but, after the re-integration of ABB Alstom Power into Alstom and the subsequent end of EWC negotiations, he resigned from his EMF function.

22. Namely, Belgium, the Czech Republic, Denmark, England, France, Germany, Greece, Italy, the Netherlands, Poland, Portugal, Romania, Spain, Sweden, Switzerland, and Turkey (Braud 2003a, 2003b; Gow 2003; Kotitschke 2003).

23. Bilger started his career, like many French business leaders, due to his insertion into political networks. His experiences as a senior advisor to several right-wing ministers in the 1970s and 1980s preceded his Alstom career (*Who's Who in France* 2006). Between 1978 and 1981, Bilger even headed the *cabinet* of the infamous budget minister Maurice Papon (Whitney 2007).

24. The Alstom disaster, however, did not end the career of Bilger—while the British-French Eurotunnel SA co-opted him onto its board of directors, he also started working as a consultant and as a blogger with a special interest in European integration and corporate ethics (www.blogbilger.com/).

25. It is worth recalling that Nicole Fontaine actively supported the ABB Alstom unionists during her previous mandate as president of the European Parliament.

26. The German government initially intended to snub Paris over the Alstom rescue plan (Hulverscheidt, Benoit, and Arnold 2003).

27. See http://europa.eu.int/comm/employment_social/news/2001/may/121_en.html.

28. See the European Industrial Relations Dictionary. Available at www.eurofound.europa.eu/areas/industrialrelations/dictionary/.

Chapter 10. A Euro-Technocratization Union Strategy

1. The APA project included only the aluminum activities of the companies, and Algroup (Alusuisse Lonza Group) announced the instant spin-off of its fine chemical and energy subsidiary, Lonza.

2. The Alcan and Algroup EWC had adopted a German EWC model, in which employers are not part of the EWC. Hence, the EWC president is a labor representative. The Pechiney EWC had adopted the French EWC model, in which the CEO of the company acts as EWC president while a labor representative acts as EWC secretary and chair of the EWC labor group. Because the rights of a German EWC correspond to those of the labor group in the French EWC, we use here the term *EWC leader* for the leading labor representative in both EWC types.

3. Transfer pricing is not used only in the aluminum industry. In 1999, total cross-border intrafirm trade accounted for 36.3 percent of U.S. exports and for 39.4 percent of U.S. imports; aggregate OECD data for the EU are surprisingly not available (OECD 2002). This calls into question the simplistic textbook model of a free world market because a high share of global market transactions mirrors political decisions made by the multinationals rather than supply and demand

curves. If the buyer and the seller of a commodity belong to the same company, there is indeed a strong incentive for the company to manipulate the transfer price of the commodity to shift company profits to countries where they are taxed least.

4. In 1988, the Australian government eventually forced Alusuisse to pay arms-length market prices to its Australian subsidiary by threatening not to renew its mining license (Indermaur 1989).

5. The socialist French President François Mitterrand did not aim to break the domination of capital but saw the nationalizations as an instrument to defend French interests in an internationalizing economy (Gélédan 1993). The nationalizations led to a recapitalization and modernization of French industry. Whereas in 1982 only three of the twenty-one nationalized firms were profitable, three years later eighteen of the twenty-one corporations were making money. This success laid the foundation for their later successful reprivatization (Uterwedde 1999).

6. The owner of the BZ Bank, Ebner became in the late 1990s the largest shareholder in many big Swiss firms, including ABB, Algroup, and Credit Suisse. He was also chairman of Algroup and one of the most important ABB board members. Ebner was one of the pioneers of shareholder-value capitalism in continental Europe. In August 2002, however, Ebner was forced to sell his investment funds to resolve a serious debt crisis at his BZ Bank. Ironically, the state-owned Zürcher Kantonalbank rescued Ebner's BZ Bank from bankruptcy, although Ebner had previously stated that the state should never intervene in the economy.

7. Incidentally, only a few hours after the announcement of the APA project, Alcoa reestablished its leading role in the industry by its hostile takeover of Reynolds. In March 2007, however, Alcoa lost its position as industry leader to United Company Rusal, which resulted from a merger between the firms of two Russian oligarchs, Rusal and Sual, and the Swiss trading company Glencore. In May 2007, Alcoa tried again to become the industry leader by launching an unfriendly takeover bid against Alcan. However, Alcan agreed in July 2007 to a rival bid from the British-Australian mining multinational Rio Tinto. Whereas Alcan and Alcoa labor representatives from France, Spain, Germany, the Czech Republic, Italy, Switzerland, and the United Kingdom unanimously denounced the Alcan-Alcoa takeover at an extraordinary EMF meeting on June 21, there was—at the time of this writing—no consensus about the consequences for labor of the Rio Tinto-Alcan merger (EWC News 2007).

8. S. Marchionne, 1999 press conference statement, 11 August, Alusuisse Lonza Group Ltd., Zurich. Marchionne anglicized his company name in 1998, changing it from Alusuisse-Lonza Holding AG to Algroup (Alusuisse Lonza Group Ltd.). Issuing the International Phonetic Alphabet version of this new label (ei/el/gru:p) he even insisted on its correct pronunciation (Mrusek 1998).

9. Although Evans, Davignon, and Ebner, representing the shareholders of the APA companies, selected Bougie (Alcan) as first CEO and after two years Rodier (Pechiney) as his successor, it took much longer to designate the APA subsidiary management staff (Wright 2000).

10. Due to the absence of works councils at the holding company level at the

time, the worker representatives were neither informed nor consulted before the merger that amalgamated the two French aluminum producers, Pechiney and Ugine-Kuhlmann, in 1971 (Beaud, Danjou, and David 1975).

11. The French *comité de groupe* is composed of local works councilors who have been selected by the unions proportionally to the last works council election results (Pichot 2001).

12. In doing so, management and unions used the procedure that the *loi Auroux* foresaw for the establishment of the French GWCs.

13. Pechiney resisted the implementation of the thirty-five-hour working-week law, which had, ironically, been drafted by its former human resources director, Martine Aubry. This led to strikes in some of its French subsidiaries in the late 1990s.

14. The EWC directive covers all companies operating in the EU, regardless of their country of origin. Overall, twenty-nine Swiss multinationals signed an EWC agreement before the September 1996 deadline; of those, only seven did not include Swiss representatives (Baumann 1997; Ziltener 2000).

15. Each of the three countries represents more than 20 percent of the European workforce.

16. Davignon was chairman of the Société Générale de Belgique and had been a very influential member of the Commission (1977–1985). As Commissioner he facilitated the setup of the European Round Table of Industrialists (ERT) and the European single-market project.

17. Since 1983, the French unions have been represented on the company boards of all nationalized enterprises. Within Pechiney, the unions retained this right even after the company was privatized (Aronssohn 1999; Bischoff and Jaeger 2001).

18. French labor law allows works councils to engage a consultancy firm of their choice at the expense of management in order to acquire an autonomous analysis of the annual accounts of the company and its extraordinary collective dismissals plans (Clavel-Fauquenot and Marignier 2000). This represents an essential power resource of the French labor movement, all the more because works councils frequently appoint union-related consultancy firms. However, the use of these consultancy firms also pleases company executives. Consultancies heighten awareness of economic constraints, and this makes unions more willing to accept change. It is worth noting that the CGT-related Groupe Alpha and the CFDT-related Syndex employ more staff than the two unions combined. However, the links of these firms to a specific union are decreasing. Given its expertise in the aluminum industry, the Pechiney CFDT EWC secretary preferred to work with Groupe Alpha rather than Syndex.

19. Incidentally, the introduction of protective steel tariffs by President George W. Bush contributed to his reelection in the decisive state of Ohio (Harvey 2005).

20. The project consisted of a matrix analysis of the APA business divisions (bauxite/alumina, aluminum fabrication, health/beauty packaging, and food packaging) and production sites. It involved an analysis of quantitative data as well as qualitative interviews with union, works council, and company officials.

21. These negative consequences were the announced closure of two of the Pechiney aerosol plants in Germany and Sweden and the expected overcapacities in the aluminum-rolling sector that could threaten one of the two big rolling plants—either the Pechiney Rhenalu plant in Neuf-Brisach or the Alcan and VAW joint venture in Norf.

22. Given that EU labor law does not oblige companies to pay for such an analysis, the EMF asked the French and German APA works councils to request remuneration for this study at the national level, in accordance with French and German labor law.

23. In contrast, the EMF meeting did not envisage any collective action, although the SMUV union official, Eger, suggested considering a European day of action.

24. Two days before the Brussels meeting, SMUV union official, Eger, had already drafted an outline of such an agreement. It required a comparison of all the competitive advantages and disadvantages of each plant to be carried out jointly by management and the EMF working group. Although Eger accepted that transnational comparisons would inform postmerger company restructurings, the draft agreement aimed to limit social dumping. It stated that a transnational transfer of employment to another plant needed to have the consent of the joint working group of the three EWCs if the respective employment, wage, and social conditions differed more than plus or minus 10 percent. If collective dismissals proved to be indispensable, the compensations packages should also not differ more than plus or minus 10 percent. In the longer term, the draft agreement also required additional measures designed to increase the qualification and the flexibility of the workforce.

25. On January 25, 2000, Ford, its EWC, and Visteon representatives signed a European agreement that secured favorable employment conditions at Ford for the outsourced Visteon workers (da Costa and Rehfeldt 2006).

26. Even if compared to the refusal to distribute the statement of objections in the prior Total-Fina-Elf merger case, the very late distribution of the documents in the APA case scarcely represents progress (Liaisons Sociales Europe 2000).

Chapter 11. Conclusion

1. Incidentally, Charlie McCreevy, the internal market commissioner, refused to withdraw the draft EU services directive and tried to push it through, despite massive popular protests that rendered the draft directive politically nonenforceable (Höpner and Schäfer 2007).

2. See also Turnbull's (2006) study of the trade union campaign against the EU directive on market access to port services.

3. Alstom workers even founded a singing group, the Alstom Choir, which performed a bilingual German and French Alstom protest song at labor demonstrations: www.alstom.resistance-online.com/ALSTOM%20 Chor.htm.

4. In the 2005 French referendum, 78 percent of blue-collar workers re-

jected the EU constitution, whereas 65 percent of the professional classes supported it (Brouard and Tiberj 2006, 262).

5. Whereas the EU Treaty claims that the "Union is founded on the principles of liberty, democracy, respect for human rights and fundamental freedoms, and the rule of law, principles which are common to the Member States" (Article 6 TEU), the European Commission has acknowledged that the existing governance structures and mechanism "are not able to provide democratic legitimisation for the EU polity as a whole" (2003b, 38).

6. Incidentally, the Commission has even included the term *democratic deficit* in its official EU glossary: http://europa.eu/scadplus/glossary/democratic_deficit_en.htm.

References

Aarts, K., and H. van der Kolk. 2006. "Understanding the Dutch 'no': The euro, the east, and the elite." *PS: Political Science & Politics* 39 (2): 243–46.

A.Se. 2003. "Les raisons qui expliquent la débâcle." *Le Figaro,* 7 February. Available at: www.lefigaro.fr/eco-entreprises/0030702.FIG0045.html.

Abbott, K. 2001. "The ETUC: The growth of a European pressure group." Paper presented at the sixth IIRA European regional congress, Oslo, 25–29 June.

Abromeit, H. 1998. *Democracy in Europe: Legitimizing Politics in a Non-state Polity.* New York: Berghahn Books.

Accornero, A. 1998. "I contratti al tempo dell'Euro." *Rassegna Sindacale* 44, 21: fascicolo II.

Adler, G., and E. Webster. 1995. "Challenging transition theory: The labor movement, radical reform, and transition to democracy in South Africa." *Politics & Society* 23 (1): 75–106.

Alcan-Pechiney-Algroup (APA). 1999. *Die Schaffung des weltweit größten Aluminium- und Verpackungsunternehmens: Hintergrundinformationen zur vorgeschlagenen Fusion.* Montreal: APA.

Allen, K. 2000. *The Celtic Tiger: The Myth of Social Partnership.* Manchester, UK: Manchester University Press.

———. 2007. *The Corporate Takeover of Ireland.* Dublin: Irish Academic Press.

Altmeyer, W. 2001a. "Deutsch-französische Arbeitnehmerpolitik: Über die Restrukturierungsvarianten bei Alstom-Power." *Die Mitbestimmung* 47 (5): 54–57.

———. 2001b. *Die Interessenmanager vor Neuen Herausforderungen: Eine Em-*

pirische Studie über Belegschaftsvertretungen in Deutschland, Frankreich, Spanien und Großbritannien. Baden Baden: Nomos.

Altvater, E. 1995. "Economic policy and the role of the state." In *Toward a Global Civil Society,* edited by M. Walzer, 149–58. Providence: Berghahn.

Altvater, E., and B. Mahnkopf. 1993. *Gewerkschaften vor der Europäischen Herausforderung: Tarifpolitik nach Mauer und Maastricht.* Münster: Westfälisches Dampfboot.

———. 1999. *Grenzen der Globalisierung: Ökonomie, Ökologie und Politik in der Weltgesellschaft.* 4th ed. Münster: Westfälisches Dampfboot.

Amernic, J. H., and R. J. Craig. 2001. "Three tenors in perfect harmony: 'Close readings' of the joint letter by the heads of aluminium giants Alcan, Pechiney, and Alusuisse announcing their mega-merger plan." *Critical Perspectives on Accounting* 12: 763–95.

Anner, M., I. Greer, M. Hauptmeier, N. Lillie, and N. Winchester. 2006. "The industrial determinants of transnational solidarity: Global interunion politics in three sectors." *European Journal of Industrial Relations* 12 (1): 7–27.

Archibugi, D., and D. Held. 1995. *Cosmopolitan Democracy.* Cambridge, UK: Polity Press.

Ardondel, P. 1999. "Doorn, ou la pédagogie de la reconquête." *CFTC Magazine* (May): 14–15.

Aronssohn, D. 1999. "Aventis: Un pari franco-allemand." *Alternatives Économiques* 176 (December): 46–49.

Artus, I., R. Schmidt, and G. Sterkel. 2000. *Brüchige Tarifrealität: Der Schleichende Bedeutungsverlust Tariflicher Normen in der Ostdeutschen Industrie.* Berlin: Ed. Sigma.

Assemblée Nationale. 2000. "Rapport d'information déposé par la délégation de l'Assemblée nationale pour l'Union européenne, sur le dumping social en Europe et présenté par M. Gaëtan Gorce, Député. 25 mai." Available at www.assemblee-nationale.fr/europe/rap-info/i2423.pdf.

Baccaro, L. 2002. "The constitution of 'democratic' corporatism in Italy." *Politics & Society* 30 (2): 327–57.

Barnouin, B. 1986. *The European Labour Movement and European Integration.* London: F. Pinter.

Barrat, O., C. Yakubovich, and J. Maurice. 2002. "Evolutions of collective bargaining in France." In *Wage Policy in the Eurozone,* edited by P. Pochet, 255–81. Brussels: P.I.E.-Peter Lang.

Bartolini, S. 2000. *The Political Mobilization of the European Left, 1860– 1980.* Cambridge, UK: Cambridge University Press.

———. 2005. *Restructuring Europe: Centre Formation, System Building, and Political Structuring between the Nation State and the European Union.* Oxford: Oxford University Press.

Baumann, H. 1997. "Schweiz und Europäische Betriebsräte—eine Zwischenbilanz." *Die Volkswirtschaft* 9: 60–63.

——. 2000. "Nasce il più grande cantiere d'Europa." *Rassegna Sindacale* 46 (12): 15.

Baumann, H., E.-L. Laux, and M. Schnepf. 1996. "Collective bargaining in the European building industry—European collective bargaining?" *Transfer* 2 (2): 321–33.

Beaud, M., P. Danjou, and J. David. 1975. *Une Multinationale Française: Pechiney Ugine Kuhlmann.* Paris: Seuil.

Behrens, M. 2002. "ECJ upholds German law on posted workers." Available at www.eiro.eurofound.eu.int/2002/02/feature/de0202208f.html.

Bélanger, J. 2001. "Autorégulation du travail et division sociale: Observation dans une aluminerie québécoise." *Sociologie du Travail* 43: 159–77.

Bélanger, J., and T. Björkman. 1999. "The ABB attempt to reinvent the multinational corporation." In *Being Local Worldwide: ABB and the Challenge of Global Management,* edited by J. Bélanger, C. Berggren, T. Björkman, and C. Köhler, 248–68. Ithaca: Cornell University Press.

Bélanger, J., and M. Dumas. 1998. "Teamwork and internal labor markets: A study of a Canadian aluminium smelter." *Economic and Industrial Democracy* 19 (3): 417–42.

Bélanger, J., P. Edwards, and M. Wright. 1999. "Best HR practice and the multinational company." *Human Resource Management Journal* 9 (3): 53–70.

Bellemare, G. 2000. "End users: Actors in the industrial relations system?" *British Journal of Industrial Relations* 38 (3): 383–405.

Bercusson, B. 1994. "The dynamic of European labour law after Maastricht." *Industrial Law Journal* 31: 1–31.

——. 2002. "The European social model comes to Britain." *Industrial Law Journal* 31 (3): 209–44.

Berggren, C. 1999. "Introduction: Between globalization and multidomestic variation." In *Being Local Worldwide: ABB and the Challenge of Global Management,* edited by J. Bélanger, C. Berggren, T. Björkman, and C. Köhler, 1–15. Ithaca: Cornell University Press.

Béthoux, É., R. Brouté, and C. Didry. 2006. "De l'Europe au territoire: Information, consultation et mobilisations des travailleurs dans les restructurations d'Alstom." Available at www.idhe.ens-cachan.fr/Eurocap/workingpapers.html.

Betts, P., and D. Dombey. 2003. "Brussels and banks back Alstom rescue." *Financial Times,* 23 September, p. 34.

Bieler, A., 2006. *The Struggle for a Social Europe: Trade Unions and EMU in Times of Global Restructuring.* Manchester: Manchester University Press.

Bieling, H.-J., and J. Steinhilber, eds. 2000. *Die Konfiguration Europas: Di-*

mensionen einer Kritischen Integrationstheorie. Münster: Westfälisches Dampfboot.

Bierbaum, H., J. Kischewski, S. Kischewski, and M. Schmidt. 2001. *Analysis of the Organizational Reorientation of the ABB Group.* Geneva: International Metalworkers' Federation.

Bischoff, W., and R. Jaeger. 2001. "AVENTIS: Verhandlungsmarathon ins Neuland." *Die Mitbestimmung* 47 (5): 52–53.

Bispinck, R. 2000. "Abschied von falscher Bescheidenheit: Eine Bilanz des Tarifjahres 1999." *WSI Mitteilungen* 53 (2): 81–94.

——. 2007. "Tarifpolitischer Halbjahresbericht. Eine Zwischenbilanz der Lohn- und Gehaltsrunde 2007." WSI Informationen zur Tarifpolitik. July. Available at www.boeckler.de/pdf/p_ta_hjb_2007.pdf.

Bispinck, R., and T. Schulten. 2000. "Alliance for Jobs—is Germany following the path of 'competition corporatism'?" WSI discussion paper no. 84. Available at www.boeckler.de/ebib/index.cgi?showdokument =172.

——. 2002. "Germany: Problems of a competition-oriented collective bargaining policy." In *Wage Policy in the Eurozone,* edited by P. Pochet, 239–53. Brussels: P.I.E.-Peter Lang.

——. 2003. "Decentralisation of German collective bargaining?: Current trends and assessments from works and staff council perspective." *WSI Mitteilungen* 56 (special issue): 24–33.

Björkman, T. 1999. "ABB and the restructuring of the electrotechnical industry." In *Being Local Worldwide: ABB and the Challenge of Global Management,* edited by J. Bélanger, C. Berggren, T. Björkman, and C. Köhler, 16–35. Ithaca: Cornell University Press.

Blanche, F. 2003. "Ne pas laisser le champ libre à la direction." Available at www.humanite.presse.fr/journal/2003-09-22/2003-09-22-379258.

——. 2007. "Recapitaliser pour quoi faire?" Available at www.humanite .fr/2007-03-10_Politique_-Recapitaliser-pour-quoi-faire.

Bohle, D. 2006. "Neoliberal hegemony, transnational capital and the terms of the EU's eastward expansion." *Capital & Class* 88 (Spring): 57–88.

Bonnand, R. 1999. "Métallurgie: Obtenir des garanties sociales." Interview. *CFDT Magazine* 246 (March): 12–13.

Boot, H. 2000. "Ausgrenzung streng nach Tarif: Bündnis für Arbeit in den Niederlanden." *Ak—Analyse & Kritik* 437 (April): 13. Available at www.akweb.de/ak_s/ak437/21.htm.

Braud, M. 2003a. "Alstom rescue plan agreed." Available at www.eiro .eurofound.eu.int/2003/10/inbrief/fr0310101n.html.

——. 2003b. "Alstom restructuring continues." Available at www.eiro .eurofound.ie/2003/08/inbrief/fr0308101n.html.

——. 2003c. "Collective bargaining in 2002 examined. Available at www .eiro.eurofound.ie/2003/09/Feature/FR0309101F.html.

Bray, M., and R. Lansbury. 2001. "The conditions for convergence in employment relations in multinationals: The case of Asea Brown Boveri." Paper presented at the sixth IIRA European regional congress, Oslo, 25–29 June.

Brouard, S., and V. Tiberj. 2006. "The French referendum: The not so simple act of saying nay." *PS: Political Science & Politics* 39 (2): 261–68.

Brumlop, E. 2002. "Internationale Arbeitersolidarität." *Express: Zeitung für Sozialistische Betriebs- und Gewerkschaftsarbeit* 40 (10): 12.

Bruun, N., and J. Hellsten, eds. 2001. *Collective Agreements and Competition Law in the EU: The Report of the COLCOM-Project.* Uppsala: Iustus Förlag.

Büchi, R. 1995. "Sozialer Habitus und Demokratie." In *Transnationale Demokratie: Impulse für ein Demokratisch Verfasstes Europa,* edited by R. Erne, A. Gross, B. Kaufmann, and H. Kleger, 109–38. Zürich: Realotopia.

Budge, I. 1996. *The New Challenge of Direct Democracy.* Cambridge, UK: Polity Press.

Busch, G. K. 1983. *The Political Role of International Trade Unions.* New York: St. Martin's Press.

Busch, K. 1994. *Europäische Integration und Tarifpolitik: Lohnpolitische Konsequenzen der Wirtschafts- und Währungsunion.* Cologne: Bund Verlag.

Cachón, L., and M. S. Valles. 2003. "Trade unionism and immigration: Reinterpreting old and new dilemmas" *Transfer* 9 (3): 469–83.

Calmfors, L. 2001. "Wages and wage bargaining institutions in the EMU—a survey of the issues." Institute for International Economic Studies seminar paper no. 690, Stockholm.

Calmfors, L., and J. Driffill. 1988. "Bargaining structure, corporatism and macroeconomic performance." *Economic Policy* 6: 14–61.

Carley, M. 2001. *Bargaining at European Level?: Joint Text Negotiated by European Works Councils.* Luxembourg: European Foundation for the Improvement of Living and Working Conditions and Office for Official Publications of the European Communities.

Castles, S., and G. Kosack. 1973. *Immigrant Workers and Class Structures in Western Europe.* London: Oxford University Press.

Catrina, W. 2003. *ABB: Die Verratene Vision.* Zürich: Orell Füssli.

Cerny, P. G. 1990. *The Changing Architecture of Politics Structure, Agency, and the Future of the State.* London: Sage.

Chaterlety, P. 2002. "Enjeux économiques et financiers des fusions et acquisitions : État des lieux et ampleur du phénomène en Europe et dans le monde." *Les Cahiers de la Fondation Europe et Société* 51–52 (Jan–June): 7–13.

Chauvel, J-P. 1999. "L'aluminium entre en fusions." *L'Hebdo/V.O.* 2869: 5–6.

Chevènement, J.-P. 2007. "La vérité de M. Monti sur l'affaire Alstom: mensonges, bras de fer et coups tordus." Available at www.chevene ment.fr.

Ciampani, A. 2000. *La Cisl tra Integrazione Europea e Mondialisazzione: Profilo Storico del "Sindacato Nuovo" nelle Relazioni Internazionali, dalla Conferenza di Londra al Trattato di Amsterdam.* Rome: Edizioni Lavoro.

Clavel-Fauquenot, M.-F., and N. Marignier. 2000. *Les Experts du Comité d'Entreprise.* Paris: Liaisons Sociales.

Cochet, A. 2002. "Strengthening the Doorn process." *AGORA, Quarterly Newsletter of the Education Institution of the European Trade Union Confederation* (June): 3.

Coldrick, P. 1998. "The ETUC's role in the EU's new economic and monetary architecture." *Transfer* 4 (1): 21–35.

Confédération des Syndicats Chrétiens (CSC). 2000. *La Coordination Transnationale des Négociations Collectives: Expériences en 2000.* Bruxelles: CSC Service d'Etudes.

Cowen, R. 2000. "Cartels, and various metal cans of worms." Available at www.geology.ucdavis.edu/~GEL115/115CH15diamonds.html.

Cowles, M. G. 1995. "Setting the agenda for a new Europe: The ERT and EC 1992." *Journal of Common Market Studies* 33 (4): 501–26.

Craig, P., and G. de Búrca. 2003. *EU Law.* Oxford: Oxford University Press.

Cremers, J., and P. Donders, eds. 2005. *Free Movement of Workers in the EU.* Brussels: CLR Studies.

Crouch, C. 1982. *Trade Unions: The Logic of Collective Action.* London: Fontana.

——. 1993. *Industrial Relations and European State Traditions.* Oxford: Oxford University Press.

——. 1999. *Social Change in Western Europe.* Oxford: Oxford University Press.

——, ed. 2000a. *After the Euro: Shaping Institutions for Governance in the Wake of European Monetary Union.* Oxford: Oxford University Press.

——. 2000b. "National wage determination and the European monetary union." In *After the Euro: Shaping Institutions for Governance in the Wake of European Monetary Union,* edited by C. Crouch, 203–27. Oxford: Oxford University Press.

——. 2000c. "The snakes and ladders of twenty-first-century trade unionism." *Oxford Review of Economic Policy* 16 (1): 70–83.

——. 2004. *Post-Democracy.* Cambridge, UK: Polity Press.

——. 2005. *Capitalist Diversity and Change: Recombinant Governance and Institutional Entrepreneurs.* Oxford: Oxford University Press.

Crouch, C., and A. Pizzorno, eds. 1978. *The Resurgence of Class Conflict in Western Europe since 1968.* London: Macmillan.

da Costa, I., and U. Rehfeldt. 2006. "European Unions and American

Automobile Firms." Available at www.press.uillinois.edu/journals/ irra/proceedings2006/dacosta.html.

Dahl, R. A. 1989. *Democracy and Its Critics*. London: Yale University Press.

D'Art, D., and T. Turner. 2007. "Trade unions and political participation in the European Union: Still providing a democratic dividend?" *British Journal of Industrial Relations* 45 (1): 103–26.

Davies, P. 1997. "Posted workers: Single market or protection of national labour law systems?" *Common Market Law Review* 34: 571–602.

Della Porta, D., and L. Mosca (2007) "*In movimento:* 'Contamination' in action and the Italian Global Justice Movement." *Global Networks* 7 (1): 1–27.

Diamond, L., and M. F. Plattner. 1996. *The Global Resurgence of Democracy*. Baltimore: Johns Hopkins University Press.

Dicken, P. 2003. *Global Shift: Reshaping the Global Economic Map in the 21st Century*. London: Sage.

Die Mitbestimmung. 1999. "Betriebsräte Special: Was tun bei Fusionen?" 45 (June–July).

Dispersyn, M., P. Van der Vorst, M. De Falleur, Y. Guillaume, C. Hecq, B. Lange, and D. Meulders. 1991. *The Construction of a European Social Snake: Feasibility Study*. Brussels: Ministère de la Prévoyance sociale.

Doellgast V., and I. Greer. 2007. "Vertical disintegration and the disorganization of German industrial relations." *British Journal of Industrial Relations* 45 (1): 55–76.

Dølvik, J. E. 1997. *Redrawing the Boundaries of Solidarity?: ETUC, Social Dialogue and the Europeanisation of Trade Unions in the 1990s*. Oslo: ARENA and Fafo.

———. 1999. *An Emerging Island?: ETUC, Social Dialogue and the Europeanisation of the Trade Unions in the 1990s*. Brussels: ETUI.

———. 2001. "Industrial relations in EMU: Re-nationalization and Europeanization two sides of the same coin?" Paper presented at the sixth IIRA European regional congress, Oslo, 25–29 June.

Donaghey, J., and P. Teague. 2006. "The free movement of workers and social Europe: Maintaining the European ideal." *Industrial Relations Journal* 37 (6): 652–66.

Drago, M. E. 1998. The institutional base of Chile's economic "miracle": Institutions, government discretionary authority, and economic performance under two policy regimes. PhD thesis, European University Institute.

Dribbusch, H. 2003a. "German and Polish unions cooperate over seasonal workers in agriculture." Available at www.eiro.eurofound.eu.int/ about/2003/10/inbrief/de0310204n.html.

———. 2003b. *Gewerkschaftliche Mitgliedergewinnung im Dienstleistungssektor: Ein Drei-Länder-Vergleich im Einzelhandel*. Berlin: Edition Sigma.

———. 2004. "European Migrant Workers' Union founded." Available at www.eurofound.europa.eu/eiro/2004/09/feature/de0409206f .html.

Dubbins, S. 2002. Towards Euro-corporatism: A study of relations between trade unions and employers' organisations at the European sectoral level. PhD thesis, European University Institute.

Due, J., J. S. Madsen, K. F. V. Petersen, and C. S. Jensen. 1998. "Denmark." In *Collective Bargaining in Western Europe 1997–1998,* edited by G. Fajertag, 71–108. Brussels: ETUI.

Dufour, C., and A. Hege. 1999. Quelle coordination syndicale des négociations en Europe? *Chronique Internationale de l'IRES* 60 (September): 108–27.

Dufresne, A. 2002. "Oskar Lafontaine's dream: An opportunity for economic policy coordination?" In *Social Developments in the European Union,* edited by C. Degryse and P. Pochet, 85–113. Brussels: ETUI/ OSE.

——. 2006. Les stratégies de l'euro-syndicalisme sectoriel: Etude de la coordination salariale et du dialogue social. PhD thesis, Université Paris X–Nanterre.

Dufresne, A., C. Degryse, and P. Pochet, eds. 2007. *The European Sectoral Social Dialogue: Actors, Developments and Challenges.* Brussels: P.I.E.-Peter Lang.

Duisenberg, W., and C. Noyer. 2002. "ECB press conference." Available at www.ecb.int/key/02/sp020502.htm.

Dyson, K., and K. Featherstone. 1996. "Italy and EMU as a 'Vincolo esterno'?: Empowering the technocrats, transforming the state." *South European Society & Politics* 1 (2): 272–99.

Ebbinghaus, B., and J. Visser. 2000. *Trade Unions in Western Europe since 1945.* London: Macmillan.

Eberwein, W., J. Tholen, and J. Schuster. 2001. *The Europeanisation of Industrial Relations: National and European Processes in Germany, UK, Italy and France.* Aldershot, UK: Ashgate.

Edwards, T. 1999. "Cross-border mergers and acquisitions: The implications for labour." *Transfer* 5 (3): 320–43.

Eichhorst, W. 1999. "Europäische marktgestaltende Politik zwischen Supranationalität und nationaler Autonomie: Das Beispiel der Entsenderichtlinie." *Industrielle Beziehungen* 3: 341–59.

——. 2000. *Europäische Sozialpolitik zwischen Nationaler Autonomie und Marktfreiheit: Die Entsendung von Arbeitnehmern in der EU.* Frankfurt: Campus.

Engels, F. 2007 [1895]. "Introduction to Karl Marx: The class struggles in France." Available at www.marx.org/archive/marx/works/1850/ class-struggles-france/index.htm.

Epifani, G. 2003. "Una sfida ancora attuale: Protocollo 23 Luglio 1993." Available at www.rassengna.it/2003/speciali/conzertazione/epifani .htm.

Eriksen, E. O., and J. E. Fossum. 2007. "Europe in transformation: How to reconstitute democracy?" Available at www.arena.uio.no/events/seminarpapers/2007.

Erne, R. 2006. "A contentious consensus: The establishment of the national minimum wage in Ireland." In *Minimum Wages in Europe*, edited by T. Schulten, R. Bispinck, and C. Schäfer, 65–83. Brussels: ETUI.

Erne, R., A. Gross, B. Kaufmann, and H. Kleger, eds. 1995. *Transnationale Demokratie: Impulse für ein Demokratisch Verfasstes Europa.* Zürich: Realotopia.

Escande, C. 1996. "Alcatel Alsthom: Les organisations syndicales essayent de mobiliser à l'échelon européen." *Les Echos*, 23 May, 8.

Esping-Andersen, G. 1990. *The Three Worlds of Welfare Capitalism.* Cambridge, UK: Polity Press.

Esping-Andersen, G., and W. Korpi. 1984. "Social policy as class politics in post-war capitalism: Scandinavia, Austria, and Germany." In *Order and Conflict in Contemporary Capitalism*, edited by John H. Goldthrope, 179–208. Oxford: Clarendon.

Etty, T. 1978. "Gewerkschaftliche Weltkonzernausschüsse—ein Überblick." In *Einführung in die Internationale Gewerkschaftspolitik: Ansatzpunkte Gewerkschaftlicher Internationalisierung*, edited by W. Olle, Vol. 1, 68–78. Berlin: Olle & Wolter.

European Commission. 1998. *EURO 1999: Report on the Situation Regarding the Convergence and Relevant Recommendations Concerning Transition to the Third Phase of EMU.* Luxembourg: Office for the Official Publications of the European Communities.

——. 2003a. "Commission clears Alcan takeover bid for Pechiney, subject to conditions." Press release no. IP/03/1309. Available at www.europa.eu.int/rapid/start/cgi/guesten.ksh?p_action.gettxt=gt&doc=IP/03/1309|0|RAPID&lg=EN.

——. 2003b. *Report from the Commission on European Governance.* Luxembourg: Office for Official Publications of the European Communities.

——. 2006. *Special Eurobarometer 251 "The Future of Europe."* Available at www.ec.europa.eu/public_opinion/futur_en.htm.

European Metalworkers' Federation (EMF). 1993. "Collective bargaining policy in a changing Europe." Statement of Principle on Collective Bargaining, adopted at the 1st EMF Collective Bargaining Conference, Luxembourg, 11–12 March.

——. 1995. *Secretariat's Report on Activities 1991–1994.* Brussels: EMF.

——. 1996. "Leitlinien und Schwerpunkte der Tarifpolitik des EMB." Brussels: EMF.

——. 1998a. "Collective bargaining with the euro." Resolution adopted at the 3rd EMF collective bargaining conference on 9–10 December 1998 in Frankfurt and confirmed at the EMF Congress, Copenhagen, 17–18 June 1999.

———. 1998b. "EMF charter on working time." Adopted at the EMF General Assembly, Luxembourg, 1–2 July.

———. 2000. "Erklärung des EMB zur Rolle der Gewerkschaftskoordinatoren und den nationalen Organisationen in den bestehenden Europäischen Betriebsräten." Verabschiedet vom Exekutivausschuss, 15–16 June. Brussels.

———. 2001a. *Eucob@ REPORT 2000/2001*. Brussels: EMF.

———. 2001b. *Report on the European Coordination Rule*. EMF Collective Bargaining Conference, Oslo, 20–21 June. Brussels: EMF.

European Migrant Workers' Union (EMWU). 2007. "Collective agreements." Available at www.emwu.org/englisch/gesetze/gesetze.htm.

European Parliament. 2000. "On restructuring of European industry, with special attention for the closure of Goodyear in Italy and the problems of ABB-Alstom." B5–0124, 0128, 0134/2000. Strasbourg.

———. 2001. "Report on the application of the directive on the establishment of a European works council or a procedure in community-scale undertakings and community-scale groups of undertakings for the purposes of informing and consulting employees." Council directive 94/45/EC of 22 September 1994. Rapporteur: W Menrad. A5–0282/2001 final. Strasbourg.

European Round Table of Industrialists (ERT). 2002. *Competition Policy Task Force: Response to the "Green Paper on the Review of Council Regulation (ECC) No 4064/89."* Brussels: ERT.

European Trade Union Confederation (ETUC). 2001a. *Annual Report on the Coordination of Collective Bargaining in Europe*. ETUC Executive Committee. Brussels: JL/EM/PSC.

———. 2001b. "EBR und Unternehmenszusammenschlüsse." EGB working paper no. 46 (2 Fassung, November 2000). In *Materialien für Euro Betriebsräte: Praktischer Leitfaden*, 22–47. Frankfurt: IG BAU.

———. 2002a. *Position of the ETUC on the Green Paper on the Review of Council Regulation (EEC) No. 4064/89*. Brussels: ETUC.

———. 2002b. *Third Annual Report on the Coordination of Collective Bargaining in Europe*. Brussels: ETUC Executive Committee.

———. 2006. "Declaration for the Doorn Group political meeting of 6 October 2006." *ETUC Collective Bargaining Information Bulletin* 4: 1–6.

EWC News 2007. "Case studies: Aluminium and household appliances industry." Available at www.ewc-news.com/eno22007.htm#7.

Falkner, G. 2003. "The interprofessional social dialogue at European level: Past and future." In *Industrial Relations and European Integration: Trans- and Supranational Developments and Prospects*, edited by B. Keller and H.-W. Platzer, 11–29. Aldershot, UK: Ashgate.

Ferner, A., and J. Quintanilla. 1998. "Multinationals, national business systems and HRM: The enduring influence of national identity or a process of 'Anglo-Saxonization'." *International Journal of Human Resource Management* 9 (4): 710–31.

Ferrera, M., and E. Gualmini. 1999. *Salvati dall' Europa? Welfare e Lavoro in Italia fra Gli Anni '70 e Gli Anni '90: Le Riforma Già Fatte e Quelle Che Restano da Fare.* Bologna: Il Mulino.

Ferrera, M., A. Hemerijck, and M. Rhodes. 2000. *The Future of Social Europe: Recasting Work and Welfare in the New Economy.* Oeiras: Celta Editora.

Ferron, A. 2002. "Aides d'etat: La concurrence n'est plus le critère unique." *La Lettre de Confrontations* 57: 4–5.

Financial Times. 2003a. "Aiding Alstom." Editorial. 11 September, p. 14.

———. 2003b. "High noon over state aid: Brussels' credibility rides on taking a firm stand on Alstom." 19 September, p. 20.

Flassbeck, H. 1997. "Und die Spielregeln für die Lohnpolitik?" *Frankfurter Rundschau,* 31 October, p. 12.

———. 1998. "Reallöhne und Arbeitslosigkeit—eine einfache empirische Widerlegung der neoklassischen Beschäftigungstheorie." *WSI Mitteilungen* 51 (4): 226–32.

Flassbeck, H., and F. Spiecker. 2000. "Real wages and unemployment: There is no trade-off. Neoclassical employment theory fails to explain the different labor market developments in the United States and Europe." English version of an article from *WSI-Mitteilungen* 53 (11). Available at www.flassbeck.de/pdf/wagesandeuro.pdf.

Florek, L. 1994. "The impact of industrial relations on political transformation in Poland." In *The Future of Industrial Relations: Global Change and Challenges,* edited by H. R. Niland, R. D. Lansbury, and C. Verevis, 307–16. Thousand Oaks, Calif.: Sage.

Fluder, R. 1996. *Interessenorganisationen und Kollektive Arbeitsbeziehungen im Öffentlichen Dienst in der Schweiz: Entstehung, Mitgliedschaft, Organisation und Politik seit 1940.* Zürich: Seismo.

Fluder, R., H. Ruf, W. Schöni, and M. Wicki. 1991. *Gewerkschaften und Angestelltenverbände in der Schweizerischen Privatwirtschaft.* Zürich: Seismo.

Foot, P. 2005. *The Vote: How It Was Won and How It Was Undermined.* London: Viking.

Force Ouvrière. 2000. "Rapports 2000: XIXème Congrès, Marseille, 6–10 March." *Force Ouvrière Hebdo* 2461: 564–65.

Foster, J. B. 2000. "Marx and internationalism." *Monthly Review* 52 (3). Available at www.monthlyreview.org/700jbf.htm.

Frege, C. M., and J. Kelly. 2004. *Varieties of Unionism: Strategies for Union Revitalization in a Globalizing Economy.* Oxford: Oxford University Press.

Freyssinet, J. 1999. "L'euro, l'emploi et la politique sociale." *Chronique Internationale de l'IRES* 56: 3–9.

Fuchs, M., and F. Marhold. 2001. *Europäisches Arbeitsrecht.* Vienna: Springer.

Fulton, L., and F. Lefresne. 1999. "Royaume-Uni: Un rôle encore actif de la négociation salariale." *Chronique Internationale de l'IRES* 60: 78–86.

Galin, A. 1994. "Myth and reality: Trade unions and industrial relations in the transition to democracy." In *The Future of Industrial Relations: Global Change and Challenges,* edited by H. R. Niland, R. D. Lansbury, and C. Verevis. 295–306. Thousand Oaks, Calif.: Sage.

Geary, J. F., and W. K. Roche. 2001. "Multinationals and human resources practices in Ireland: A rejection of the new conformance thesis." *International Journal of Human Resource Management* 12 (1): 109–27.

Gélédan, A., ed. 1993. *Le Bilan Économique des Années Mitterrand (1981–1994).* Paris: Le Monde Éditions.

General, Municipal, Boilermakers and Allied Trade Union (GMB). 2002. *GMB Trade Union Response to European Commission Green Paper on the Review of Council Regulation (ECC) No 4064/89.* London: GMB.

Généreux, J. 2005. *Manuel Critique de Parfait Européen : Les Bonnes Raisons de Dire "Non" à la Constitution.* Paris: Seuil.

Gennard, J., and K. Newsome. 2001. "European coordination of collective bargaining: The case of UNI-Europa graphical sector." *Employee Relations* 23 (6): 599–613.

Gester, J. 1997. "Der Weg von BBC zu ABB: Die 'multi domestic enterprise' Strategie als sozialer Konfliktstoff." Mimeo. Freie Universität Berlin.

Gewerkschaftliche Monatshefte. 1999. "Bewegte Zeiten—Arbeit an der Zukunft: Dokumentation der wissenschaftlichen Konferenz des DGB '50 Jahre DGB.'" 40 (12).

Gill, S. 1998. "European governance and new constitutionalism: Economic and monetary union and alternatives to disciplinary neo-liberalism in Europe." *New Political Economy* 3 (1): 5–26.

Giotakos, D. 2000. "The commission's review of the aluminium merger wave." *Competition Policy Newsletter* [of the European Commission] 2: 8–23.

Giugni, M. G., Doug McAdam, and C. Tilly, eds. 1998. *From Contention to Democracy.* Lanham: Rowman & Littlefield.

Gobin, C. 1996. Consultation et concertation sociales à l'échelle de la Communauté économique européenne: Étude des positions et stratégies de la confédération européenne des syndicats (1958–1991). PhD thesis, Université Libre de Bruxelles.

———. 1997. *L'Europe Syndicale entre Désir et Réalité: Essai sur le Syndicalisme et la Construction Européenne a l'Aube du XXIe Siècle.* Bruxelles: Labor.

———. 2005. "La démocratie, le syndicalisme et la gouvernance de l'Union Européenne: La mémoire du conflit démocratique en péril?" Available at www.unige.ch/ieug/publications/euryopa/module2005.pdf.

Goldstein, L. F. 2001. *Constituting Federal Sovereignty: The European Union in Comparative Context.* Baltimore: Johns Hopkins University Press.

Gollbach, J. 2000. *Grenzüberscheitende Tarifpartnerschaften in der Metallindustrie.* Essen: Klartext Verlag.

Gollbach, J., and T. Schulten. 2000. "Cross-border collective bargaining networks in Europe." *European Journal of Industrial Relations* 6 (2): 161–79.

Gorz, A. 1967. *Strategy for Labor: A Radical Proposal.* Boston: Beacon Press.

Gottschalk, B., and E.-L. Laux. 2000. *Tarifpolitik der Baugewerkschaften in Europa.* Frankfurt: IG BAU.

Gow, D. 2003. "Alstom unearths €51m black hole." *The Guardian,* 1 July, p. 16.

Graham, R., and M. Arnold. 2003. "France justifies Alstom bailout." *Financial Times,* 7 August, p. 19.

Gramsci, A. 1992. *Gefängnishefte: Kritische Gesamtausgabe.* Vol. 4. Hamburg: Argument.

Gray, J. 2000. "The passing of social democracy." In *The Global Transformations Reader: An Introduction to the Globalization Debate,* edited by D. Held and A. McGrew, 328–31. Cambridge, UK: Polity Press.

Greven, M. T. 1998. "Mitgliedschaft, Grenzen und politischer Raum: Problemdimensionen der Demokratisierung der Europäischen Union." In *Politische Vierteljahresschrift, Vol. 249: Regieren in Entgrenzten Räumen,* edited by B. Kohler-Koch, 249–70. Opladen: Westdeutscher Verlag.

Greven, T. 2003. "Gewerkschaften in der Globalisierung: Die Herausforderung transnationaler Gewerkschaftspolitik." In *Das Ende der Politik?: Globalisierung und der Strukturwandel des Politischen,* edited by A. Scharenberg and O. Schmidtke, 336–54. Münster: Westfälisches Dampfboot.

Grimm, D. 1995. "Does Europe need a constitution?" *European Law Journal* 1 (3): 282–302.

———. 1999. "Es besteht Aushöhlungsgefahr." *Süddeutsche Zeitung,* 4 June, p. 10.

Gross, A. 1998. "Föderalismus und direkte Demokratie." *Die Union: Vierteljahresschrift für Integrationsfragen* 4: 99–114.

Grote, J. R., and P. C. Schmitter. 1999. "The renaissance of national corporatism: Unintended side effect of European economic and monetary union or calculated response to the absence of European social policy?" *Transfer* 5 (1–2): 34–63.

Groux, G., and R. Mouriaux. 1992. *La CGT: Crises et Alternatives.* Paris: Economica.

Gubian, A., S. Jugnot, F. Lerais, and V. Passeron. 2004. "Les effets de la RTT sur l'emploi: Des simulations *ex ante* aux évaluations *ex post.*" *Économie et Statistique* 376–77: 25–54. Available at www.insee.fr/fr/ffc/docs_ffc/es376377b.pdf.

Guéhenno, J.-M. 1994. *La Fin de la Démocratie.* Paris: Flammarion.

Gumbrell-McCormick, R. 2000. "Quel internationalisme syndical?: Passé, présent, avenir." *Les Temps Modernes* 55 (607): 178–206.

References

Gutiérrez, E., and C. Martín Urriza. 1998. "Spain." In *Collective Bargaining in Western Europe: 1997–1998*, edited by G. Fajertag, 313–36. Brussels: ETUI.

Haas, E. B. 1968. *The Uniting of Europe: Political, Social, and Economic Forces 1950–1957*. Stanford: Stanford University Press.

Habermas, J. 1992. *Faktizität und Geltung: Beiträge zur Diskurstheorie des Rechts und des Demokratischen Rechtsstaats*. Frankfurt: Suhrkamp.

———. 1996a. *Between Facts and Norms: Contributions to a Discourse Theory of Law and Democracy*. Cambridge, Mass.: MIT Press.

———. 1996b [1990]. "Citizenship and national identity." In *Between Facts and Norms: Contributions to a Discourse Theory of Law and Democracy*, 491–515. Cambridge, Mass.: MIT Press.

Hamann, K., and J. Kelly. 2004. "Unions as political actors: A recipe for revitalization?" In *Varieties of Unionism: Struggles for Union Revitalization in a Globalizing Economy*, edited by C. Frege and J. Kelly, 93–116. Oxford: Oxford University Press.

Hammarström, O. 1994. "Local and global: Trade unions in the future." In *The Future of Industrial Relations: Global Change and Challenges*, edited by J. R. Miland, R. D. Lansbury, and C. Verevis, 152–63. Thousand Oaks, Calif.: Sage.

Hancké, B. 2000. "European works councils and industrial restructuring in the European motor industry." *European Journal of Industrial Relations* 6 (1): 35–59.

———. 2002. *Large Firms and Institutional Change. Industrial Renewal and Economic Restructuring in France*. Oxford: Oxford University Press.

Hancké, B., and D. Soskice. 2003. "Wage-setting and inflation targets in EMU." *Oxford Review of Economic Policy* 19: 149–60.

Hardiman, N. 2000. "Social partnership, wage bargaining, and growth." In *Bust to Boom?: The Irish Experience of Growth and Inequality*, edited by B. Nolan, P. J. O'Connell, and C. T. Whelan, 286–309. Dublin: Institute of Public Administration.

———. 2001. "Kieran Allen—The Celtic Tiger: The myth of social partnership." Book review. *Economic and Social Review* 32 (2): 183–87.

Harrod, J. 1972. *Trade Union Foreign Policy: A Study of British and American Trade Union Activities in Jamaica*. New York: Anchor Books.

Harrod, J., and R. O'Brien. 2002. *Global Unions?: Theory and Strategies of Organized Labour in the Global Political Economy*. London: Routledge.

Harvey, D. 2005. *A Brief History of Neoliberalism*. Oxford: Oxford University Press.

Hassel, A. 1999. "Bündnisse für Arbeit: Nationale Handlungsfähigkeit im Europäischen Regimewettbewerb." MPIfG discussion paper no. 99/5, MPIFG, Cologne.

Hebauf, R. 2002. "ABB-Konzern: Rastlose Restrukturierung." *Die Mitbestimmung* 48 (5): 19–21.

Hege, A., and U. Rehfeldt. 1999. "Une modération salariale qui vient de loin." *Chronique Internationale de l'IRES* 60: 62–71.

Heller, J.-M. 2000. "Faire reculer la direction." *Vivre le Territoire: Le Magazine du Conseil Général du Territoire de Belfort* 43: VIII.

Héritier, A. 1999. "Elements of democratic legitimation in Europe: An alternative perspective." *Journal of European Public Policy* 6 (2): 269–82.

Hirschman, A. O. 1970. *Exit, Voice and Loyalty: Responses to Decline in Firms, Organizations and States.* Cambridge, Mass.: Harvard University Press.

Hirst, P., and G. Thompson. 1996. *Globalisation in Question.* Cambridge, UK: Polity Press.

Hobsbawm, E. 1984. *Worlds of Labour: Further Studies in the History of Labour.* London: Weidenfeld & Nicolson.

Hooghe, L., and G. Marks. 2006. "Europe's blues: Theoretical soul-searching after the rejection of the European Constitution." *PS: Political Science & Politics* 39 (2): 247–50.

Höpner, M. 2003. "Was trennt Gewerkschaften und Sozialdemokratie?" *Die Mitbestimmung* 49 (1–2): 48–51.

Höpner, M., and G. Jackson. 2003. "Besteht ein Markt für Unternehmenskontrolle?: Der Fall Mannesmann." In *Alle Macht dem Markt?* edited by W. Streeck and M. Höpner, 147–68. Frankfurt: Campus.

Höpner, M., and A. Schäfer. 2007. "A new phase of European integration: Organized capitalisms in post-Ricardian Europe." MPIfG discussion paper no. 07/4. Available at www.mpi-fg-koeln.mpg.de/pu/mpifg_dp/dp07-4.pdf.

Hulverscheidt, C., B. Benoit, and M. Arnold. 2003. "Berlin snubs Paris over Alstom rescue plan." *Financial Times,* 8 August, p. 26.

Hunger, U. 2001. "Globalisierung auf dem Bau." *Leviathan* 29 (March): 70–82.

Hyman, R. 1999. "Imagined solidarities: Can trade unions resist globalisation?" In *Globalisation and Labour Relations,* edited by P. Leisink, 94–115. Cheltenham, UK: Edward Elgar.

——. 2000. "European industrial relations: From regulation to deregulation to re-regulation? The end of an Old Regime and the struggle for a New Order." In *Europa 2000+: Auf dem Weg zu einem Europäischen Sozialmodell,* edited by Zukunfts- und Kulturwerkstätte and Fritz Verzetnitsch, 71–82. Vienna: SPÖ Zukunfts- und Kulturwerkstätte.

——. 2001. *Understanding European Trade Unionism: Between Market, Class and Society.* London: Sage.

IG Metall and European Metalworkers' Federation. 2002. "Frankfurt Declaration. Strike in the German metal-working industry—Solidarity between the European metal-working trade unions," 10 May, Frankfurt.

Imig, D., and S. Tarrow, eds. 2001. *Contentious Europeans: Protest and Politics in an Emerging Polity.* Lanham: Rowman & Littlefield.

Indermaur, P. 1989. "Silbersonne am Horizont." In *Alusuisse—Eine*

Schweizer Kolonialgeschichte, edited by T. Bauer, G. J. Crough, et al., 17–87. Zürich: Limmat Verlag.

Initiative and Referendum Institute Europe. 2007. "Our mission." Available at www.iri-europe.org/.

International Metalworkers' Federation (IMF). 1993. *Report of the Secretariat.* 28th IMF World Congress, Zurich, Switzerland, June 13–18. Geneva: IMF.

Jobert, A. 2000. *Les Espaces de la Négociation Collective.* Toulouse: Octares.

Joerges, C. 2001. "'Deliberative supranationalism'—a defence." Europe Integration Online Papers 5 (8). Available at www.eiop.or.at/eiop/texte/2001–088a.htm.

Joerges, C., and J. Falke, eds. 2000. *Das Ausschusswesen der Europäischen Union: Praxis der Risikoregulierung in Binnenmarkt und Ihre Rechtliche Verfassung.* Baden-Baden: Nomos.

Joerges, C., and E. Vos. 1999. *EU Committees: Social Regulation, Law and Politics.* Oxford: Hart.

Juquel, G., and R. Metz. 2001. "Peut-on coordonner les revendications salariales en Europe?" *Le Peuple* 1542: 10–11.

Juravich, T., and K. Bronfenbrenner. 1999. *Ravenswood: The Steelworkers' Victory and the Revival of American Labor.* Ithaca: ILR Press.

Karch, H. 2000. "Weder Dogmen noch neue Beliebigkeit Anmerkungen zum System 'IG Metall-Tarifpolitik' am Beispiel der Metall-Tarifrunde 2000." *Gewerkschaftliche Monatshefte* 51 (5): 257–67.

Karlin, D., and R. Lainé. 1994. *La Multinationale: Voyage au Coeur du Group Pechiney.* Paris: Albin Michel and ARTE/La Sept Editions.

Kaufmann, B. 1995. "Unterwegs zur transnationalen Demokratie." In *Transnationale Demokratie: Impulse für ein Demokratisch Verfasstes Europa,* edited by R. Erne, A. Gross, B. Kaufmann, and H. Kleger, 17–33. Zürich: Realotopia.

Keller, B. 2000. "Book review: T. Schulten/R. Bispinck (Eds.), Tarifpolitik unter dem EURO—Perspektiven einer europäischen Koordinierung: das Beispiel Metallindustrie." *WSI Mitteilungen* 53 (2): 145–47.

——. 2003. "Social dialogues at sectoral level: The neglected ingredient of European industrial relations." In *Industrial Relations and European Integration: Trans- and Supranational Developments and Prospects,* edited by B. Keller and H.-W. Platzer, 30–57. Aldershot, UK: Ashgate.

Kelly, J. E. 1998. *Rethinking Industrial Relations: Mobilization, Collectivism, and Long Waves.* London: Routledge.

Keune, M. 2004. *The Coordination of Collective Bargaining in Europe: Annual Report 2004.* Brussels: ETUC/ETUI.

——. 2005. *The Coordination of Collective Bargaining in Europe: Annual Report 2005.* Brussels: ETUC/ETUI.

——. 2006. *The Coordination of Collective Bargaining in Europe: Annual Report 2006.* Brussels: ETUC/ETUI.

Kirby, P. 2002. *The Celtic Tiger in Distress: Growth with Inequality in Ireland.* Basingstoke: Palgrave.

Klandermans, B., H. P. Kriesi, and S. Tarrow. 1988. *From Structure to Action: Comparing Social Movement Research across Cultures.* Greenwich, Conn.: JAI Press.

Klebe, T., and S. Roth. 2000. "Die Gewerkschaften auf dem Weg zu einer internationalen Strategie?: Am Beispiel der Automobilindustrie." *Arbeitsrecht im Betrieb* 12: 749–59.

Kleger, H. 1997. "Bausteine transnationaler Demokratie." In *Transnationale Staatsbürgerschaft*, edited by Heinz Kleger, 287–335. Frankfurt: Campus.

Köbele, B., and G. Leuschner, eds. 1995. *Dokumentation der Konferenz "Europäischer Arbeitsmarkt Grenzenlos Mobil?" 6–8 March, Bonn.* Baden-Baden: Nomos.

Kochan, T. A., and P. Osterman. 1994. *The Mutual Gains Enterprise.* Boston: Harvard Business School Press.

Kocka, J. 2000. "Zivilgesellschaft als historisches Problem und Versprechen." In *Europäische Zivilgesellschaft in Ost und West,* edited by M. Hildermeier, J. Kocka, and C. Conrad, 13–40. Frankfurt: Campus.

Kolehmainen, E. 2002. The posted workers directive: European reinforcement of national labour protection. PhD thesis, European University Institute.

Koselleck, R., and K. Schreiner, eds. 1994. *Bürgerschaft: Rezeption und Innovation der Begrifflichkeit vom Hohen Mittelalter bis ins 19. Jahrhundert.* Stuttgart: Klett-Cotta.

Kotitschke, A. 2003. "Les personnels sont déterminés à entrer en résistance." Interview. *L'Humanité,* 2 July.

Kowalsky, W. 2000. *Focus on European Social Policy: Countering Europessimism.* Brussels: ETUI.

Kreimer-de Fries, J. 1999. "Tarifkorporation der Gewerkschaftsbünde BeNeLux-Deutschland: Die Erklärung von Doorn." In *Tarifpolitik unter dem EURO, Perspektiven einer Europäischen Koordinierung: Das Beispiel der Metallindustrie,* edited by T. Schulten and R. Bispinck, 185–96. Hamburg: VSA Verlag.

Kriesi, H-P. 1995. *Le Système Politique Suisse.* Paris: Economica.

———. 2007. "The role of European integration in national election campaigns." *European Union Politics* 8 (1): 83–108.

Labbé, C. 1999. "Un objectif purement financier." Interview. *L'Hebdo/ V.O.* 2869 (20 August): 7.

Langneau, E., and P. Lefébure. 1999. "La spirale de Vilvorde: Médiatisation et politisation de la protestation, un cas d'européanisation des mouvements sociaux." *Les Cahiers du CEVIPOF* 22.

Lascoumes, P., and P. Le Gales. 2007. "Introduction: Understanding public policy through its instruments—from the nature of instruments to the sociology of public policy instrumentation." *Governance* 20 (1): 1–21.

L.B. 2003. "Alstom: Les syndicats européens pour un moratoire." *L'Humanité*, 9 October. Available at www.humanite.fr/2003-10-09_Politique_-Alstom-Les-syndicats-europeens-pour-un-moratoire.

Lecher, W., H.-W. Platzer, S. Rüb, and K.-P. Weiner. 2001. *European Works Councils: Developments, Types and Networking.* Aldershot, UK: Gower.

Lefébure, P. 2002. "Euro-manifs, contres-sommets et marches européennes." In *L'Opinion Européenne 2002 (Annuaire)*, edited by B. Cautrès and D. Reynié, 109–30. Paris: Presses de Sciences Po.

Leibfried, S., and P. Pierson. 2000. "Social policy: Left to courts and markets?" In *Policy-Making in the European Union*, edited by H. Wallace and W. Wallace, 267–92. Oxford: Oxford University Press.

Lemaître, P. 2000. "Les salariés d'ABB Alstom Power interpellent Bruxelles sur les conséquences des restructurations." *Le Monde*, 12 April, p. 16.

Lenin, V. 1917. "The chain is no stronger than its weakest link." *Pravda*, 27 May. Available at www.marxists.org/archive/lenin/works/1917/may/27.htm.

Léonard, E., R. Erne, S. Smismans, and P. Marginson. 2007. *New Structures, Forms and Processes of Governance in European Industrial Relations.* Luxembourg: Office for the Official Publications of the European Communities.

Lepsius, M. R. 1990. "'Ethnos' oder 'Demos'." In *Interessen, Ideen und Institutionen*, edited by M. R. Lepsius, 247–55. Opladen: Westdeutscher Verlag.

———. 1993a. "Die europäische Gemeinschaft und die Zukunft des Nationalstaates." In *Demokratie in Deutschland: Soziologisch-Historische Konstellationsanalysen, Ausgewählte Aufsätze*, 249–64. Göttingen: Vandenhoeck & Ruprecht.

———. 1993b. "Nationalstaat oder Nationalitätenstaat als Modell für die Weiterentwicklung der Europäischen Gemeinschaft." In *Demokratie in Deutschland: Soziologisch-Historische Konstellationsanalysen, Ausgewählte Aufsätze*, 265–85. Göttingen: Vandenhoeck & Ruprecht.

Le Queux, S., and G. Fajertag. 2001. "Towards a Europeanisation of collective bargaining?: Insights from the European chemical industry." *European Journal of Industrial Relations* 7 (2): 117–36.

Levinson, C. 1972. *International Trade Unionism.* London: Allen & Unwin.

Lévy, G-P. 2002. "Le Comité d'entreprise européen: Une instance d'écoute." *Les Cahiers de la Fondation: Europe et Société* 51–52: 45–49.

Liaisons Sociales Europe. 2000. "Fusions d'entreprise: Les syndicats s'invitent à Bruxelles." *Liaisons Sociales Europe* 3: 1–2.

Linz, J., and A. C. Stepan. 1996. *Problems of Democratic Transition and Consolidation: Southern Europe, South America, and Post-Communist Europe.* Baltimore: Johns Hopkins University Press.

Lipset, S. M. 1969. *Political Man: The Social Basis of Politics.* London: Heinemann.

Lo Faro, A. 2000. *Regulating Social Europe: Reality and Myth of Collective Bargaining in the EC Legal Order.* Oxford: Hart.

Loth, W. 1996. *Stalins Ungeliebtes Kind: Warum Moskau die DDR Nicht Wollte.* München: Deutscher Taschenbuch Verlag.

Macaire, S., U. Rehfeldt, M. Braud, C. Sauviat, and M. Carley. 2002. "Industrial relations aspects of mergers and takeovers." Available at www .eiro.eurofound.eu.int/2001/02/study/tn0102401s.html.

Magraw, R. 1992. *A History of the French Working Class, Vol. 1: The Age of Artisan Revolution 1815–1871.* Oxford: Blackwell.

Mair, P. 2006. "Ruling the void? The hollowing of Western democracy." *New Left Review* 42: 25–51.

Majone, G. 1994a. "The rise of the regulatory state in Europe." *West European Politics* 17 (3): 77–101.

——. 1994b. "Understanding regulatory growth in the European Community." EUI working paper no. SPS 94/17, EUI, Florence.

Mania, R., and G. Sateriale. 2002. *Relazioni Pericolose: Sindacati e Politica Dopo la Concertazione.* Bologna: Il Mulino.

Marginson, P. 2000. "The euro company and euro industrial relations." *European Journal of Industrial Relations* 6 (1): 9–34.

Marginson, P., and K. Sisson. 1996. "Multinational companies and the future of collective bargaining: Review of the research issues." *European Journal of Industrial Relations* 2 (2): 173–98.

——. 2004. *European Integration and Industrial Relations: Multi-level Governance in the Making.* Basingstoke, UK: Palgrave Macmillan.

Marginson, P., K. Sisson, and J. Arrowsmith. 2003. "Between decentralisation and Europeanisation: Sectoral bargaining in four countries and two sectors." *European Journal of Industrial Relations* 9 (2): 163–87.

Marin, B. 1990. *Generalised Political Exchange.* Frankfurt: Campus.

Marks, G., and D. McAdam. 1996. "Social movements and the changing structure of political opportunity in the European Union." In *Governance in the European Union,* edited by G. Marks, F. W. Scharpf, P. C. Schmitter, and W. Streeck, 95–120. London: Sage.

Marks, G., F. W. Scharpf, P. C. Schmitter, and W. Streeck, eds. 1996. *Governance in the European Union.* London: Sage.

Marshall, T. H. 1992. "Citizenship and social class." In *Citizenship and Social Class,* edited by T. H. Marshall and T. Bottomore, 3–51. London: Pluto Press.

Martin, A. 1996. "European institutions and the Europeanisation of trade unions: support or seduction." ETUI working paper no. DWP 96.04.01, ETUI, Brussels.

——. 1999. "Wage bargaining under EMU: Europeanization, re-nationalization or Americanization?" ETUI working paper no. DWP 99.01.03, ETUI, Brussels.

——. 2000. "Social pacts, unemployment, and EMU macroeconomic policy." EUI working paper no. RSC 2000/32, EUI, Florence.

Martin, A., and G. Ross. 1999. "In the line of fire: The Europeanization of labor representation." In *The Brave New World of European Labor: European Trade Unions at the Millennium,* edited by A. Martin, G. Ross, et al., 312–67. New York: Berghahn.

——, eds. 2004. *Euros and Europeans: Monetary Integration and the European Model of Society.* Cambridge, UK: Cambridge University Press.

Marx, K. 1999 [1887]. *Capital, Volume One.* Available at http://marxists .org/archive/marx/works/1867–c1/index.htm.

Maschino, D., J.-F. Boivin, and R. Laflamme. 2001. "Les conventions collectives de longue durée dans le contexte des nouvelles approches en relations de travail au Québec." Available at www.travail.gouv.qc.ca/ quoi_de_neuf/actualite/APEC.pdf.

Maurice, J. 1999. *Emploi, Négociations Collectives, Protection Sociale: Vers quelle Europe Sociale? Rapport du Groupe Présidé par Joël Maurice.* Paris: Commissariat Général du Plan and La Documentation Française.

——. 2001. "Analyse comparative des politiques salariales: Allemagne, Pays-Bas, Belgique." *La Revue de la CFDT* 44: 3–14.

McBrearty, L. 2002. "Notes pour le discours d'ouverture." Available at www.uswa.ca/fr/confrnce/ndspeech.htm.

McGowan, F. 2000. "Competition policy: The limits of the European regulatory state." In *Policy-Making in the European Union,* 4th ed., edited by H. Wallace and W. Wallace, 115–47. Oxford: Oxford University Press.

Meardi, G. 2006. "'Multinationals' heaven?: Uncovering and understanding worker responses to multinational companies in post-communist central Europe." *International Journal of Human Resource Management* 17 (8): 1366–78.

Megale, A., G. D'Aloia, and L. Birindelli. 2003. *La Politica dei Redditi negli Anni '90: Potere d'Acquisto, Contrattazione e Produttività in Italia e in Europa.* Roma: Ediesse.

Menz, G. 2005a. *Varieties of Capitalism and Europeanization: National Response Strategies to the Single European Market.* Oxford: Oxford University Press.

——. 2005b. "Old bottles—new wine: The new dynamics of industrial relations." *German Politics* 14 (2): 196–207.

Mermet, E. 1999. "Wage formation in the European Union: A comparative study." Mimeo. ETUI, Brussels.

——. 2001. *Wage Formation in Europe.* Brussels: ETUI.

Mestmäcker, E.-J. 1991. "Die Wiederkehr der bürgerlichen Gesellschaft und ihres Rechts." *Rechtshistorisches Journal* 10: 177–92.

Michels, R. 1999. *Political Parties: A Sociological Study of the Oligarchical Tendencies of Modern Democracy.* New Brunswick, N.J.: Transaction Publishers.

Miguélez, F. 2000. "CC.OO holds seventh congress." Available at www
.eiro.eurofound.ie/2000/05.

Milkman R., and K. Wong. 2001. "Organising immigrant workers." In
Rekindling the Movement, edited by L. Turner, H. C. Katz, and R. W.
Hurd, 99–128. Ithaca: Cornell University Press.

Miller, D., B. Tully, and I. Fitzgerald. 2000. "The politics of language and
the European Works Councils: Towards a research agenda." *European
Journal of Industrial Relations* 6 (3): 307–23.

Miller, J. 1978. "Perspektiven internationaler Gewerkschaftsarbeit auf
Branchenebene." In *Einführung in die Internationale Gewerkschaftspolitik:
Ansatzpunkte Gewerkschaftlicher Internationalisierung,* edited by W. Olle,
Vol. 1, 235–42. Berlin: Olle & Wolter.

Milward, A. S. 2000. *The European Rescue of the Nation-State.* London: Routledge.

Ministère de l'Emploi et de Solidarité. 1999. "L'initiative de Doorn." In
La Négociation Collective en 1998, Vol. 1, 288–92. Paris: Éditions legisla-
tives.

Ministère des Affaires Sociales, du Travail et de la Solidarité. 2001.
Dossier de Presse: Bilan 2000 de la Négociation Collective. Paris: Ministère
des Affaires Sociales, du Travail et de la Solidarité.

———. 2003a. *La Négociation Collective en 2002, Vol. 1.* Paris: Éditions légi-
slatives.

———. 2003b. *La Négociation Collective en 2002, Vol. 2.* Paris: Éditions légi-
slatives.

Molina, Ó., 2006. "Trade union strategies and change in neo-corporatist
concertation: A new century of political exchange?" *West European Politics,* 29 (4): 640–64.

Monti, M. 2002. "Review of the EC Merger Regulation—roadmap for
the reform project." Speech/02/252. Available at www.europa.eu.int/
rapid/.

———. 2007a. "Ma vérité sur l'affaire Alstom" *Le Figaro,* March 23. Available at w3.nexis.com/sources.

———. 2007b. "Sakozy, l'Europe et la concurrance" *Le Figaro,* July 30.
Available at: w3.nexis.com/sources.

Moody, K. 1997. *Workers in a Lean World: Unions in the International Economy.* New York: Verso.

Moore, B. 1969. *Social Origins of Dictatorship and Democracy: Lord and Peas-
ant in the Making of the Modern World.* Harmondsworth, UK: Penguin.

Moore, H. 1978. "Dunlop-Pirelli: Internationalen Shop Stewards-Komi-
tee versus Weltkonzernausschuss." In *Einführung in die Internationale
Gewerkschaftspolitik,* edited by W. Olle, Vol. 1, 97–106. Berlin: Olle &
Wolter.

Moravcsik, A. 2001. "Federalism in the European Union: Rhetoric and
reality." In *The Federal Vision: Legitimacy and Levels of Governance in the*

United States and the European Union, edited by K. Nicolaidis and R. Howse, 161–89. Oxford: Oxford University Press.

———. 2006. "What can we learn from the collapse of the European constitutional project?" *PVS Politische Vierteljahresschrift* 47 (2): 219–41.

Möschel, W. 2000. "Megafusionen ohne Ende—besteht ordnungspolitischer Handlungsbedarf?" IFO discussion paper no. 76, IFO Institute for Economic Research, Munich.

Mouriki, A. 1998. "Greece." In *Collective Bargaining in Western Europe: 1997–1998,* edited by G. Fajertag, 167–86. Brussels: ETUI.

Müller, T., and A. Hoffmann. 2001. "EWC Research: A review of the literature." Warwick papers in industrial relations, no. 65. University of Warwick: Coventry.

Müller-Jentsch, W. 1986. *Soziologie der Industriellen Beziehungen.* Frankfurt: Campus.

Münch, K. 1994. *History of the EMF: The Key Concerns, Continuity and Change.* Brussels: European Metalworkers' Federation.

Munck, R. 2002. *Globalisation and Labour.* London: Zed Books.

Narr, W.-D. 1999. *Die Zukunft des Sozialstaats als Zukunft einer Illusion?* Neu-Ulm: AG-SPAK-Bücher.

Noé, C. 1998. "The euro—wages—employment." *Transfer* 4 (1): 36–47.

Nolan, B., and T. M. Smeeding. 2005. "Ireland's income distribution in comparative perspective." *Review of Income and Wealth* 51 (4): 537–60.

Northrup, H. R., and R. L. Rowan. 1979. *Multinational Collective Bargaining Attempts: The Record, the Cases, and the Prospects.* Philadelphia: Industrial Research Unit, The Wharton School, University of Philadelphia.

O'Donnell, G., and P. C. Schmitter. 1986. "Tentative conclusions about uncertain democracies." In *Transitions from Authoritarian Rule: Prospects for Democracy,* edited by G. O'Donnell, P. C. Schmitter, and L. Whitehead, chap. 4. Baltimore: Johns Hopkins University Press.

O'Donnell, G., P. C. Schmitter, and L. Whitehead, eds. 1986. *Transitions from Authoritarian Rule: Prospects for Democracy.* Baltimore: Johns Hopkins University Press.

Offe, C. 1985. *Disorganized Capitalism: Contemporary Transformations of Work and Politics.* Cambridge, UK: Polity Press.

———. 1998. "Demokratie und Wohlfahrtsstaat: Eine europäische Regimeform unter dem Stress der europäischen Integration." In *Internationale Wirtschaft, Nationale Demokratie: Herausforderungen für die Demokratietheorie,* edited by W. Streeck, 99–135. Frankfurt: Campus.

Organisation for Economic Cooperation and Development (OECD). 1983. *Aluminium Industry: Energy Aspects of Structural Change.* Paris: OECD.

———. 2002. "Intra-industry and intra-firm trade and the internationalisation of production." *OECD Economic Outlook* 71: 159–70.

Pasture, P. 2000. "The flight of the robins: European trade unionism at the beginnings of the European integration process." *The Past and Future of International Trade Unionism,* edited by B. De Wilde, 80–103. Ghent: IALHI.

———. 2002. "Has European integration led to Europeanization or rather re-nationalization of the trade union movement?" Paper presented at the interdisciplinary workshop Trade Unions in the Transnational Sphere, Florence, European University Institute, 26 October,.

Pasture, P., and J. Verberckmoes, eds. 1998. *Working-Class Internationalism and the Appeal of National Identity: Historical Debates and Current Perspectives.* Oxford: Berg.

Pearsall, J., ed. 1998. *New Oxford Dictionary of English.* Oxford: Oxford University Press.

Peillon, L. 2000. "Les salariés d'Alstom dans l'incertitude." *Syndicalisme Hebdo* 2818: 9.

Penninx, R., and J. Roosblad, eds. 2000. *Trade Unions, Immigration, and Immigrants in Europe, 1960–1993.* New York: Berghahn Books.

Perlmutter, H. V. 1965. "L'entreprise internationale: Trois conceptions." *Revue Economique et Sociale* (Lausanne) 22 (May): 151–65.

Pernot, J.-M. 1998. "Une université européenne du syndicalisme?: L'Europe des syndicats." *Politix* 43 (3): 53–78.

———. 1999. "Portugal: Un rattrapage salarial encore modeste." *Chronique Internationale de l'IRES* 60 (September): 72–77.

———. 2001. Dedans, dehors, la dimension internationale dans le syndicalisme français. PhD thesis, Université Paris-X-Nanterre.

———. 2005. *Syndicats: Lendemains de crise?* Paris: Editions Gallimard.

Piazza, J. 2001. "De-linking labour: Labour unions and social democratic parties under globalisation." *Party Politics* 7 (4): 413–35.

Pichot, E. 2001. *L'Europe des Représentants du Personnel et de Leurs Attributions Économiques.* Luxembourg: Commission Européenne, DG Emplois & Affaires Sociales.

———. 2002. "La politique de concurrence—quelle cohérence avec les objectifs économiques et sociaux?" *L'Option de Confrontations* 17: 121–30.

Pizzorno, A. 1978. "Political exchange and collective identity in industrial conflict." In *The Resurgence of Class Conflict in Western Europe since 1968,* edited by C. Crouch and A. Pizzorno. London: Macmillan.

Pochet, P. 1999a. "Monetary union and collective bargaining in Belgium." In *Monetary Union and Collective Bargaining in Europe,* edited by P. Pochet, 187–217. Brussels: P.I.E.-Peter Lang.

———, ed. 1999b. *Monetary Union and Collective Bargaining in Europe.* Brussels: P.I.E.-Peter Lang.

Pochet, P., and B. Vanhercke, eds. 1998. *Les Enjeux Sociaux de l'Union Économique et Monétaire.* Bruxelles: Presses Interuniversitaires Européennes.

Pulignano, V. 2006. "The diffusion of employment practices of US-based multinationals in Europe: A case study comparison of British- and Italian-based subsidiaries." *British Journal of Industrial Relations* 44 (3): 497–518.

Putzhammer, H. 1999. "Aspekte einer europäischen Beschäftigungspolitik." *Gewerkschaftliche Monatshefte* 40 (5): 263–69.

Quaderni Rassegna Sindacale. 2002. "La struttura della contrattazione: Caratteri e tendenze." 40 (4): 1–170.

Rakovsi, C. 2002. "Le rôle de la Commission dans le contrôle des opérations de concertations dans l'Union européenne." *Les Cahiers de la Fondation: Europe et Société* 51–52: 15–22.

Ravaioli, C., and M. Agostinelli. 1998. *Le 35 Ore: La Sfida di un Nuovo Tempo Sociale.* Rome: Editori Riuniti.

Régin, T., and S. Wolikow, eds. 2002. *Les Syndicalismes en Europe: A l'Épreuve de l'International.* Paris: Editions Syllepse.

Rehfeldt, U. 1998. "Arbeitsbeziehungen und Europäische Betriebsräte in Frankreich." In *Europäische Betriebsräte und Arbeitsbeziehungen—zur Lage und Entwicklung in Großbritannien, Frankreich und Italien,* edited by W. Lecher, 27–60. Düsseldorf: Hans Böckler Stiftung.

———. 2000. "Les stratégies syndicales européenne." In *Le Syndicalisme dans la Mondialisation,* edited by A. Fouquet, U. Rehfeldt, and S. Le Roux, 77–86. Paris: Les Éditions de l'Atelier.

Rhodes, M. 1997. "Globalisation, labour markets and welfare states a future of 'competitive corporatism'?" EUI working paper no. RSC 97/36, European University Institute, Florence.

Risse, T., and M. Kleine. 2007 "Assessing the legitimacy of the EU's treaty revision methods." *Journal of Common Market Studies* 45 (1): 69–80.

Roche, W. K., and T. Cradden. 2003. "Neo-corporatism and social partnership." In *Public Administration and Public Policy in Ireland: Methods and Theory,* edited by M. Adshead and M. Millar, 69–90. London: Routledge.

Rodier, J.-P. 1999. "Un groupe différent qui ne sera ni canadien, ni français, ni suisse." *La Tribune,* 10 November, pp. 1, 22–23.

———. 2003. "Pechiney ne sera pas une simple filiale d'Alcan." Interview. *Le Monde,* 14 September, p. 14.

Royle, T. 2000. *Working for McDonald's in Europe: The Unequal Struggle.* London: Routledge.

Rüb, S. 2002. *World Works Councils and Other Forms of Global Employee Representation in Transnational Undertakings: A Survey.* Düsseldorf: Hans Böckler Stiftung.

Rueschemeyer, D., E. Huber Stephens, and J. D. Stephens. 1992. *Capitalist Development and Democracy.* Cambridge, UK: Polity Press.

Ruigrok, W., and R. Van Tulder. 1995. *The Logic of International Restructuring.* London: Routledge.

Rustow, D. 1970. "Transitions to democracy." *Comparative Politics* 2: 337–63.

Sabel, C. 1991. "Moebius-strip organizations and open labor markets: Some consequences of the reintegration of conception and execution in a volatile economy." In *Social Theory for a Changing Society*, edited by J. Coleman and P. Bourdieu, 23–63. Boulder: Westview Press.

Samyn, B. 2001. "Tarifpolitik zwischen Europäischer Koordinierung und nationalen Bündnissen." In *Interventionen wider den Zeitgeist: Für eine Emanzipatorische Gewerkschaftskritik in 21. Jahrhundert, Festschrift für Helmut Schauer zum Übergang in den Un-Ruhestand*, edited by H. Wagner, 347–59. Hamburg: VSA.

Sarkozy, N. 2006. *Testimony. The English Version of the Bestselling Témoinage.* Harriman House: Petersfield.

——. 2007. "Mon projet: Ensemble tout devient possible." Available at www.sarkozy.fr/lafrance/.

Sassoon, D. 1997. *One Hundred Years of Socialism: The West European Left in the Twentieth Century.* London: Tauris.

Sauerborn, W. 2001. "Flächentarif und Globalisierung: Nachforschungen zur Krise der Gewerkschaften." In *Jenseits der Bescheidenheit: Löhne und Einkommen im Kasinokapitalismus*, edited by W. Sauerborn, M. Schlecht, and M. Wendl, 111–46. Hamburg: VSA.

Sauramo, 2000. "Finland." In *Collective Bargaining in Europe 2000*, edited by G. Fajertag, 125–139. Brussels: ETUI.

Sauviat, C. 2003. "Alstom announces Europe-wide restructuring." Available at www.eiro.eurofound.eu.int/2003/06/inbrief/fr0306101n .html.

Scharpf, F. W. 1975. *Demokratietheorie zwischen Utopie und Anpassung.* Kronberg: Scriptor-Verlag.

——. 1999. *Governing in Europe: Effective and Democratic?* Oxford: Oxford University Press.

Schartau, H. 1998. "Von den nationalen Interessenvertretungen zur Euro-Gewerkschaft: Grenzüberschreitende Zusammenarbeit in der Tarifpolitik." *Frankfurter Rundschau*, 8 October.

Schiesser, R. 1999. "Interview." *Die Neue Gewerkschaft*, 18 May, vol. 9, p. 3.

Schiller, T., and V. Mittendorf, eds. 2002. *Direkte Demokratie: Forschung und Perspektiven.* Wiesbaden: Westdeutscher Verlag.

Schmidt, V. A. 2006. *Democracy in Europe: The EU and National Polities.* Oxford: Oxford University Press.

Schmitter, P. C. 2000. *How to Democratize the European Union — and Why Bother?* Lanham: Rowman & Littlefield.

Schmitter, P. C., and G. Lehmbruch, eds. 1979. *Trends toward Corporatist Intermediation.* Beverly Hills: Sage.

Schneider, M. 1989. *Kleine Geschichte der Gewerkschaften.* Bonn: Verlag JHW Dietz Nachf.

Schnepf, M., E.-L. Laux, and H. Baumann. 1997. *Projekt Europäische Tarif-*

politik im Baugewerbe, Schlussbericht. Brussels: Friedrich Ebert Foundation and European Federation of Building and Woodworkers.

Schönhoven, K., and H. Weber. 1996. *Quellen zur Geschichte der Deutschen
Gewerkschaftsbewegung im 20 Jahrhundert, Vol. 11: Der Deutsche Gewerkschaftsbund 1949–1956.* Cologne: Bund Verlag.

Schroeder, W., and R. Weinert. 2003. "New institutional arrangements
after EMU: 'Actors' rather than 'structure' in the process of Europeanization of trade union politics." Paper presented at the IIRA 13th
World Congress, Free University of Berlin, Germany, September 8–12.

Schulten, T. 1998. "Collective bargaining policy under European Monetary Union." In *Third EMF Collective Bargaining Conference: Current Results of the WSI Research Project, "Collective Bargaining in the Light of the
European Monetary Union,"* edited by EMF, chap. 2. Brussels: EMF.

———. 1999a. "Auf dem Weg in die Abwärtsspirale?: Tarifpolitik unter
den Bedingungen der europäischen Währungsunion in Schulten." In
Tarifpolitik unter dem EURO, edited by T. Schulten and R. Bispinck, 16–
37. Hamburg: VSA Verlag.

———. 1999b. "German and Polish construction unions sign cooperation
agreement." Available at www.eiro.eurofound.eu.int/about/1999/
11/inbrief/de9911223n.html.

———. 2000a. "Agreements in chemicals and metalworking shape 2000
bargaining round." Available at www.eiro.eurofound.eu.int/2000/04/
FEATURE/DE0004255F.html.

———. 2000b. "Zwischen nationalen Wettbewerbskorporatismus und sym-
bolischem Euro-Korporatismus—zur Einbindung der Gewerkschaften
in die neoliberale Restrukturierung Europas." In *Die Konfiguration Europas: Dimensionen einer Kritischen Integrationstheorie,* edited by H.-J. Bieling and J. Steinhilber, 222–42. Münster: Westfälisches Dampfboot.

———. 2002a. "A European solidaristic wage policy?" *European Journal of
Industrial Relations* 8 (2): 173–96.

———. 2002b. "Pilot agreements signed in metalworking after strike."
Available at www.eiro.eurofound.ie/2002/05/Feature/DE0205206F
.html.

———. 2003. "Europeanisation of collective bargaining: Trade union initiatives for the transnational coordination of collective bargaining." In
*Industrial Relations and European Integration: Trans- and Supranational De-
velopments and Prospects,* edited by B. Keller and H.-W. Platzer, 112–36.
Aldershot, UK: Ashgate.

Schulten, T., and R. Bispinck, eds. 2001. *Collective Bargaining under the
Euro: Experiences from the European Metal Industry.* Brussels: ETUI.

Schulten, T., R. Bispinck, and W. Lecher. 1998. "Introduction." In *Third
EMF Collective Bargaining Conference: Current Results of the WSI Research
Project, "Collective Bargaining in the Light of the European Monetary Union
2,"* edited by EMF, chap. 1. Brussels: EMF.

Schulten, T, R. Bispinck, and C. Schäfer, eds. 2006. *Minimum Wages in Europe*. Brussels: ETUI.

Schumpeter, J. A. 1954. *Capitalism, Socialism and Democracy*. London: Allen & Unwin.

Secafi Alpha. 2003. "Alcan Pechiney: Quels enjeux?" Available at http://perso.wanadoo.fr/lacgtpechiney/doc14.htm.

Siebert, H. 1997. "Labor market rigidities: At the root of unemployment in Europe." *Journal of Economic Perspectives* 11 (3): 37–54.

Silver, B. J. 2003. *Forces of Labor: Workers' Movements and Globalization since 1870*. Cambridge, UK: Cambridge University Press.

Sinyai, C. 2006. *Schools of Democracy: A Political History of the American Labor Movement*. Ithaca: Cornell University Press.

Sklair, L. 2001. *The Transnational Capitalist Class*. Oxford: Blackwell.

Skocpol, T. 2003. *Diminished Democracy: From Membership to Management in American Civic Life*. Norman: University of Oklahoma Press.

Smelser, N. 1995. "Reflections on the methodology of comparative studies." Mimeo. European University Institute.

Smismans, S. 2000. "The European Economic and Social Committee: Towards deliberative democracy via a functional assembly." Available at http://ideas.repec.org/a/erp/eiopxx/p0055.html.

——. 2004. *Law, Legitimacy, and European Governance: Functional Participation in Social Regulation*, Oxford: Oxford University Press.

——, ed. 2006. *Civil Society and Legitimate European Governance*. Cheltenham, UK: Edward Elgar.

Stedman Jones, G. 1983. *Languages of Class: Studies in English Working Class History 1832–1982*. Cambridge, UK: Cambridge University Press.

Steinauer, J., and M. Von Allmen. 2000. *Changer la Baraque: Les Immigrés dans les Syndicats Suisses 1945–2000*. Lausanne: Editions d'en bas.

Stiglitz, J. E. 2002. "Employment, social justice and societal well-being." *International Labour Review* 141 (1–2): 9–29.

Stråth, B. 1990. "Union strategies in historical perspective Sweden and Germany." EUI working paper no. HEC 90/5, EUI, Florence.

Streeck, W. 1997. "Industrial citizenship under regime competition: The case of European Works Councils." *Journal of European Public Policy* 4 (4): 643–64.

——. 1998a. "Gewerkschaften zwischen Nationalstaat und Europäischer Union." *WSI Mitteilungen* 51 (1): 1–14.

——. 1998b. "Industrielle Beziehungen in einer internationalisierten Wirtschaft." In *Politik der Globalisierung*, edited by U. Beck, 169–202. Frankfurt: Suhrkamp.

——, ed. 1998c. *Internationale Wirtschaft, Nationale Demokratie*. Frankfurt: Campus.

——. 1999. "Competitive solidarity: Rethinking the 'European Social

Model'." MPIfG working paper no. 99/8, Max Plank Institute for the Study of Societies, Cologne.

———. 2000. "Die Bürgergesellschaft als Lernzielkatalog." *Die Mitbestimmung* 46 (6): 28–31.

Streeck, W., and P. C. Schmitter. 1991. "From national corporatism to transnational pluralism." *Politics & Society* 19 (2): 133–64.

Tarrow, S. 1994. *Power in Movement: Social Movements, Collective Action and Politics.* Cambridge, UK: Cambridge University Press.

———. 1995. "Bridging the quantitative-qualitative divide in political science." *American Political Science Review* 89 (2): 471–74.

Taylor, G., and A. Mathers. 2004. "The European Trade Union Confederation at the crossroads of change?" *European Journal of Industrial Relations* 10 (3): 267–85.

Teulings, C. N., and J. Hartog. 1998. *Corporatism or Competition?: Labour Contracts, Institutions, and Wage Structures in International Comparison.* Cambridge, UK: Cambridge University Press.

Thibaud, P. 1992. "L'Europe par les nations (et réciproquement)." In *Discussion sur l'Europe,* edited by J.-M. Ferry and P. Thibaud, 11–126. Paris: Calman-Lévy.

Thiéry, S., and J. Bass. 2001. "Une nouvelle dynamique de la négociation salariale." *La Revue de la CFDT* 5 (October): 21–28.

Thompson, C. 1994. "Strategy and opportunism: Trade unions as agents for change in South Africa." In *The Future of Industrial Relations: Global Change and Challenges,* edited by H. R. Niland, R. D. Lansbury, and C. Verevis, 349–66. Thousand Oaks, Calif.: Sage.

Thompson, E. P. 1980. *The Making of the English Working Class.* London: Penguin.

Tilly, C. 2004. *Contention and Democracy in Europe, 1768–2004.* Cambridge, UK: Cambridge University Press.

Tomasi di Lampedusa, G. 1998. *The Leopard.* Translated from the Italian by A. Colquhoun. London: Everyman's Library.

Traxler, F. 1998. "Nationale Tarifsysteme und wirtschaftliche Internationalisierung: Zur Positionierung des Modell Deutschland im internationalen Vergleich." *WSI Mitteilungen* 51 (4): 249–55.

———. 2002. "Wage policy, bargaining institutions and monetary policy: Empirical findings and policy implications for European Monetary Union." In *Wage Policy in the Eurozone,* edited by P. Pochet, 111–30. Brussels: P.I.E.-Peter Lang.

Traxler. F., B. Brandl, V. Glassner, and A. Ludwig. 2007. "Can cross-border bargaining coordination work?: Analytical reflections on its feasibility and evidence from Germany's and Austria's metal industry." *European Journal of Industrial Relations* (forthcoming).

Traxler, F., and E. Mermet. 2003. "Coordination of collective bargaining: The case of Europe." *Transfer* 9 (2): 229–46.

Trentin, B. 1994. *Il Coraggio dell'Utopia.* Milan: Rizzoli.

Trogrlic, J.-F. 1999. "L'euro pour vivre ensemble." *Syndicalisme Hebdo* 2727: 3.

Turnbull, P. 2006. "The war on Europe's waterfront—repertoires of power in the port transport industry." *British Journal of Industrial Relations* 44 (2): 305–26.

Turner, L. 1996. "The europeanisation of labour: Structure before action." *European Journal of Industrial Relations* 2 (3): 325–44.

Turner, L., and D. B. Cornfield. 2007. *Labor in the New Urban Battlegrounds: Local Solidarity in a Global Economy.* Ithaca: Cornell University Press.

UG. 2003. "Entsetzen in Paris über Alstom-Ultimatum: Furcht vor einem sozialen und industriellen Waterloo." *Neue Zürcher Zeitung,* 19 September. Available at www.nzz.ch.

Usher, A. 2001. "The implications of the EMU for collective bargaining in French metalworking: The exception proves the rule?" In *Collective Bargaining under the Euro: Experiences from the European Metal Industry,* edited by T. Schulten and R. Bispinck, 129–62. Brussels: ETUI.

Uterwedde, H. 1999. "Abschied vom französischen Modell?" In *Länderbericht Frankreich,* edited by M. L. Christadler and H. Uterwedde, 201–27. Opladen: Leske & Budrich.

Uyterhoeven, H. 1993. "Leadership in a multidomestic organization (reflections on the ABB experience)." In *Führen von Organisationen: Konzepte und Praktische Beispiele aus Privaten und Öffentlichen Unternehmen,* edited by J. S. Krulis-Randa, B. Staffelbach, and H.-P. Wehrli, 180–204. Berne: Verlag Paul Haupt.

Van Apeldoorn, B. 2000. "Transnational class agency and European governance: The case of the European Round Table of Industrialists." *New Political Economy* 5 (2): 157–81.

Van Bael, I., and J.-F. Bellis. 1994. *Competition Law of the European Community.* 3rd ed. Bicester: CCH Europe.

Vanhulle, S., and T. Van Grop. 1998. *Le Choc Renault Vilvorde.* Paris: VO Éditions and EPO.

Veneziani, B. 2006. "Right of collective bargaining and action." In *European Labour Law and the EU Charter of Fundamental Rights,* edited by B. Bercusson, 291–336. Baden-Baden: Nomos Verlagsgesellschaft.

Verdier, C. 2000. "L'exemple Péchiney: Histoire inachevée des comités européens." *Le Peuple* 1521: 6–7.

Verzetnitsch, F. 2000. "Einleitung." In *Europa 2000+: Auf dem Weg zu einem Europäischen Sozialmodell,* edited by Zukunfts- und Kulturwerkstätte and Fritz Verzetnitsch. Vienna: SPÖ Zukunfts- und Kulturwerkstätte.

Vincenzi, C., and J. Fairhurst. 2002. *Law of the European Community.* 3rd ed. Harlow: Pearson Education Limited.

Visser, J. 1996. "Internationalism in European trade unions: A lost perspective or a new agenda?" In *The Lost Perspective?: Trade Unions between Ideology and Social Action in the New Europe,* edited by P. Pasture, J. Verberckmoes, and H. De Witte, Vol. 2, 176–99. Aldershot, UK: Ashgate.

——. 2002. "Unions, wage bargaining and coordination in European labour markets—the past twenty years and the near future." In *Wage Policy in the Eurozone,* edited by P. Pochet, 39–77. Brussels: P.I.E.-Peter Lang.

Visser, J., and A. Hemerijck. 1997. *A Dutch Miracle: Job Growth, Welfare Reform and Corporatism in the Netherlands.* Amsterdam: Amsterdam University Press.

Vousden, S. 2000. "Albany, market law and social exclusion." *Industrial Law Review* 29: 181–91.

Waddington, J. 2003. "Heightening tension in relations between trade unions and the Labour government in 2002." *British Journal of Industrial Relations* 41 (2): 335–58.

Waddington, J., R. Hoffmann, and J. Lind. 1997. "European trade unionism in transition?: A review of the issues." *Transfer* 3 (3): 464–97.

Wagner, A.-C. 2004. "Syndicalistes européens: Les conditions sociales et institutionnelles de l'internalisation des militants syndicaux." *Actes de la Recherche en Sciences Sociales* 155: 13–33.

——. 2005. *Vers une Europe syndicale: Une enquête sur la confédération européenne des syndicats.* Bellecombe-en-Bauges: Croquant.

Wagner, P. 2001. "Modernity, capitalism, and critique." *Thesis Eleven* 66: 1–31.

Weiler, J. H. H., U. Haltern, and F. C. Mayer. 1995. "European democracy and its critique." In *Special Issue on the Crisis of Representation in Europe,* edited by Jack Hayward. *West European Politics* 18 (4): 4–39.

Wets, J., ed. 2000. *Cultural Diversity in Trade Unions: A Challenge to Class Identity?* Aldershot, UK: Ashgate.

Whitney, C. R. 2007 "Maurice Papon, French Nazi Collaborator, Dies at 96," *New York Times,* February 19, section B, p. 8.

Who's Who in France. 2006. "Pierre Bilger." Available at http://web.lexis-nexis.com/professional.

Wiesehügel, K., and K.-H. Sahl, eds. 1998. *Die Sozialkassen der Bauwirtschaft und die Entsendung Innerhalb der Europäischen Union.* Cologne: Bund Verlag.

Wolton, D. 1993. *La Dernière Utopie: Naissance de l'Europe Démocratique.* Paris: Flammarion.

Woolfson, C., and J. Sommers. 2006. "Labour mobility in construction: European implications of the Laval un Partneri dispute with Swedish labour." *European Journal of Industrial Relations* 12 (1): 49–68.

Wright, C. 2000. "The world's first three-way cross-border merger rolls out." *Corporate Finance: Global M&A Yearbook 2000:* 44–48.

Wright, M., and P. Edwards. 1998. "Does teamworking work, and if so, why?: A case study in the aluminium industry." *Economic and Industrial Democracy* 19 (1): 59–90.

Zagelmeyer, S., and T. Schulten. 1997. "Collective bargaining on employment in Europe." Available at www.eiro.eurofound.eu.int/1997/10/study/tn9710201s.html.

Ziltener, P. 1999. *Strukturwandel der Europäischen Integration.* Münster: Westfälisches Dampfboot.

———. 2000. "Interaktionen und Integration: Das europäische Mehrebenensystem als Handlungsfeld der Schweizer Gewerkschaften." In *Gewerkschaften in der Schweiz,* edited by K. Armingeon and S. Geissbühler, 219–89. Zürich: Seismo.

Index

Page numbers with an *f* indicate figures; those with a *t* indicate tables.

Index